Quality of Life and Public Management

Quality of Life and Public Management explores the possibility for a dramatic and significant improvement in quality of life for all population groups and sub-groups in the UK. Strongly evidence-based, the book draws on case study data and comparisons into local and central government structure, funding, policy, cultures and outcomes from a number of EU countries, such as Denmark, Germany and Switzerland. It shows that quality of life on a number of important criteria is superior in these other countries compared to the UK. The book makes a strong argument that it is possible to replicate this success in the UK and that failure to do so has been the result of failed political institutions, in particular local government.

John Whitelegg examines the impact of better central and local governance on the welfare of children and older people. He also looks at the built environment, air quality, resilience and renewable energy in the UK and gives suggestions for practical and implementable policies based on evidence and best practice from other EU cities.

The book is rooted in the belief that every locality can and should have the best possible standards of health, quality of life, environment, climate change protection and transport choices that can be found anywhere in the world.

This book will be of great value to students and researchers in the fields of public management, politics, social work, planning and public services in general. It also has direct relevance for professionals in central and local government, councillors, community groups and NGOs.

John Whitelegg is Professor of Sustainable Development at the Stockholm Environment Institute, University of York, UK. He worked at Lancaster University for 20 years as a teacher, researcher and activist on transport and the environment. He was a city councillor for eight years and from 2008 to 2010 was deputy chair of the Local Government Association Regeneration and Transport Board.

Quality of Life and Public Management

Redefining development in the local environment

John Whitelegg

LONDON AND NEW YORK

from Routledge

First published 2013
by Routledge
2 Park Square, Milton Park, Abingdon, Oxon, OX14 4RN

Simultaneously published in the USA and Canada
by Routledge
711 Third Avenue, New York, NY 10017

Routledge is an imprint of the Taylor & Francis Group, an informa business

British Library Cataloguing in Publication Data
A catalogue record for this book is available from the British Library

Library of Congress Cataloging-in-Publication Data
Whitelegg, J. (John)
  Quality of life and public management : redefining development in the
  local environment / John Whitelegg.
  p. cm.
  1. Quality of life—Great Britain. 2. Local government—Great Britain. I. Title.
  HN386.W47 2013
  306—dc23
  2012006862

ISBN13: 978–0–415–50955–8 (hbk)
ISBN13: 978–0–203–10156–8 (ebk)

Typeset in Times New Roman
by Swales & Willis Ltd, Exeter, Devon

Printed and bound in Great Britain by the MPG Books Group

This book is dedicated with love to Jacob, Teo, Lauren, Fynn, Kilian, Rebecca, Henry and Hedda

Contents

Figures

Tables

Preface

This book has been growing as an idea for approximately three decades. During this very long gestation period several other books have been written, but all of them have dodged the central questions that are dealt with in this book. The author's background is in the kind of geography that was normal in the 1960s and was passionate about the differences between places and the explanations that could be marshalled to explain differences. A key influence on thinking was the book by David Harvey with the title *Explanation in Geography*, but even that did not satisfy the desire to know why there were such important differences between places. In the 1960s geographers were categorised as 'human' or 'physical', and those who took the 'human' route were given a very firm grounding in urban, social, economic and rural geography and given the empirical, statistical and conceptual tools to deal with reflection and explanation. I decided to be 'human' and not to draw attention to my fascination with fluvial geomorphology, glaciation, soil science and other delights of a geography department at University College of Wales, Aberystwyth in the late 1960s.

Following this modest, thorough and detailed grounding in human geography the author went on to investigate ways of improving the flow of steel exports from South Wales ports to the Great Lakes ports of North America, and then moved to a post as transport and economic development officer in the Outer Hebrides with responsibility for ferries, air services, seaweed processing, tweed and crab processing as well as building new jetties to help lobster fishermen develop their businesses. This was followed by 18 years in the geography department at Lancaster University, finishing in 1993 as head of department. During this period the author developed undergraduate courses on transport and the European Union that emphasised the importance of comparing cities, regions and nations and looking for best practice examples of planning, urban design, public transport and economic performance to inform explanation of what was going on (or not going on) in the UK and more importantly identify the ingredients of success. This development was greatly assisted by a three-year period on secondment as a researcher working with the Institut fuer Landes- und Stadtentwicklungsforschung des Landes Nordrhein-Westfalen in Dortmund, Germany (ILS). ILS was part of the Ministry of City Development, Housing and Traffic of the State of North Rhine-Westphalia, headquartered in Düsseldorf in Germany. This was a period of intense learning and personal development that led to the conclusion that UK problems variously described as transport problems, urban problems, rural problems or housing problems were all capable of being solved within the kind of governance, budgeting and commitment to quality culture of a German ministry with responsibility for 16 million people in the most populous state of pre-unification Germany.

This learning and development was not limited to Germany. Two periods of time as visiting professor of transport at Roskilde University in Denmark and visits to Lund in Sweden to teach on courses at the university provided very similar learning experiences, and all of these influences can be detected in this book.

In 1993 I left Lancaster University to set up a transport consultancy and take on the role of managing director. In the transport consultancy it became abundantly clear that many of the problems we were asked to investigate could benefit enormously from mainland European experience across a wide spectrum of social, economic, environmental and organisational case studies. Seventeen years of consultancy have poured vast amounts of this experience into transport plans and strategies, travel plans, walking and cycling promotion strategies and interventions to reduce greenhouse gases, improve air quality and improve the economic performance of city regions, and this work continues.

The consultancy work was balanced with a very productive 10 years working for a global science policy research institute, the Stockholm Environment Institute (SEI). This introduced me to yet more perspectives on rigorous scientific work embedded in a commitment to improve public policy through the quality of the scientific analysis, and that has heavily influenced this work. It also took me to India and China to contribute to sustainable urbanisation work in Beijing and air quality policy discussions in India and other Asian cities. This work continues in the cities of Africa south of the Sahara.

In 2003 I was elected as a Green Party city councillor on Lancaster City Council, representing 6,000 people in a densely populated area to the east of the city centre (Bulk ward). Eight years of experience as a city councillor and three years of that as deputy chair of the national Regeneration and Transport Board of the Local Government Association in London have had an even bigger influence on my thinking than three years in the state government of North Rhine-Westphalia in Germany and 10 years with SEI. The three sets of experiences have been perfectly complementary. The German experience showed me how it is possible to think carefully and modestly about quality outcomes and actually make them happen, the Swedish experience taught me the importance of high-quality scientific work as an aid to better policy formulation and delivery, and the Lancaster councillor experience has shown me how easy it is to lose the plot and get lost in a fug of useless policy and process debate with very little to show for it at the end of that process. Local authorities in England operate within a system that has very little real power to change things, very little budgetary independence, very few resources and a strong central control imperative that makes innovation and experimentation almost impossible.

This combination of these very different experiences has triggered the writing of this book. The book is about quality, excellence, desirable places and positive outcomes and how to recognise them, learn from other places on how to design and deliver them, and explain the differences in outcomes so that we can all focus effort on eliminating any systematic tendencies in the direction of poor quality. It is about significant and serious improvement in the way we do things in the UK so that comparison, analysis and delivery focus on real outcomes of value to real people and do not get lost in useless bureaucracy. It is not an attack on English local or central government. It is a book very much in the spirit of 1960s geography about explaining the differences between places and moving rapidly to using that explanation to make suggestions on what needs to be changed to ensure that in the UK we get the high-quality outcomes and sense of joy from living in wonderful places that every citizen deserves. It is a celebration of high-quality places and a distillation of what needs to be done to isolate the virtuous virus that replicates quality and excellence and releases it into the DNA of local and central government in the UK.

John Whitelegg
Staufen im Breisgau
Baden-Württemberg
Germany

Acknowledgements

I am very grateful to a large number of friends and colleagues who have helped me with this book. The contributions they have made are invaluable and range from background moral support through the sharing of really good ideas about how to make things better in Britain to detailed information and insights on the complicated nature of public transport subsidy in Germany, Denmark, Austria, Switzerland and Sweden. Those who have helped and made writing this book a pleasurable experience, when it could have been very different, include Midge Whitelegg, Per Homan Jespersen, Helmut Holzapfel, Martin Haag, Tomas Björnsson, Bjoern Frauendienst, Ulrike Reutter, Tricia Grove-Smith, David Merrett, Paul Raynes, Nick Williams, Lynn Sloman, Eric Britton, Pedro Abrantes, Matt Brunt, Alistair Kirkbride, Rod King, Holger Robrecht, Wolfgang Teubner, Stefan Kuhn, Peter Newman, Jeff Kenworthy, Anchoret Stevens, Paul Tranter, Andreas Hildebrandt, Uwe Schade, Michael Glotz-Richter, Oliver Dümmler, Jim Barclay, Sarah Dewar, Brian Hansen, Anton Geyer, Yvonne Meier-Bukowiecki, Martin Demmeler and Felix Laube.

I would like to thank Dr Dieter Salomon, the Lord Mayor of Freiburg, for spending time with me to answer my questions about that city and explaining how it has achieved such a remarkable record of success across so many policy areas.

I am very grateful to my colleagues at the Stockholm Environment Institute (SEI), University of York (UK) for providing a stimulating environment in which to work over a 10-year period. It has been a great pleasure to work with Gary Haq, Howard Cambridge, Steve Cinderby, Harry Vallack and many others. This period of time and the opportunity to work in China, on transport issues in Africa south of the Sahara and on European Environment Agency projects sharpened my thinking about many of the topics in this book.

I am very grateful for the opportunity to spend two months living in Staufen im Breisgau in southern Germany in 2010 in an idyllic setting provided by Herr Max and Frau Claudia Mueller. Much of this book was written in Staufen whilst experiencing the very high quality of life to be found there.

I am grateful for all those who have generously given permission for the reproduction in this book of their original material:

Figures I.1 and I.2 reproduced with the permission of UNICEF
Figure 1.1 reproduced with the permission of the North West Public Health Observatory, Liverpool

Figure 3.1 reproduced with the permission of UNICEF

Figure 3.2 reproduced with the permission of the OECD

Figure 3.3 reproduced with the permission of Paul Tranter

Figure 3.4 reproduced with the permission of Jan Garrard

Figure 3.5 reproduced with the permission of Bruce Whyte and NHS Greater Glasgow and Clyde

Figures 4.1 and 4.2 reproduced with the permission of John Hills under the UK National Archives Open Government Licence

Figure 4.3 reproduced with the permission of Eurostat

Figure 4.4 reproduced with the permission of the *Lancet*

Figure 4.5 reproduced with the permission of Pluto Press

Figure 4.6 reproduced with the permission of Eurostat

Figure 5.1 reproduced with the permission of Routledge

Figure 5.2 reproduced with the permission of Joshua Hart and Eco-Logica Ltd

Figures 5.3 and 5.4 reproduced with the permission of Jeff Kenworthy

Figures 7.1 and 7.5 reproduced with the permission of the European Commission

Figure 7.2 reproduced with the permission of Bettina Kampman and CE Delft

Figure 7.3 reproduced with the permission of the Passivhaus Institut

Figure 7.4 reproduced with the permission of Freiburg Wirtschaft Touristik und Messe GmbH & Co. KG, Rathausgasse 33, 79098 Freiburg, Germany

Figure 7.6 reproduced with the permission of the European Environment Agency

Figures 7.7 and 7.8 reproduced under the UK National Archives Open Government Licence

Figure 8.1 reproduced with the permission of Freiburg City Council

Figure 8.2 reproduced with the permission of the Peak Oil Centre

Figure 8.3 reproduced with the permission of Taylor & Francis

Figure 8.4 reproduced with the permission of Debbie Greenfield and the Lewes Pound organisation

Figure 8.5 reproduced with the permission of Eco-Logica Ltd

Figures 8.6 and 8.7 reproduced with the permission of Martin Demmeler

Figure 9.1 reproduced with the permission of the Equality Trust

Figures 9.3 and 9.4 reproduced with the permission of Ipsos MORI

Figure 9.5 reproduced with the permission of Eurostat

Figure 9.6 is an original graphic produced by Alistair Kirkbride and reproduced with his permission

Figure 10.1 reproduced with the permission of the European Commission

The author and publisher have made every effort to contact authors/copyright holders. In those cases where copyright holders could not be traced or did not reply to requests for permission to reproduce diagrams we welcome correspondence from those individuals and companies.

I am very grateful to my editorial assistant at Routledge, Charlotte Russell, who was very patient when I announced more than one delay in submitting the final manuscript, and to Erik Willis at the Stockholm Environment Institute, who did the excellent work on the diagrams.

If I have made errors of fact, interpretation or logic then this is entirely my fault and not the fault of any of the people listed here.

Abbreviations

ADT	American District Telegraph
AQMA	air quality management area
BESTUFS	Best Urban Freight Solutions
BMA	British Medical Association
BUND	Bund fuer Umwelt und Naturschutz Deutschland
CABE	Commission for Architecture and the Built Environment
CAL	Campaign for Clean Air in London
CfIT	Commission for Integrated Transport
Civitas	City–Vitality–Sustainability, or 'Cleaner and Better Transport in Cities'
CTC	Cyclists' Touring Club
DECC	Department of Energy and Climate Change
DEFRA	Department for Environment, Food and Rural Affairs
DfT	Department for Transport
DTI	Department of Trade and Industry
EEA	European Environment Agency
EIU	Economist Intelligence Unit
ELTIS	European Local Transport Information Service
EPEE	European Partnership for Energy and the Environment
EPOMM	European Platform on Mobility Management
ERSO	European Road Safety Observatory
ESAW	European Study of Adult Well-Being
EU	European Union
FES	Friedrich Ebert Stiftung
GOD	green-oriented development
IEA	International Energy Agency
IEE	Intelligent Energy Europe
IEEP	Institute for European Environmental Policy
IPCC	Intergovernmental Panel on Climate Change
ISTAT	Italian National Institute of Statistics
ITDP	Institute for Transportation and Development Policy
LGA	Local Government Association
NEF	New Economics Foundation
NFER	National Foundation for Educational Research

NICE	National Institute for Health and Clinical Excellence
NWPHO	North West Public Health Observatory
ODAC	Oil Depletion Analysis Centre
OECD	Organisation for Economic Co-operation and Development
PM	particulate matter
POD	pedestrian-oriented development
PPS	purchasing power standard
SACTRA	Standing Advisory Committee on Trunk Road Assessment
SDC	Sustainable Development Commission
SEI	Stockholm Environment Institute
SEU	Social Exclusion Unit
TfL	Transport for London
TOD	transit-oriented development
UKERC	United Kingdom Energy Research Centre
UNFCCC	United Nations Framework Convention on Climate Change
UNICEF	United Nations Children's Fund
VTPI	Victoria Transport Policy Institute
WHO	World Health Organization

Introduction

The UK is the sixth richest country in the world (World Bank, 2011) and yet seems to have settled at or near the bottom of European rankings on quality of life, health, child poverty, obesity, recycling, percentage of journeys made by bicycle, the quantity and quality of public transport and many other indicators of social progress. The UK has become more like the USA and less like its European neighbours in its social evolution, and this is at odds with history and with the perception that the UK is a progressive, socially responsible and innovative nation.

The UK has a long tradition of stable government and social progress ranging over a very wide spectrum of issues and topics and 200 years of achievements. Table I.1 is an impressive catalogue of social progress and of the capacity of the state and its institutions to innovate and improve the lives of ordinary citizens, especially those who fall into vulnerable groups.

There is evidence that this long-term social progress and state activity to protect all citizens is now at an end and we have entered a period of decline on outcomes that matter to most citizens. Two figures illustrate the degree of more recent deviation from this long-term progressive trend. Figure I.1 shows the percentage of children living in households with equivalent income less than 50 per cent of the median, and Figure I.2 shows subjective well-being of young people.

Table I.1 Key events and dates in British social progress

	Key legislative dates
Abolition of slavery	1807 and 1833
Compulsory schooling for children aged 5–13	1870
Compulsory schooling for children aged up to 14	1918
Employment of children under the age of 10 in factories made illegal	1878
Pensions for the retired	1907
Universal suffrage for men over the age of 21	1918
Universal suffrage for women over the age of 21	1928
Sanitation and drinking water in cities	1848, 1866 and 1875
The National Health Service	1948
Clean Air Acts to deal with smog	1956

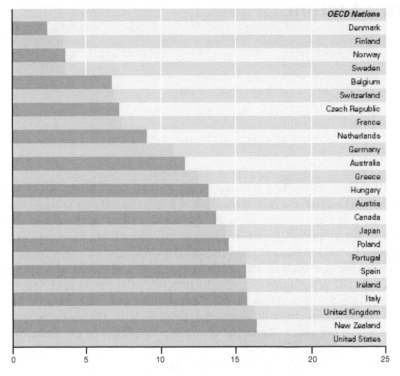

Figure I.1 Relative income poverty: percentage of children (0–17 years) in households
with equivalent income less than 50 per cent of the median

Source: UNICEF (2007).

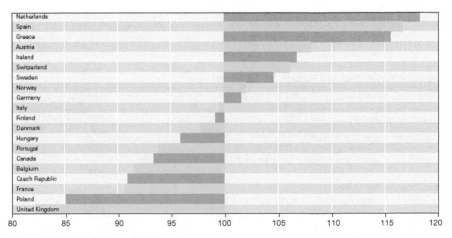

Figure I.2 Subjective well-being of young people

Source: UNICEF (2007).

Figure I.1 reveals that the UK is third from the bottom in terms of this measure of relative poverty. The USA is at the bottom. Children in the UK are far more likely to live in poverty than children in Denmark, Norway and Finland. Figure I.2 shows that the UK is bottom in the rankings when children are asked questions about well-being in a consistent way across several countries. Subjective well-being is a self-reported measure of the child's own view of health status and well-being, and the UK performs worse than any other country in this UNICEF comparison of 'rich countries'.

The UNICEF study compares 21 countries on six indicators (subjective well-being is one of these indicators). The rankings for the UK are summarised in Table I.2. The overall average ranking for the UK is 18.2, with the USA at 18.0. The UK is the worst performer of all 21 countries.

This poor performance on child welfare in a wealthy country is an indicator of a more general malaise, which we explore in Chapter 3. Freeman and Tranter (2011) explore the idea that children are an 'indicator species'. If our children thrive then society as a whole is working in the right direction to deliver benefits for all age groups and all sections of the community. Child-friendly cities are likely to be low-carbon cities and resilient cities, and healthy children are likely to grow into healthy adults capable of interacting with other adults and confidently solving many of the problems that are central to creating a sustainable, socially just and ecologically efficient world. If our children are stressed, isolated, suffering mental health problems and deprived of safe spaces in which to move around and play then society as a whole is the poorer.

UNICEF (2007) put this very succinctly: 'The true measure of a nation's standing is how well it attends to its children – their health and safety, their material security, their education and socialisation, and their sense of being loved, valued, and included in the families and societies into which they are born.'

Improving the environment and space in which children play and move around is an important part of this book because it is important in itself and because if we succeed with children we will also succeed with other groups and begin the process of improving overall quality of life for everyone.

The first two chapters of this book describe the evidence base and the rankings that clearly show the UK as a poor performer across a wide range of social, economic, environmental and quality-of-life indicators. National-level comparisons

Table I.2 UK rankings on six indicators of child welfare

Indicator	Rank
Material well-being	18
Health and safety	12
Educational well-being	17
Family and peer relationships	21
Behaviour and risk	21
Subjective well-being	20

Note: A ranking at number 21 means the 'worst' and at number 1 the 'best'.

are used, but where the data are up to the task city- and regional-level comparisons are used.

Chapters 3 to 8 give a detailed examination of six key areas of quality-of-life outcomes and public policy and the international variation in the quality of those outcomes. This examination utilises published data to establish clear rankings that can be used to explore the place of the UK in those international comparisons and the reasons for differences in performance.

Chapters 9 and 10 are about the exploration of factors that have a part to play in explaining the UK's poor performance. Why does the UK perform less well than many other countries? There are some intriguing possibilities that can explain these international differences, and they include budgets, the age and gender characteristics of politicians, and governance. Chapter 9 looks at budgets and assesses whether or not we spend less on policies and interventions that improve quality of life than other countries. It also looks at politicians and the possibility that gender and age representativeness distorts outcomes in ways that do not happen when there is a closer fit between age and gender and the populations that elected politicians represent. Governance is important. The UK is one of the most centralised countries in the world, and local authorities have less ability to raise funds and spend resources on projects that benefit the local population than many other countries enjoy. Governance is discussed in Chapter 10.

The book concludes (Chapter 11) with clear recommendations about what has to change in order to trade up to the best in Europe. The UK can do much better than current performance levels, and the conclusion paints a picture of what the UK could look like with Swiss public transport, Swedish child welfare, Danish and Dutch levels of cycling and German renewable energy. The overall conclusion is very clear. We can do better, and we must do better. There is no excuse for poor-quality outcomes and no excuse for bumping along in the bottom 10 per cent of the rankings. The book is a zero-tolerance manual for poor-quality outcomes and a clear signposting exercise that guides cities, regions and nations to the top of the rankings in a very short amount of time.

1 A tale of three cities and two rural areas

Recent years have seen an explosion in international surveys of quality of life in world cities, which apply various methodologies to rank cities in terms of liveability, environmental quality, transport, attraction to inward investors, crime and cultural attributes. The report of the Economist Intelligence Unit (2011) is more rigorous than most:

> The Economist Intelligence Unit's liveability rating quantifies the challenges that might be presented to an individual's lifestyle in any given location, and allows for direct comparison between locations. Every city is assigned a rating of relative comfort for over 30 qualitative and quantitative factors across five broad categories: stability; healthcare; culture and environment; education; and infrastructure. Each factor in a city is rated as acceptable, tolerable, uncomfortable, undesirable or intolerable. For qualitative indicators, a rating is awarded based on the judgement of in-house analysts and in-city contributors. For quantitative indicators, a rating is calculated based on the relative performance of a number of external data points. The scores are then compiled and weighted to provide a score of one–100, where one is considered intolerable and 100 is considered ideal. The liveability rating is provided both as an overall score and as a score for each category. To provide points of reference, the score is also given for each category relative to New York and an overall position in the ranking of 140 cities is provided.

The rankings cover 140 cities, and the top 10 cities in the 2011 report are listed in Table 1.1.

Similar exercises were conducted by Cushman & Wakefield (2011) from a business perspective and rank cities in terms of their attraction for inward investment and business location. The top 20 cities in the 2011 rankings are listed in Table 1.2.

Whilst primarily a business ranking, the Cushman & Wakefield data include assessments of quality of life for employees and freedom from pollution. The business ranking puts London at number one on the list, but quality-of-life, pollution and public transport components in both ranking exercises put Swiss and Scandinavian cities together with Barcelona higher up the list than UK cities. The Economist Intelligence Unit rankings are dominated by Australia and Canada, with only two cities, Vienna and Helsinki, in the top 10 from Europe.

Table 1.1 Top 10 cities in world ranking of cities on 'liveability'

City	Rank	Overall rating (100 = ideal)
Melbourne	1	97.5
Vienna	2	97.4
Vancouver	3	97.3
Toronto	4	97.2
Calgary	5	96.6
Sydney	6	96.1
Helsinki	7	96.0
Perth	8	95.9
Adelaide	9	95.9
Auckland	10	95.7

Table 1.2 Top 20 cities in terms of attractiveness for inward investment and business location

Location	2011 rank	2010 rank
London	1	1
Paris	2	2
Frankfurt	3	3
Amsterdam	4	6
Berlin	5	7
Barcelona	6	5
Madrid	7	8
Brussels	8	4
Munich	9	9
Zurich	10	13
Geneva	11	14
Milan	12	11
Stockholm	13	16
Dusseldorf	14	10
Hamburg	15	15
Manchester	16	12
Lisbon	17	17
Birmingham	18	18
Lyon	19	19
Dublin	20	20

Both rankings open up the debate about the possibility that excellence across all the main dimensions of everyday life can be located and ranked. It is of course methodologically impossible to capture all the dimensions of quality of life, collapse them into a ranking and be confident that the ranking is robust and credible, but a pattern is emerging, and that pattern includes the absence of UK cities in top 10 or 20 rankings.

Environmental policy in 31 OECD countries has been evaluated and ranked (Bertelsmann Foundation, 2011a). The evaluation addressed the question 'Does environmental policy protect and preserve resources and the quality of the environment?' Britain is ranked lower than the high performers, Denmark, Finland,

Germany, Norway, Sweden, Switzerland, the Czech Republic, Hungary, Japan and Luxembourg but ahead of France, Italy, Spain, the USA and Australia.

On another key indicator, the United Kingdom is ranked 23 out of 31 countries on public expenditure on early childhood education (Bertelsmann Foundation, 2011b). Twenty-two countries spend more on children on this measure than the UK. The relatively poor outcomes of UK policy in the area of child welfare, child poverty and inequality that flow from this under-resourcing are discussed in more detail in Chapter 3.

The UK is a very unequal country and far more unequal than most other OECD countries. Income inequality as measured by the Gini coefficient (Bertelsmann Foundation, 2011b) ranks the UK at 26 out of 31 countries. Twenty-five countries are more equal than the UK. This indicator has been linked to a large number of negative social outcomes (Wilkinson and Pickett, 2009) and is discussed in more detail in Chapter 2.

In this chapter we attempt to paint a picture of excellent places in countries that figure highly in all the international rankings reviewed above. This is deliberately qualitative and subjective. What do excellent places look like and how do the components of excellence impact on the senses? This is a necessary foundation for what follows in the remainder of the book, where we examine individual components of excellence at different scales and state very clearly how the UK can achieve excellence and deliver improvements in quality of life that are clearly better than the current situation. The existence of excellent places is itself a stimulus to delivering the changes in quality of life in the UK that we wish to stimulate.

For the purposes of this discussion and stimulating an appetite for change we have selected three urban areas and two rural areas and tried to capture what makes them so attractive. The urban areas are Freiburg im Breisgau in Germany, Basel in Switzerland and Roskilde in Denmark. The rural areas are Arlesheim in Switzerland and North Rhine-Westphalia in Germany.

Freiburg im Breisgau (Germany)

Freiburg is a city in southern Germany with a population of 240,000. It has a strong reputation as a 'green' city, with large and successful solar energy and wind components in its energy production. It is a European centre for photovoltaic (PV) research, development and manufacturing employing 10,000 people (Stadt Freiburg, 2010). It has clear strategies in place to deal with climate change, air pollution and energy-efficient housing and has a local law requiring all new residential building to operate to the 'Passivhaus' standard of energy use (Passivhaus Institut, 2011). This standard results in very low energy consumption levels per square metre of living space, and this is discussed in more detail in Chapter 5.

Climate change policy is a hugely important political priority in Freiburg. By 2009, on a 1992 base Freiburg had reduced per capita CO_2 emissions by 25.6 per cent (Stadt Freiburg, 2011).

Freiburg has an international reputation for its successful sustainable transport system (Whitelegg, 2011a). Walking and cycling around Freiburg make a very strong impression on the senses. Walking accounts for 24 per cent of all trips every day, cycling 28 per cent, public transport 20 per cent and the car 28 per cent (Stadt Freiburg, 2010). There is very little congestion. The streets are relatively calm, with large numbers of pedestrians and cyclists; the speed of the traffic, where it is allowed, is below 20 mph; there is a profusion of small retail outlets, cafés and restaurants and an absence of large supermarkets with large car parks. The streets convey a strong sense of calmness, smooth-flowing traffic, and high standards of design of footways, bike paths, tree planting and cleanliness, and the whole experience generates feelings of satisfaction and pleasure in sampling the delights of an urban environment. Moving around by any mode of transport could not be easier. Quiet trams make their way through city centre streets and out to the suburbs and integrate seamlessly with buses. The main railway station is an integrated transport hub with direct access to buses, a major tram stop that is located at the southern end of the platforms, and a cycling centre with parking for 1,000 bikes, repair facilities and public transport information. Public transport fares are reasonable, and there are generous offers for commuters and families to make the cost of travel affordable as well as enjoyable. Visitors staying in the hotels of Freiburg are given a totally free-of-charge travel pass for all forms of public transport within a large region around Freiburg for the duration of their stay. The trams and buses are clean and tidy; the systems are legible and easy to use and in a quiet, non-intrusive manner send the very strong message that car use is not really necessary or desirable when choices and experiences are so rich without a car.

The Freiburg experience

After attending a splendid concert in an old church in the centre of Freiburg which ended at 9.30 p.m. we decided to go for a meal and then to make our way back home to a small village about 25 kilometres from Freiburg (Staufen im Breisgau). We do not have a car. We walked through very pleasant traffic-free streets to the main Freiburg railway station, caught a modern, warm, comfortable double-deck train that was serving a large number of towns and villages on the way to Basel in Switzerland, and got off at Bad Krozingen at 10.45 p.m. Unfortunately the last train and last bus from Bad Krozingen to Staufen had left, but whilst eating a meal in Freiburg we had phoned the Anrufsammeltaxi (AST) and requested a pick-up at Bad Krozingen. The AST is part of the overall public transport offer provided by the regional public transport company and is available for a very small charge to any holder of a public transport ticket who needs to complete a journey when buses or trains have stopped running. On arrival at Bad Krozingen the taxi was there, we paid the driver €4, and he took us to our front door in Staufen. A wonderful evening, a perfect journey and no hint of rural isolation or inaccessibility, and not having a car is not in any way an obstacle to the enjoyment of Freiburg's rich cultural opportunities.

Basel (Switzerland)

Basel has a population of 166,173. It is a border city with Germany and France and is the headquarters of several multinational companies. In Basel the Freiburg sense of calm, integration and a highly attractive public realm is repeated. There is very little, if any, traffic congestion. Trams move quietly through attractive streets and cross the River Rhine to connect city centre and suburbs. Buses, trams and trains link with each other to produce a highly integrated system that works so well that no one talks about integration as a policy objective. It just exists. The main railway station gives direct access to buses and trams in the square directly in front of the station. Modal split statistics (EPOMM, 2011) reveal a high level of sustainability in transport choices based on high-quality alternatives. Of all trips every day, 24 per cent are on foot, 17 per cent by bicycle, 32 per cent by public transport and 27 per cent by car. The streets have wide pavements, easy crossing facilities for pedestrians and a high standard of public realm in terms of tree planting, attractive building frontages, generous squares and numerous pavement cafés.

Roskilde (Denmark)

Roskilde has a population of approximately 47,000. It served as the capital of Denmark in the Middle Ages and is the burial place of Danish monarchs. Today it is a small market town but with very fine public spaces, cycling facilities, public transport and train connections to Copenhagen, which is about 30 kilometres from Roskilde. Roskilde does not have trams, but main bus routes are directly accessible in front of the railway station and serve an extensive suburban and rural area around Roskilde. Roskilde University has its own railway station (Trekroner) on the line to Copenhagen. The Basel and Freiburg picture is once again repeated. Excellent cycling facilities dominate the geography of the urban area, giving a quality of cycling that is one of the best in Europe and makes the choice of a bike for all ages and both genders a natural one. High levels of walking and cycling in attractive streets backed up by high-quality public transport give the town a rich texture of transport choices, high levels of accessibility, high levels of safety and comfort for the non-motorised modes and high levels of air quality. Once again the main impact of experiencing Roskilde lies in the tempo or cadence of the place. It is calm, friendly, free of dense amounts of polluting traffic and free of rapidly accelerating and decelerating vehicles.

All three cities and urban areas have created an exceptionally high quality of life for residents and visitors alike and one that goes far beyond transport, air quality, street design and accessibility. The highly visible clues of quality and excellence are quite naturally to be found in the public realm, the street, the transport systems and feelings of calm, but these are the outward signs of inner excellence that embraces education, provision for the elderly and the young, waste minimisation and recycling and many other characteristics of a civilised society delivering unequivocal high quality to its citizens.

This quality is not limited to the atmosphere, services and facilities available to urban dwellers. Rural dwellers are particularly well served by a whole raft of public services and attention to detail in Denmark, Germany, Sweden and Switzerland, and the idea that this might not be the case or that there is a rural 'problem' is not recognised in any of these four countries.

Arlesheim (Switzerland)

Arlesheim in Switzerland is a large village (*Dorf*) of 8,900 people. It has a tram service to the main railway station in Basel (Basel SBB), which takes 25 minutes. The first tram of the day is at 4.55 a.m., and the last tram of the day is at 12.48 a.m. For most of the day the trams run at 15-minute intervals.

Gempen is a small village near Arlesheim with a population of 738. It has a regular bus service from the post office (it even has a post office), which connects with rail services directly at platform level at Dornach. The journey from Gempen to Basel SBB, including the connection at Dornach, takes 26 minutes. The first bus of the day from Gempen is at 5.24 a.m., and the last bus is at 10.24 p.m.

There is no debate in Gempen or Arlesheim about a 'rural transport problem'. There is no rural transport problem.

North Rhine-Westphalia (NRW)

Sloman (2003) illustrates her account of what rural transport 'should be like' with examples from several parts of Europe, including NRW. She sets out a very clear picture and policy agenda: 'Its vision [the report] is of a future in which an interconnecting web of train services, buses, door-to-door buses, safe cycle routes, and, when needed, cars enables people to make journeys in rural areas efficiently at reasonable cost and without damaging the very thing that makes the countryside special' (p. 7).

Sloman singles out the Duerener Kreisbahn (country railway) in NRW as a particularly good example of a high-quality rural railway service connecting 'cheek to cheek' with bus services. New track and new trains on this rural railway line and the introduction of an hourly service have led to a huge increase in passenger numbers.

NRW is Germany's largest state (*Land*) with a population of 16 million. Whilst well known for its successes in reinventing towns and cities that used to rely on coal and steel, including Dortmund, Essen and Bochum, the state has also delivered over 50 years of consistent year-on-year investment in sustainable transport modes and rural transport infrastructure. Rural areas are well served by modernised rural railway lines and integrated bus services but also by the innovative 'Citizens' Bus' or 'Buerger Bus'. This is a community minibus scheme funded by the state government with the objective of providing over 60 communities with minibuses and the infrastructure needed by the community to develop its own timetabled minibus services to link in with existing bus routes, destinations that matter to local residents, and rail services. The Citizens' Bus is complemented by the Anrufsammeltaxi (AST) system (Sloman, 2003: 30). The AST is a taxi that can be requested by a phone call to meet a bus or a train when a public transport journey is no longer possible because the last service has departed. A small charge is made, and the availability of the AST enables complete reliance on public transport even late into the evenings. Once again, in rural parts of NRW there is no such thing as a rural transport problem.

Successful cities

In 2010 Mercer (Mercer Consulting, 2010) produced a ranking of 221 world cities. The results do not reveal high rankings for UK cities:

> Europe has 16 cities amongst the world's top 25 cities for quality of living. Vienna retains the highest ranking both for the region and globally and is again followed by Zurich (2), Geneva (3) and Düsseldorf (6). The lowest-ranking Western European cities are Leipzig (64) and Athens (75). In the UK, London is the highest-ranking city at 39, followed by newcomer to the list Aberdeen (53), Birmingham (55), Glasgow (57) and Belfast (63).
>
> In the eco-city index, Nordic cities fare particularly well with Helsinki (3) the highest-ranked in the region, followed by Copenhagen (8) and Oslo in joint ninth place with Stockholm. 'Nordic cities do particularly well because the modern parts of most of them have been designed with potential environmental impacts in mind,' said Mr Parakatil. Aberdeen (19) is the highest-ranking UK eco-city, followed by Belfast (30), Glasgow (47), London (63) and Birmingham (64).

Mercer said that a high-ranking eco-city optimised its use of renewable energy sources and generated the lowest possible quantity of pollution (air, water, noise, etc.). The researchers added:

> A city's eco-status or attitude toward sustainability can have significant impact on the quality of living of its inhabitants. As a consequence these are also pertinent issues for companies that send employees and their families on long-term assignments abroad, especially considering the vast majority of expatriates are relocated to urban areas.

The emphasis on German-speaking cities and Scandinavian cities will be reflected in subsequent chapters in this book, as these cities and countries perform well by comparison with the UK.

UK cities

UK cities have many admirable qualities, and it is important to try to understand why they do not achieve high rankings in international surveys. We will explore this further by focusing on Liverpool. Liverpool is chosen because it is particularly well documented (Health Is Wealth Commission, 2008), has a major initiative under way to boost its fortunes and attractiveness (Liverpool Vision, 2009), and in mid-2011 saw the appointment, by the prime minister, of Michael Heseltine in a special role to support and promote the economic and social revival of this city.

The Liverpool city region is one of the most exciting, creative, dynamic, culturally rich, architecturally significant and physically attractive city regions in the UK. It is also a city region with a number of problems. A recent report from the Centre for Cities (2008) expressed confidence in the importance of city regions as engines of growth and development for the UK economy as a whole and described Liverpool's achievements as follows:

- Liverpool has added significant numbers of new jobs (61,200 jobs added in the period 1995–2005).
- Liverpool was ranked number one in the national city earnings growth rate in the period 2002–06.

The same report identifies a number of problems and challenges:

- Liverpool is the third most unequal city in the UK (the gap between wealthy and not-so-wealthy residents is very large).
- Twenty-three per cent of working-age adults in Liverpool have no qualifications.
- Liverpool displayed the steepest population decline in a four-city comparison (Newcastle, Sunderland, Stoke and Liverpool). There was a decline of 26,600 in the period 1996–2006, described as losing 'the most people'.
- Liverpool is described as a 'less successful untapped potential' city.
- Liverpool's employment rate is 65.7 per cent (2006 data). This is ranked at 58 out of 60, with 60 being the bottom of the league table.
- Liverpool has the highest percentage of those claiming benefits (26 per cent).
- Liverpool, Hull, Sunderland and Blackburn are listed as 'most deprived'.
- Over 60 per cent of people drive to work in Liverpool compared to 40 per cent in the economically successful cities of Oxford and Cambridge.

The World Health Organization (WHO, 2008) has made the connection between many aspects of ordinary everyday life and health outcomes and identified the importance of high-quality housing, the built environment and transport choices in removing health inequalities and improving the health of the population as a whole:

The daily conditions in which people live have a strong influence on health equity. Access to quality housing and shelter and clean water and sanitation are human rights and basic needs for healthy living. Growing car dependence, land use change to facilitate car use, and increased inconvenience of non-motorized modes of travel, have knock-on effects on local air quality, greenhouse gas emission, and physical inactivity. The planning and design of urban environments has a major impact on health equity through its influence on behaviour and safety.

(WHO, 2008: 6)

The Liverpool city region is a relatively poor performer in rankings of the health of its population. This poor performance has persisted over two decades of traditional economic development and suggests that wider issues around the built environment, cycles of deprivation and poverty, and low levels of spending on early-years education have all conspired to define Liverpool as a place with poor health, high dependence on state benefits, poverty and unemployment. The Centre for Cities in a report (Shaheen, 2008) on cities and worklessness said: 'If cities like Liverpool continue to have a quarter of their population on benefits both the city and the national economy will suffer.'

In the North West Public Health Observatory 2011 Health Profiles (NWPHO, 2011) Liverpool is shown to have a large number of serious health problems. These are summarised in Figure 1.1, which shows the health performance of the city. Of the 32 categories of health outcomes, 21 are reported as significantly worse than the England average.

The report *Health Is Wealth* from the Liverpool city region's Health Is Wealth Commission (2008: 55) concluded that health in the city region was poor: 'People live shorter, unhealthier lives, there are higher levels of premature death from preventable causes and higher proportions of residents claiming incapacity benefits due to ill health or disability than elsewhere.'

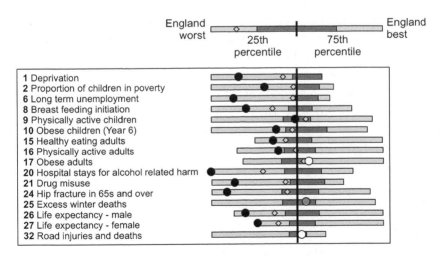

Figure 1.1 A summary of health outcomes in Liverpool (2011)

A more rigorous assessment of the performance of European cities (European Commission, 2007) has characterised Liverpool as a 'transformation pole' and compared its economic performance with other transformation poles in the EU.

A 'transformation pole' is a city that has seen industrial decline and is now working hard to reinvent itself with new strategies and initiatives. Table 3.7 of this European Commission report (p. 66) compares all the 'transformation poles' in the EU in terms of GDP per capita. Liverpool is the lowest of all UK cities in this list at 85 (against an EU average of 100). This can be compared with the German city region of Bremen with a nearby port and a population of 540,950, which has a GDP per capita of 128. The UK rankings together with those of four German cities are shown in Table 1.3.

UK cities perform less well than comparable German cities on the GDP per capita indicator. Dortmund, Bochum and Essen have all experienced serious industrial decline and loss of basic industries and have all received substantial new investment in housing, knowledge-based industries, parks and green spaces, and transport. The national picture in Germany is characterised by better outcomes for child poverty, the elderly, the built environment and public transport funding, and these dimensions are discussed in more detail in later chapters. Transport systems are not the sole determinant of economic success at city spatial scales, but the vast majority of EU cities with relatively high GDP per capita figures have transport systems that are better funded and more integrated and operate as a coherent, integrated whole, which is not the case in the UK.

The European Commission report concludes with some observations on the UK and comparisons with other EU member states. The main points are:

- Many of Europe's high performers (in terms of GDP per capita) are in Denmark, Sweden, Finland, the Netherlands and the western parts of Germany.
- The performance of a number of English cities is disappointing.

Table 1.3 GDP per capita for a selection of EU cities

	GDP per capita
Belfast	119
Birmingham	117
Cardiff	101
Glasgow	115
Leeds	143
Liverpool	**85**
Manchester	113
Newcastle	109
Bremen	128
Dortmund	119
Bochum	124
Essen	141

Source: European Commission (2007, table 3.7).

Note: The EU city average GDP per capita is set at 100.

• Cities in Italy, the UK and Belgium feature in both the strongest and the weakest categories.

Reinventing cities

The former mayor of New York Rudolph Giuliani established a clear link between quality of life and environment and economic progress. In his book *Leadership* (Giuliani, 2002) he says: 'Nearly all my principal concerns – quality of life, economic redevelopment, child protection, even crime reduction – were enhanced by well-tended, safe, beautiful parks. During the 8 years of my administration, New York City gained 2038 acres of new parkland' (p. 124).

There is now a global trend in the direction of reinventing cities so that they celebrate parks, open spaces, walking, cycling and public transport, and whilst the car is still welcome the clear direction of travel is towards reduced vehicle numbers and a much more pleasant living and working environment dominated by people, public spaces and non-motorised transport. Jan Gehl, a Danish architect based in Copenhagen, is in the vanguard of this new approach to city life. Summarising key aspects of his work Gehl says:

> In January 2007 Gehl Architects was invited to cast a critical look at how the public spaces in Sydney are performing in terms of public life. The findings are presented in this report and in an additional public life data part. The analysis performed pointed towards a city which is choking in vehicular traffic and where there is no balance between the various transport modes. Pedestrians and cyclists are consequently at the bottom of the agenda and as a result conditions are quite poor for the people choosing the most sustainable transport modes, discouraging some and excluding others.
>
> An equally problematic consequence is the fact that there are a number of problems in relation to the visual environment and the general lack of celebration of the waterfront. Thus the extra-ordinary physical qualities are not cherished and the city is gradually being downgraded.
>
> Looking to other cities in the world it is evident that change is happening in a number of cities. Thus Melbourne, Portland in the US and Lyon in France are remarkable examples of cities which have radically transformed. Common for all of them is a movement towards a more balanced traffic system, a strong focus at public space and an understanding of how a high quality public realm can invite more people to use the city in a variety of ways.
>
> Changing the current situation in Sydney demands a change of mindset. A more holistic approach needs to be used where traffic planning and public space planning are thought of as a whole. Visions need to be formulated looking at what ought to be achieved to celebrate Sydney as a world class city. Strategies then need to be put in place to gradually change the current course and deal with how the visions can be achieved on practical terms. Looking at practicalities first and then formulating visions will set the bar too low.

Sydney will no doubt change dramatically during the coming years. The spirit is there, the knowledge is there and the potential is there. How the process and the end result will be is still to be seen.

(Gehl Architects, 2007)

These comments apply with equal force to Liverpool. Liverpool has as many positive attributes as does Sydney, but has suffered from severe deterioration in its public realm and lack of attention to the importance of green space and parks, and it has suffered more than most cities from national policies that have embedded poverty and cycles of deprivation in the psyche of this city through regressive spending decisions.

Liverpool is a microcosm of what has gone wrong in UK cities. Its cultural attributes and heritage are first-class and are not outranked by those cities identified earlier in this chapter that come out well in international rankings, for example Stockholm, Copenhagen and Vienna. Its listed buildings, iconic buildings, fine waterfront and place distinctiveness stand comparison with any European city. It fails on the practicalities around the quality of the public realm, environmental quality and the degree to which it is dominated by vehicular traffic. It is difficult and unpleasant to walk and cycle around Liverpool, and decades of local authority prioritisation have given Liverpool ugly car parks, wide roads that are difficult to cross and a lack of permeability for the pedestrian and the cyclist. It feels unpleasant. Quiet squares in the orbit of fine buildings are rare. The exceptionally fine waterfront is cut off by an ugly, noisy and dirty road, and moving around is as unpleasant as remaining in one place with the intention of enjoying the architectural and cultural heritage. These city attributes have been exceptionally well summarised by Jan Gehl and others in a recent report (Institute for Transportation and Development Policy, 2010). The report describes in vivid detail what is wrong with a car-dominated city and how easy it is to put it 'right'. Gehl's report for the Queensland government on Brisbane (Gehl Architects, 2008) is very relevant indeed to all UK cities searching for excellence and debating ways of reinventing themselves. The reinvention that Gehl recommends is system-wide place transformation to prioritise the public realm, walking, cycling and permeability and the significant downgrading of car-centric thinking, planning and spending. There are no technical, organisational or financial problems associated with his recommended paradigm shift in city planning. The problem lies in the heads of those senior people in charge of city planning who are terrified of choosing system-wide place quality thinking and retreat into a car-centric model of 1960s economic growth with all its place-destroying consequences and prioritising of the sterile.

The picture that emerges from this brief exploration of excellent places and a comparison with Liverpool does not paint a flattering picture of the UK or of quality of life in its cities. There is clear evidence of systemic failure to deliver high-quality outcomes for all UK citizens. A nation with high levels of child poverty, low levels of participation in employment, education and training, low levels of use of sustainable means of transport and low levels of economic performance of its city regions is a nation that is failing to engage with a high-quality twenty-first-century place agenda. This does not mean that the UK is a failing state or a 'basket case', but it does mean that it is letting down millions of its citizens and missing significant opportunities to redirect policies, focus on high-quality outcomes and deliver social, economic and quality-of-life improvements. Nor does it mean that Liverpool is a place to be avoided or a place that is so drenched in problems that it is irredeemable. It means that there is something out of focus and not quite right in the overall process of thinking, willing and doing in the UK, and the fact that there is evidence of better outcomes elsewhere should ring alarm bells. The remainder of this book is about the detail of sorting out how we create place excellence in the UK, how to get things into focus and how to deliver an absolute, no-excuses, high-quality commitment to better outcomes.

2　You can't compare us with them

Explaining differences between places is not easy. In the nineteenth and early twentieth centuries geographers embraced environmental determinism to assist the business of explanation. If a group of people or a nation lived in a slightly cool, ever-changing climate and in a place with a challenging environment, for example a mountainous area, then they would develop great skills and ingenuity and be a more successful 'people' than those without these conditions. This concept lost ground in the first two to three decades of the twentieth century and was replaced by 'possibilism', which argued that there were many possible routes that could be taken for the development of a people or a region and the options were not limited by the environment. These early experiments with explanation have lost favour, but we still struggle with how to explain the huge economic success of Hamburg (for example) and the relatively poor performance of Liverpool when compared with Hamburg (Whitelegg, 2009a). Hamburg has a GDP per capita of 158, when the average for the EU is standardised at 100 and Liverpool's performance is 85. It is of more than curiosity value to explore the reasons why this difference should exist, if only to steal some good ideas from Hamburg and 'do' the whole regeneration, urban revival, reinvention strategy in a different way with the intention of closing the gap with Hamburg.

It is, of course, possible that there is nothing to learn from Hamburg and things are so different between Hamburg and Liverpool that it would be a huge waste of time to try to learn. This view is rejected in this book. There is a curious irony in debates around learning from elsewhere (benchmarking) in the private sector and the public policy realm. A large IT corporation, pharmaceutical company or logistics organisation will search intensively and constantly for any good ideas from anywhere. If there is a smidgeon of evidence that these good ideas could reduce costs, improve profits, open new markets, steal a march on competitors, get the upper hand in Asia and so on, they will be adopted and implemented on the kind of time scale that local and central government cannot match. Any corporate executive who denied the value of this process would not be employed for very long. Nor would the business last for very long. In the public policy sector this model is not used, and the hundreds of examples of city twinning, for example Freiburg (Germany) with Guildford or Lancaster with Aalborg (Denmark), very rarely go beyond an exchange of dignitaries and civic receptions.

Many research projects on transport systems and outcomes in mainland Europe have shown that the outcomes in mainland Europe are much better than in the UK (Pucher *et al.*, 2010b; Sloman, 2003). These findings have been presented to ministers and key decision takers, but the direction of travel in the UK remains fixed on emphasising, perpetuating and justifying the status quo, which often equates with poor performance. Even within the UK there is very little evidence of learning. The growth of bus use in London over the last few years sits alongside the decline of bus use in cities outside London. One of these situations is a deregulated free-for-all and receives far less funding than the other. Success in London is closely associated with a degree of regulation and additional resourcing, but this has not leaked across to Manchester, Leeds, Liverpool or Newcastle, and the absence of a coordinated approach to public transport provision in these 'provincial' cities is a major obstacle to creating the high-quality systems that are taken for granted in Basel, Vienna or Freiburg. To the person on the Clapham omnibus it looks as though there is a block on learning and a rule against benchmarking. It very much looks as though we do not wish to see good ideas widely adopted. There is a block on the diffusion of innovation.

The first stage of explanation is to be very clear about the evidence, the data and the facts on what we are trying to explain. This is the subject of Chapters 3–8 of this book, and the objective is to present and discuss the case that has to be answered. Chapters 9–11 turn to explanation and how we might begin to change things to promote quality of life and place excellence.

Before moving on to detailed evidence we need to be very clear about the conceptual and methodological basis on which this book is constructed. The fact that there are substantial international differences in outcomes that matter to citizens is self-evidently true and dealt with in the next six chapters. What is not yet clear is whether or not these differences can be interrogated to inform new ways of doing things or are simply manifestations of 'cultural differences'. The references to cultural differences is usually associated with an underlying view that whilst they may be present and interesting they should really be categorised in the same way as an Italian fascination with opera or a Spanish love of tapas or a German liking for the music of Wagner or an English love of cricket and rugby union. These are cultural differences, and they sit there and they are interesting, but they are not part of a public policy debate about how we can 'up our game' in the UK and improve the quality of the built environment, health or the way we provide for children and the elderly.

This is not a new problem, and we can gain some understanding from previous attempts to look at international variations and deal with explanations. We can then locate the approach adopted in this book on the significance of international variation and the degree to which this variation can be used to stimulate new approaches to long-standing problems in the UK. There is a large literature on international variations in outcomes, and most of the studies can be located on a 'variation–explanation continuum'. This continuum has at one extreme those studies that describe the variation and do not attempt any explanation at all. At the opposite extreme, there are very thoughtful reviews of international variation followed by an attempt to explain the variation and associated with an attempt to identify policies and interventions that will bring about an improvement in outcomes. This book attempts to locate itself towards this extreme, with as much explanation as can be supported by the evidence and with as much policy discussion and suggestions for new direction in policy as can be supported by the outcomes in different countries.

At the purely descriptive end of this variation–explanation continuum we have the example of a large European study of anti-social behaviour and how it is perceived and where it happens (ADT Europe, 2006). The authors concluded: 'This survey has provided some fascinating insights into the public perception of anti-social behaviour across Europe; it provides food for thought.'

This lack of explanation is very disappointing. Anti-social behaviour is a huge problem for many citizens, and it varies a great deal across Europe. It costs a great deal of money to police and to put right (e.g. removing graffiti, repairing street furniture, bus stops and railway equipment), and it leads to self-imposed isolation and consequent health damage, as many elderly citizens are afraid to leave their homes after dark. From a public policy perspective we need to know if any EU country is sorting this out with some flair and ingenuity and inspect the interventions to see if they can be applied in the UK. This is not done in this study.

The same study reports that in Germany 60 per cent of those questioned would definitely or probably intervene to challenge a group of 14-year-old boys who were vandalising a bus stop. The UK result was 30 per cent. This finding cries out for explanation. Why are Germans twice as likely to intervene when compared with UK citizens? The authors are silent on this question.

The anti-social behaviour study has a degree of resonance with a study of children's independent mobility carried out in Germany and the UK in 1989 (Hillman *et al.*, 1990). This study had its origins in earlier work carried out by Mayer Hillman on the degree to which children were able to move around independently (i.e. without an adult being present) and the erosion of this independent mobility in the period 1970–90. The study found that German children had more independent mobility than an English peer group, and this was carefully measured and quantified and was then discussed. The authors concluded that German children had more independent mobility and freedom because there was a higher level of mutual surveillance in the German case studies (more people were using streets, buses, trams, etc.) and more people were willing to take an interest in what was going on around them. This is very close to the anti-social behaviour observation reported above, but with an attempt to explain what had been observed. These higher levels of street use and surveillance were in turn prevalent because of higher levels of investment in the public realm (wider pavements, safer streets, extensive 20 mph enforced speed limits) and higher levels of investment in buses, trams and local trains. The environment in which children moved around was of higher quality than in the UK and was part of a virtuous cycle of consequences. More people used the public realm because it was safer and attractive, and more people felt even safer because more people were around. Parents then felt more confident they could 'release' their children, and more children were able to associate with each other and gain confidence in their ability to negotiate an urban environment and interact with others in a way simply not possible in a car.

More recently, in 2010, this study was updated (Shaw *et al.*, 2012) with a repeat of the earlier work on child freedom and mobility in both Germany and England. In the 2010 survey the differences between Germany and England were still pronounced. One of the measures used to describe child freedoms was the percentage of children of different ages in the two countries allowed to travel home from school independently:

- For 7-year-olds it was 5 per cent of English children and 50 per cent of German children.
- For 9-year-olds it was 20 per cent of English children and 85 per cent of German children.
- For 12-year-olds it was 82 per cent of English children and 98 per cent of German children.

In 1990 German children had more independent mobility than English children, and that was still the same in 2010, though German levels had reduced in the 20-year period separating the two surveys. The reason for the German levels of independent mobility remain the same. The quality of the built environment and the positive signals from that environment to both parents and children are strong enough to create a 'culture' that encourages independent mobility. In England this is not the case, and worried parents take their children to school by car far more than in any other EU country.

Moving further along the variation–explanation continuum there are a number of systematic, evidence-based cross-national studies that set out to explain variations by reference to public policy interventions that are associated with those variable outcomes. Pucher *et al.* (2010b) carried out a systematic survey of 139 studies into international variations in cycling levels and looked in more detail at 14 case studies. They concluded that increases in cycling levels on the scale of those achieved in Copenhagen, Freiburg, Berlin and Groningen had been achieved by detailed, systematic, integrated and coordinated efforts to provide high-quality cycling infrastructure and create a land use system more conducive to cycling and by restraining car use. Interestingly all the countries involved had seen a decline in cycling with the advent of large-scale motorisation in the 1950s and 1960s but then responded to public policy interventions designed to halt the decline of cycling and give priority to cycling in the whole process of urban and transport planning. The fact that cycling had been in decline and this decline was then reversed to give us some very impressive best practice results goes a long way to refute the reductionist argument that cycling in Denmark and the Netherlands is something to do with 'culture' and hence is not replicable in the UK. More detailed information on policy interventions in these countries can be found in Pucher and Buehler (2007), and there is a detailed comparison of New York, London, Paris and Tokyo in Pucher and Buehler (2012) identifying the factors that produce high rates of cycling.

In another contribution to the discussion of international, US state and city variation and expansion Pucher *et al.* (2010a) studied 14 countries, all 50 US states and 47 of the 50 largest US cities to explain the variations in obesity levels by reference to measures of physical activity (cycling and walking). The conclusions are of considerable relevance to public health and transport planning and show that measures that encourage active travel are associated with lower levels of obesity. This study demonstrates the power of national and international comparisons to identify relationships that can then be converted into policy interventions to produce the outcomes that are already identifiable in policy but not yet achieved in reality. All EU countries actively want to reduce obesity levels, and this study shows how that can be done.

At the very ambitious end of the comparison spectrum, but sadly with very little explanation, is a European Commission study of current social and economic conditions in 258 cities in the 27 EU member states covering over 300 variables (European Commission, 2007). The report is a valuable data compendium and graphic display medium but disappointingly avoids explanation and the possibility that this mass of data might actually be informative for public policy formulation. Intriguingly, and something returned to in Chapter 10, there is an 'index of city power', which raises the possibility that successful outcomes might be related to the administrative and constitutional powers available to deliver solutions and improve outcomes.

A study of obesity in the European region of the World Health Organization (WHO, 2007) is very clear indeed on comparison between countries on the prevalence of obesity and on the factors that contribute to raised prevalence. These include diet, sedentary lifestyles, lack of physical activity and the marketing of foods with a high salt, sugar and fat content. The study also emphasises the importance of 'obesogenic environments'. An obesogenic environment is one that through a combination of urban design, low densities, lack of access to green space, longer distances, and road traffic danger promotes lifestyle and behavioural choices that contribute to raised obesity prevalence. The 'most active' countries are the Netherlands and Denmark, and these also have the highest rates of cycling. The study recommends cross-sectoral work to change both transport and health policy to eliminate obesogenic environments and encourage more physical activity, including walking and cycling. This is in addition to recommendations about healthy diets. The WHO study actively uses international comparisons to identify factors that contribute to reducing obesity prevalence and then uses this information to frame recommendations for all 57 countries in the European region. This is at the extreme 'explanation-rich' end of the continuum, and that is where this book is located. This book will follow the WHO model in the way it interrogates international comparative data on quality-of-life factors and uses this information to suggest ways of improving outcomes in the UK.

The WHO obesity report fully engages with policy, especially those policies that appear to produce results in terms of reducing the scale of the problem. It identifies the key components of the national obesity strategies and comments on their effectiveness. There appears to be no systematic cross-national study of policy effectiveness in terms of a quantifiable impact (e.g. policy X is likely to reduce obesity prevalence in group Y by Z per cent), but the pointers to what should be done to sharpen a national obesity strategy are very clear indeed. As a result of the WHO study there are no excuses for not getting on with the job of reducing obesity utilising clearly identified policies and interventions that deal with diet, awareness raising, actions in workplaces and schools, and changes in transport policy and the built environment to promote walking and cycling.

Cities, regions and nations

For over 100 years geographers have worried about scale. The answers to many questions depend on scale. There are important differences between countries on things like obesity prevalence, child poverty, inequality and health, but there are also differences between cities that sit 'Russian doll'-like within the national-level variations, and even more variations within a given city. Glasgow is frequently reported as a very unhealthy place (NHS, 2008), but any Glaswegian knows that if you move two or three kilometres across the city you can find areas of excellent health, affluence and life expectancy that are equal to any in the well-endowed urban areas of Surrey or Cheshire, areas of the UK frequently cited as very wealthy and very healthy. Glasgow reports differences in life expectancy of 12 years between the most and the least affluent communities (Hanlon *et al.*, 2006) and this in turn reflects the nature of this city, which is extremely polarised in social and economic terms, with elevated inequalities on most quality-of-life indicators. The difference in life expectancy between Bridgeton and Dennistoun (less affluent) and Annies-land, Bearsden and Milngavie (affluent) is 15 years. At an even finer geographical scale (postcode level) the difference in male life expectancy between least and most affluent reaches 20 years (Hanlon *et al.*, 2006). These differences are greater than those between many countries. Whatever story national statistics are telling has very little relevance to daily experiences and life opportunities for significant numbers of Glaswegians, and a similar story can be told for Liverpool and Manchester, where inequalities also exist though not as severe as in Glasgow.

City-level comparisons frequently tell a different story to that to be found in national-level comparisons. At the national level Germany has lower levels of poverty than the UK, and yet in a European study of perceptions of quality of life in 75 EU cities (Eurobarometer, 2009) Glasgow and Dortmund reported similar levels of concern about poverty, with 77 per cent of Glasgow respondents reporting that they are concerned about poverty in the city compared to 79 per cent in Dortmund. Both cities are experiencing problems with poverty, joblessness and insecurity, both are in relatively wealthy countries, and both city-level reports disguise a huge amount of variation within the cities. The residents of Aplerbeck in Dortmund probably have far more in common with the residents of Bearsden in Glasgow than they have with their neighbours down the road. Problems of scale and complexity across 27 countries, hundreds of cities and hundreds of thousands of small areas within cities will not be solved in this book, but all sources of evidence relevant to improving the performance of UK administrative areas at any geographical scale will be used and conclusions moderated by the recognitions that scale really does matter.

Eighty per cent of EU citizens live in urban areas, so city-to-city comparisons are important in understanding whether or not the UK performs well or badly on defined outcomes and whether or not cities in other countries perform better. The European comparison of perceptions of quality of life reported above (Eurobarometer, 2009) paints a very clear picture of variation across 75 cities and includes Manchester, Belfast, Glasgow, Cardiff, Newcastle and London. For the purposes of this discussion, perceptions are very important indeed, even if so-called objective studies of reality paint a different picture.

For the purposes of this discussion just five out of 30 topics have been selected. The wording of the selected topics is the same wording as used in the Eurobarometer report based on interviews across Europe asking respondents to reply whether they agree, strongly agree, disagree and so on with a number of statements. The statements are:

Q1 It is easy to find a job in your city.
Q2 Do you feel safe in your city?
Q3 The city is clean.
Q4 Degree of satisfaction with public spaces including pedestrian areas.
Q5 Frequency of use of public transport.

Table 2.1 shows for each question the 10 'top' cities, for example the 10 top cities reporting that it is easy to find a job or that the city is clean and so on. The list is in descending order, so the first named is the 'best' down to the city ranked 10 out of 75.

These five topics cover a wide range of economic, social, environment and quality-of-life attributes, and UK cities are poorly represented in the top 10. The selection of the top 10 is of course arbitrary, but it is not unreasonable to expect the top 10 to give a rough indication of which cities are performing well. Fifty cities are mentioned in Table 2.1 (including multiple references to the same city), and four of the 50 listings are UK cities. This includes Cardiff and Newcastle on the question about satisfaction with public spaces, Newcastle on the clean city question and London on the frequency of using public transport.

Table 2.1 Rankings from Eurobarometer study of perceptions of quality of life in EU cities

	Q1	Q2	Q3	Q4	Q5
1	Rotterdam	Oviedo	Oviedo	Oviedo	Paris
2	Amsterdam	Groningen	Piatra Neamt	Munich	London
3	Hamburg	Aalborg	Luxembourg	Groningen	Prague
4	Stockholm	Oulu	Munich	Malmo	Stockholm
5	Munich	Munich	Bialystok	Cardiff	Budapest
6	Groningen	Piatra Neamt	Vienna	Luxembourg	Helsinki
7	Antwerp	Luxembourg	Groningen	Rennes	Riga
8	Copenhagen	Bordeaux	Cluj-Napoca	Newcastle	Barcelona
9	Luxembourg	Copenhagen	Newcastle	Piatra Neamt	Madrid
10	Rennes	Helsinki	Braga	Kosice	Krakow

Source: Eurobarometer (2009).

If we look at individual UK cities across all 30 variables we find that Newcastle is mentioned 14 times in top 10 listings and Cardiff nine times, with Manchester and Glasgow attracting one mention each. These counts are out of a total of 300 possibilities for a listing. The absence of any UK city in the top 10 for the degree to which people can be trusted or the degree to which people feel safe in their city points to an unimpressive performance. Newcastle, which does better than any other UK city with 14 mentions, is not in the top 10 on these two variables.

It's the economy, stupid

Cities are increasingly described as engines of economic growth and as operating in an intensely competitive globalised environment. Economic success is expected to deal with large numbers of wider societal problems and outcomes including poverty, worklessness, welfare dependency and improved health. Whilst this is intuitively correct, Hanlon *et al.* (2006) have described a situation of persistent worklessness, inequality, poor health outcomes and social problems against a background of economic progress as Glasgow redefines itself as a retail, service and tourist economy. Economic success does not necessarily bring widespread social progress. This is also a theme in work on inequalities (Wilkinson and Pickett, 2009) and happiness (Layard, 2005).

Cities are frequently ranked in terms of economic performance (e.g. GDP per capita) and attractiveness to business (Cushman & Wakefield, 2011). One measure of attractiveness to business is summarised in Table 2.2.

Table 2.2 Best cities to locate a business today

Location	2011 rank	2010 rank	2011 score	2010 score	1990 rank
London	1	1	0.84	0.85	1
Paris	2	2	0.55	0.55	2
Frankfurt	3	3	0.32	0.36	3
Amsterdam	4	6	0.26	0.25	5
Berlin	5	7	0.26	0.24	15
Barcelona	6	5	0.25	0.27	11
Madrid	7	8	0.25	0.22	17
Brussels	8	4	0.25	0.29	4
Munich	9	9	0.19	0.22	12
Zurich	10	13	0.14	0.12	7
Geneva	11	14	0.12	0.12	8
Milan	12	11	0.12	0.13	9
Stockholm	13	16	0.12	0.11	19
Dusseldorf	14	10	0.11	0.14	6
Hamburg	15	15	0.11	0.11	14
Manchester	16	12	0.10	0.12	13
Lisbon	17	17	0.09	0.10	16
Birmingham	18	18	0.09	0.09	—
Lyon	19	19	0.08	0.09	18
Dublin	20	20	0.07	0.09	—

Source: Cushman & Wakefield (2011).

The Cushman & Wakefield (2011) ranking of 36 European cities puts London at number 1, Manchester at number 16, Birmingham at number 18, Leeds at 28, Glasgow at 30 and Edinburgh at 31. The overall ranking is intended to identify cities that are 'best to locate a business', and the final ranking is an amalgam of 12 components, including easy access to markets, availability of qualified staff, quality of telecommunications, transport links with other cities and internationally, value for money and availability of office space, languages spoken, ease of travelling around the city, business-friendly climate, quality of life for employees, and freedom from pollution.

London is clearly in the lead in rankings on easy access to markets, customers and clients, transport links with other cities and internationally, availability of qualified staff and the quality of telecommunications, and this produces its overall number 1 position in the ranking. Other UK cities do not do very well.

The quality of life for employees ranking (Table 2.3) has London, Edinburgh and Leeds in the top 20 but is dominated by Scandinavian, Northern European and Swiss cities, with Barcelona at number 1.

The Cushman & Wakefield rankings are determined by the responses of businesses and are intended to assist a business audience in making decisions on location and expansion. They represent another source of information on how we can define excellence and seek out best practice, and they also point very clearly towards the kinds of things that need to be done by city region and national governments to improve rankings and the attraction of a city for inward investment. The ability to attract inward investment is a key policy objective in all EU cities, and businesses themselves have set out a clear list of what they find attractive. In this sense the Cushman & Wakefield rankings and methodology are rich in explanation and point clearly to what needs to be done to populate the top 20 or 30 cities in the rankings with more UK examples. It is clear, for example, that quality of life and freedom from pollution are important, and we should inspect carefully the excellent performance of Stockholm, Copenhagen, Helsinki and Vienna to identify what makes these places special and then set out to replicate success in the UK. We will discuss in much more detail in later chapters the way in which many EU cities operate better internal transport systems and choices than the UK and spend more money on doing this than the UK, and this feeds directly into the business rankings based on the Cushman & Wakefield parameter 'ease of travelling around the city'. For each of the 12 dimensions of what makes cities attractive to businesses there are practical policy interventions that can be implemented in the UK to push cities higher up the rankings and make sure that cities currently not on the list will be on future lists.

The overall picture on national and city rankings and comparative surveys is that the UK does not perform well. Equally the underperformance leaves a great deal of scope for improvement and upgrading to best practice standards across the EU whether these are based on nation- or city-level survey results. In subsequent chapters we look in much more detail at six topic areas and identify best practice as well as those policies, interventions and measures that seem to work to ensure that citizens get the best possible results from government, governance and the

Table 2.3 Quality of life for employees

Location	2011 rank	2010 rank	2011 score	2010 score
Barcelona	1	1	1.08	1.08
Stockholm	2	3	0.91	0.71
Zurich	3	5	0.71	0.63
Geneva	4	9	0.69	0.56
Madrid	5	6	0.67	0.62
Munich	6	2	0.62	0.85
Copenhagen	7	7	0.56	0.59
Vienna	=8	=11	0.52	0.45
Paris	=8	4	0.52	0.64
London	10	10	0.46	0.52
Oslo	=11	=13	0.45	0.44
Edinburgh	=11	8	0.45	0.57
Amsterdam	13	17	0.44	0.37
Brussels	14	16	0.41	0.41
Hamburg	15	=11	0.39	0.45
Berlin	16	=13	0.38	0.44
Lisbon	17	=19	0.27	0.30
Leeds	=18	24	0.26	0.25
Rome	=18	=19	0.26	0.30
Lyon	=18	15	0.26	0.43
Dublin	21	=19	0.25	0.30
Milan	=22	25	0.23	0.24
Manchester	=22	23	0.23	0.26
Dusseldorf	=24	22	0.20	0.29
Helsinki	=24	18	0.20	0.33
Frankfurt	26	=26	0.17	0.18
Prague	27	28	0.15	0.17
Birmingham	28	=26	0.13	0.18
Glasgow	=29	31	0.11	0.09
Bratislava	=29	29	0.11	0.14
Istanbul	31	34	0.10	0.05
Warsaw	32	35	0.06	0.03
Budapest	33	32	0.05	0.08
Moscow	34	36	0.03	0.01
Bucharest	=35	33	0.02	0.07
Athens	=35	30	0.02	0.11

Source: Cushman & Wakefield (2011).

spending of public money. The objective is to exploit the rich evidence and experience of other places to accelerate a paradigm shift in policy development, spending and outcomes in the UK.

3   Children

Children's health and environment needs to be high on the political agenda. It is not possible to talk about health and quality of life without taking into consideration, and paying specific attention to the needs of children.

What is good for our children is good for society as a whole.

(EEA and WHO, 2002)

If we can create cities in which children are freer to playfully explore their environments, then we are likely to have overcome many of the obstacles to the creation of resilient cities.

(Freeman and Tranter, 2011)

Children are a key indicator of community health, quality of life and the success of a wide variety of governmental interventions across the whole spectrum of social, economic, built environment, transport and health policy areas. If children are experiencing symptoms of stress either in self-reported levels of mental health and happiness (UNICEF, 2007) or in objective measures of health status (Hanlon *et al.*, 2006) there is a clear case to be answered. The evidence currently available points to a failure to deal effectively with child welfare issues and problems in the UK. The evidence for the label 'failing' lies in the international comparisons. If some countries can do much better on child poverty or death and injury affecting children on the roads then this demonstrates that better outcomes are possible but they are not being achieved.

Child poverty is clearly one of the most important indicators of overall success or failure in the ability of governmental systems to provide a basic quality of life for children. High rates of childhood poverty are indicative of serious societal malfunction. They impose burdens on health and social support services that could be avoided or reduced if child poverty were eliminated, and they condemn millions of children to low educational attainment and low income in adult life.

In this chapter we first of all discuss child poverty and international comparative evidence on the relatively poor performance of the UK, and we then turn to three other dimensions of child welfare that add depth and context to our understanding of the lives of children in the UK.

Childhood poverty

The UK performs badly in childhood poverty terms (Figure 3.1).

An OECD report on child poverty in 34 countries (OECD, 2011a) has produced a ranking showing that the average across all countries was 12.6 per cent of children at risk of poverty, and the UK is 12.5 per cent (Figure 3.2). The ranking shows 22 countries with a better performance than the UK, with a clear grouping of Nordic countries coming out with the lowest rates of child poverty. Denmark

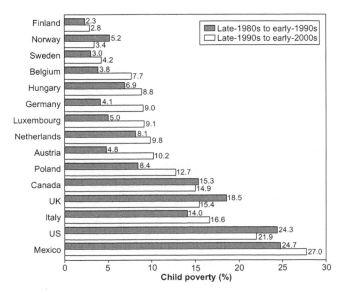

Figure 3.1 Percentage of children living in relative poverty

Source: UNICEF (2004).

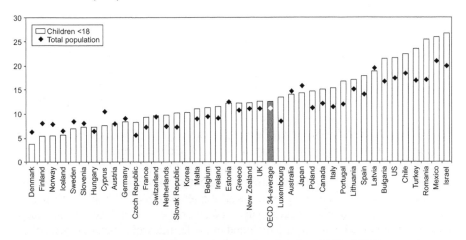

Figure 3.2 Poverty rates for children and the total population, 2008, OECD countries

at 3.7 per cent has set a high standard for achievement in this policy area, and if Denmark can achieve this so can other national jurisdictions.

The consequences of child poverty for wider social and economic welfare and feelings of safety and security in our communities are severe:

> Further the statistics presented in these pages also represent a threat to the quality of life of all citizens in those nations with high rates of child poverty. For while it is true that many poor families make sacrifices to give their children the best possible start in life, the broader picture shows that those who grow up in poverty are more likely to have learning difficulties, to drop out of school, to resort to drugs, to commit crimes, to be out of work, to become pregnant at too early an age, and to live lives that perpetuate poverty and disadvantage into succeeding generations. In other words many of the most serious problems facing today's advanced industrialised nations have roots in the denial and deprivation that mark the childhoods of so many of their future citizens.
>
> (UNICEF, 2000)

UNICEF (2000) presents a powerful argument supported by data to link child poverty with the proportion of households with children with no working adult. The UK at 20 per cent has the highest proportion of such households.

Countries with low child poverty rates are countries which in the main have a working adult member of the household. The UK has the highest percentage of households with children with no working adult. Sweden's success in combating child poverty appears to be highly correlated with its success in facilitating a high rate of working members in a household with children, which in turn is related to high rates of support for working mothers, child care and generous maternity and paternity leave arrangements.

The UK record on child poverty conveys a very strong message about the need to improve the quality of life of an important segment of the population of that country:

> A fifth of Britain's children lived in poverty in the 1990s, a rate more than twice as high as in France or the Netherlands and five times higher than in Norway or Sweden. And while child poverty has remained stable or risen only slightly in most industrial nations over the last 20 years, it tripled in Britain.
>
> (UNICEF, 2000)

Children are in many ways the 'canary in the cage' and provide clear signals if things are going wrong in society at large. A UNICEF report on children in 21 industrialised countries paints a gloomy picture of the condition and worries of children in the UK and the much better situation in other countries: 'The true measure of a nation's standing is how well it attends to its children – their health and safety, their material security, their education and socialisation, and their sense of being loved, valued, and included in the families and societies into which they were born' (UNICEF, 2007).

The UK comes out very near the bottom of all the measures used in this audit of how 'well children are doing'. When all 21 countries are ranked on the different criteria used to measure child welfare in its broadest sense the UK is:

- fourth from the bottom on material well-being;
- second from the bottom on 'relative income poverty';
- fifth from the bottom on education well-being;
- bottom on 'family and peer relationships';
- bottom on 'behaviour and risk taking of young people';
- bottom of subjective well-being.

The 'behaviour and risk taking' measure includes the degree to which young people in the UK smoke, consume alcohol, have sexual intercourse, use condoms on the last time of sexual intercourse and get pregnant.

The UK performs well on the indicator 'deaths from accidents and injuries per 100,000 people under the age of 19'. It is ranked at number 2, just below 'best in class'.

A European Union survey of poverty ranked all countries where data were available on the percentage of the population living in poverty (Eurostat, 2009). The definition of 'poverty threshold' was living on less than 60 per cent of the national median equivalised disposable income. The UK was placed in the group of poor performers, that is, those with high levels of poverty. This group had 19–21 per cent of its population living in poverty on this definition and included Lithuania, Latvia, Estonia, Greece, Spain, Italy, the UK and Romania. The best performers included Sweden, Iceland, the Netherlands and the Czech Republic and they reported 10–11 per cent poverty levels.

The Eurostat (2009) data reveal that when 29 countries are ranked on this EU poverty measure, where 1 is the best (Iceland) and 29 is the worst (Latvia), the UK is ranked at 23.

The UK's poor performance on child poverty is a serious cause for concern. The performance of Nordic countries at the opposite end of the spectrum indicates that child poverty can be substantially reduced through policies aimed at reducing worklessness, providing for child care and providing rich educational and social opportunities for children as part of a cultural shift away from an acceptance of welfare dependency. The correlation between child poverty and a range of other social problems including obesity, teenage pregnancy and drug addiction points to the need for a significant effort to reduce child poverty and one that is considerably greater than seen in the UK for several decades. It also needs to take into account the work of Wilkinson and Pickett (2009) on inequalities and the importance of reducing inequalities as a fundamental strategy for solving many interlinked social problems, especially poverty. The large-scale income inequalities in the UK described by Wilkinson and Pickett are also considered in the Eurostat (2009) report, which lists the countries of greatest inequality as 'southern countries and the UK' and those of lowest inequality as 'all Nordic countries'.

The report shows that if 29 countries are ranked from the 'best' performer, that is, the most equal society in the ranking, to the 'worst' performer, that is, the most unequal, with 1 = most equal and 29 = least equal, then the UK is ranked at 25. The UK is a very unequal society and one where inequalities are widening (Hutton, 2010).

In one UK city, Glasgow, the failure is stark, and has been thoroughly documented by Hanlon *et al.* (2006):

- 9,940 children have a 'problem alcohol use father';
- 3,360 children have a mother with drug misuse problems;
- 7,600 children have a 'problem drug use' father.

These categories are not mutually exclusive, and the authors conclude: 'In all more than 6,000 children in Glasgow are estimated to be living with at least one parent who has a substance misuse problem.' This is one in 20 children in Greater Glasgow. Glasgow's children are not very healthy. Twenty-one per cent of those born in 1998 are classified as obese or overweight, and 60 per cent of all five-year-olds have symptoms of dental decay.

The authors estimate that 100,000 children in the West of Scotland (an area bigger than Greater Glasgow) live in households where neither parent works. Worklessness is closely associated with poverty, and 18 per cent of children live in workless households in Scotland, a figure that rises to 58–64 per cent at small area (postcode) level in Glasgow itself (Hanlon *et al.*, 2006).

The Glasgow-level findings are in alignment with the UNICEF international comparisons and clearly show a systemic UK failure to deliver an overall health, employment and social infrastructure that can produce better outcomes for children.

Policy recommendations for the reduction of childhood poverty

Adopt the analysis and recommendations of Wilkinson and Pickett (2009) and reduce income inequalities.

Adopt the social welfare and child support spending policies of those countries with the lowest child poverty indicators (Iceland, Sweden, Denmark and the Netherlands).

Adopt the recommendations of Hutton (2010) on increasing spending from public funds on child care, pre-school nurturing facilities and high-quality educational provision in the primary years in areas of poverty and deprivation.

We now turn to three more dimensions of child welfare that illuminate child welfare considerations in the UK:

- road safety;
- children's independent mobility;
- obesity.

Road safety

Road traffic injuries are a major public health problem in the WHO European region and cause the premature deaths of some 120,000 people every year. They are the leading cause of death in children and young adults aged 5–29.

The evidence that road traffic injuries can be prevented is compelling.

(WHO, 2009)

The UK government Social Exclusion Unit (SEU, 2003) reported that children from lower social groups were at much greater risk than those from higher social groups from death and injury on the road: 'Children from the lowest social class are five times more likely to die in road accidents than those from the highest social class. More than one quarter of child pedestrian casualties happen in the most deprived 10 per cent of wards.'

The SEU report concludes that the British record on road safety as far as children are concerned is 'poor': 'In contrast with its relatively good record on road safety overall, Britain has a poor record compared to the rest of Europe for child pedestrian deaths; one study estimates that half of the difference could be explained by British children's greater exposure to busy roads' (SEU, 2003, para. 1.34).

In 2008 the House of Commons Select Committee on Transport investigated road safety and took evidence from a large number of witnesses (House of Commons, 2008). The Transport Select Committee specifically asked witnesses to comment on EU comparisons, and the majority of witnesses identified the excellent track records for road safety in the Netherlands, Denmark and Sweden and the fact that the UK used to be regarded as a high performer but was now falling back. The report tabulates international child pedestrian road crash fatalities as a fatality rate per 100,000 of the population group (aged 0–14). This is summarised in Table 3.1.

A number of countries are worse than the UK, including Ireland, Portugal, Austria and Greece, but it is clear that child pedestrians in the UK are subject to far worse conditions, circumstances and outcomes than obvious comparator countries such as France, Germany and Spain. It is also interesting that the UK performance is the same as the US performance.

The European Road Safety Observatory (ERSO, 2008) has tabulated actual numbers to illustrate the degree to which the UK is performing less well than

Table 3.1 International child pedestrian fatality rates per 100,000 population in this group

UK	0.56
US	0.56
Sweden	0.19
France	0.35
Germany	0.35
Switzerland	0.33
Denmark	0.29
Spain	0.43

Source: House of Commons (2008), extracts taken from table 4.

countries of comparable size. This is summarised in Table 3.2. The UK performance described in Table 3.2 is considerably worse than that of France, Spain and Italy, which also have large populations, and is worse than that of the Netherlands.

The comparison of road safety records and the actual amounts of walking and cycling was identified by the Cyclists' Touring Club (CTC) in its evidence to the House of Commons Select Committee (CTC, 2008):

> Although Britain's road safety record is in overall terms better than most EU countries, the picture is much more mixed when it comes to vulnerable road users. The UK has the highest proportion of pedestrian casualties of any of its EU peer countries but the third lowest level of walking. Britain's casualty rate of 36 cyclist deaths per billion kms travelled is three times worse than the Netherlands, where 27 per cent of journeys are made by cycle.

The Commission for Integrated Transport (2007) reported that pedestrians in the UK form a higher proportion of fatalities than in other countries: 'The rate of pedestrian fatalities per head of population is almost three times the level experienced in the Netherlands.'

Children in the UK suffer a higher level of fatality in road traffic incidents than in many other EU countries and at the same time have lower levels of exposure. This points to much higher levels of danger and further layers of detriment to quality of life as children are restricted in the journeys they can make, the facilities they can access and the amount of active play they can engage in. Road safety is part of a general syndrome of enforced 'battery children' as opposed to 'free-range children' (Hillman, 1993), and the battery version is deprived of independence, active play and active travel and sees far more of the inside of a car than the free-range groups in some other EU countries.

Table 3.2 Numbers of pedestrian and pedal cycle fatalities in the age group 0–15 in countries of comparable size to the UK, 2006 data

	Population[a] *(millions)*	*Pedestrians*	*Cyclists*
UK	62.027	77	34
France	64.716	25	17
Spain	45.989	28	6
Italy	60.340	23	13
Netherlands[b]	16.575	17	25

Notes

a Population data are from Eurostat demographic data for 2010, http://epp.eurostat.ec.europa.eu/ cache/ITY_OFFPUB/KS-SF-11-038/EN/KS-SF-11-038-EN.PDF (accessed 14 January 2012).

b The Netherlands has a much smaller population than the UK, but is included in this table to illustrate the coexistence of very low fatality rates with very high levels of cycling. The Dutch cycling rate is more than 10 times larger than that of the UK (Pucher and Buehler, 2008).

Policy recommendations for road safety

Adopt Swedish Vision Zero road safety policy, which has a target of zero deaths and serious injuries in the road traffic environment and adopts a total-systems approach to eliminating death and injury (Whitelegg and Haq, 2006).

Implement general system-wide total 20 mph (30 kph) speed limits on every residential road in every urban area without associated engineering and with zero-tolerance strategy for breaches. The new 'default speed limit' will also apply to all villages where there is currently a higher limit. Adopt the 'Graz model' (ELTIS, 2011).

Implement fully segregated cycle paths connecting all health care facilities, educational establishments and main residential and employment areas. Adopt the Freiburg, Basel, Muenster and Groningen models to achieve a 25 per cent modal share for bikes in urban areas in the UK.

Revise road traffic law and the rules and conventions applying to civil compensation to establish the principle of stricter liability so that the onus of proof in road crashes is reversed (Roadpeace, 2011). Under stricter liability the onus would be on the driver's insurance company to prove that the casualty caused the collision and not on the pedestrian or cyclist to prove negligence on the part of the car driver.

The UK should adopt the same system as applies in France and the Netherlands where pedestrians, cyclists and vulnerable groups including children, the elderly and those with disabilities receive full compensation regardless of their actions (Roadpeace, 2011).

Reduce traffic levels through intelligent land use and transport planning designed to reduce distances travelled and prioritise walking and cycling (WHO, 2004).

Redesign fiscal regimes to eliminate subsidy and financial support of motorised transport (Whitelegg, 1983).

Children's independent mobility

Hillman *et al.* (1990) identified the importance of children's independent mobility and used the language of 'licences' to emphasise the significance of the research. Over an approximately 20-year-period English children in five selected areas had experienced a large reduction in what they were allowed to do (the 'licence'). The licences were:

- children allowed to cross the main road alone;
- licences to walk to places other than school;
- licence to travel home from school independently;

- licence to use buses;
- licence to go out after dark;
- licence to cycle on main roads.

The 1990 study had two main elements. It revisited the same areas surveyed in 1970 and found that the percentages of children allowed to travel independently to and from school had declined from 80 per cent in 1970 to 8 per cent in 1990. It also carried out a comparative study of England and Germany. German children in 1990 had considerably more freedom than their English counterparts.

Tranter (1996) compared the percentage of children driven to school by car in Germany, England and Australia, and these data are shown in Figure 3.3.

The English survey work reported in Hillman *et al.* (1990) was repeated in 2010 in both England and Germany (Shaw *et al.*, 2012). For five out of six licences German primary-age children have greater levels of independent mobility than their English counterparts. For four out of these five licences older English children do attain similar (high) levels of licence holding aged 12 and above. This means that English children are granted parental licences years after their German counterparts. English children appear to have greater freedom to cycle on roads than do German children, which is an anomalous result given the overall differentials in terms of licences and freedoms.

The differences between the 7- to 10-year-olds in England and Germany are very large. More than 40 per cent of seven- and eight-year-old German children are allowed to cross main roads alone, and the equivalent English percentage is 3 for seven-year-olds, 12 for eight-year-olds and 30 for nine-year-olds. In the case of walking to places other than schools 10 per cent of English seven-year-olds have this licence, and the figure is 80 per cent in Germany, with similar differences on the licence to travel home from school independently.

The overall results comparing England and Germany in 1990 (Hillman *et al.*, 1990) and again in 2010 (Shaw *et al.*, 2012) and noting changes between the two time periods show that English independent mobility remained at roughly the same level between 1990 and 2010 (i.e. very low) but German independent

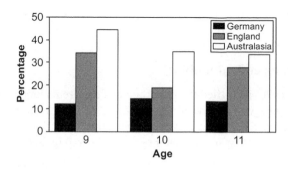

Figure 3.3 Percentage of children taken to school by car for cities in Germany, England and Australasia

Source for German and English data: Hillman *et al.* (1990: 131).

mobility fell. This raises interesting questions around explanation and interpretation, and these are explored in Shaw *et al.* (2012).

Garrard (2011) has summarised international variations in walking and cycling by children, and this reveals very significant variations, with implications for policies in those countries developing anti-obesity strategies. Her summary is reproduced in Table 3.3, and the implications for obesity are considered in the next section of this chapter.

The UK is clearly a long way behind other European countries like Germany and Switzerland on walking and even further behind on cycling. German children cycle six times the distance of UK children each year, and Dutch children manage an impressive 28 times greater distance than their UK peers.

Explaining international variation in children's independent mobility is not a straightforward matter and runs the risk of embracing very general 'cultural' explanations rather than insights derived from inspecting policy interventions and spending. We have already suggested that the explanation is likely to be located within the overall German approach (shared with Denmark, the Netherlands and Switzerland) to public space and public transport and long-standing attention to 'Tempo 30' policies (widespread 20 mph/30 kph speed-limited areas on the majority of streets in urban areas). These suggestions remain untested in a formal sense, but they lend themselves to rigorous scientific evaluation through demonstration projects. The UK is very familiar indeed with demonstration projects ranging from cycling demonstration towns through to 'personalised journey planning' and the adoption of home zones (20 mph zones). In the case of cycling demonstration towns the adoption of pro-cycling policies long prevalent in Germany, the Netherlands and Denmark produced an average 27 per cent increase in cycling levels (DfT, 2009). Home zone policies creating distinctive areas with speed limits set at 20 mph or lower have long been a feature in Germany and the Netherlands. By 1990 there were over 10,000 of these in the German state of North Rhine-Westphalia alone, and they came to Britain relatively late. When they were introduced in London there was a 54 per cent reduction in numbers of people killed and seriously injured (Grundy *et al.*, 2008). In the case of personalised journey planning,

Table 3.3 Distance walked and cycled per child (10–14 years) per year (kilometres)

Country	Distance walked per child per year (kilometres)	Distance cycled per child per year (kilometres)	Proportion of total distance travelled using active modes (%)
USA	123	—	0.8
UK	396	79	6.8
New Zealand	—	232	—
Norway	550	370	9.7
Sweden	275	424	7.4
Germany	431	518	13.8
Switzerland	773	535	14.4
Netherlands	180	2,200	33.5
Melbourne	182	26	4.6

one of the 14 demonstration projects, which was run in York, produced a 16 per cent reduction in car use amongst the 'intervention group', which had been targeted with personal advice, maps, encouragement and support to switch from car to walking, cycling and bus use (Whitelegg and Haq, 2004).

It is possible to have a scientific debate about how to explain differences in children's independent mobility between the UK and Germany, but in many ways it would be better to identify the key parameters that are associated with success in Germany, transfer these to selected areas in the UK and monitor the impact of these measures on children's independent mobility. This appears to be a far better use of time and effort and will also bring a number of co-benefits to the people who live in the test areas, including improved public transport, reduced traffic noise and air pollution, reduced level of death and injury, and healthier children. Germany demonstrated the effectiveness of pro-cycling interventions in the 1970s through its equivalent of cycling demonstration towns, the 'Farradfreundliche Staedte' project in Detmold and Rosenheim. UK policy makers ignored these results, did nothing to develop an equivalent UK programme for 25 years and then replicated the German project in the 2003–10 period. This produced similar results, but the agency doing the work (Cycling England) was closed down in late 2010.

Policy recommendations for children's independent mobility

Design child-friendly cities (Tranter, 2006; Tranter and Malone, 2008) with detailed attention to road safety (implementing all the road safety measures already listed in this chapter).

Implement detailed guidelines on child- and youth-friendly transport and land use planning (Gilbert and O'Brien, 2005).

Give detailed attention to those aspects of urban life that support children in their everyday mobility and accessibility needs. This will require significant attention to improve the number and density of play areas, green space, swimming pools and other child-centred destinations (Play England, 2011).

Implement the International Charter for Walking (Walk 21, 2011).

Reduce exposure to traffic whilst increasing the amount of active travel, physical mobility, walking and cycling. Traffic reduction can be achieved by closing streets as well as by systematic sustainable transport policies to improve walking, cycling and public transport alternatives to the car.

Obesity

> The obesity problem is especially alarming in children and adolescents. The annual rate of increase in the prevalence of childhood obesity has been growing steadily and is 10 times higher than it was in the 1970s.
>
> (WHO, 2007)

Trends in childhood obesity are now so serious that they are widely expected to lead to shorter life expectancies for today's children. That would be the first reversal in life expectancy in many developed countries since governments started keeping track in the 19th century.

(Wilkinson and Pickett, 2009: 89)

Garrard (2009, 2011) has plotted childhood obesity against the rates of active travel (Figure 3.4). As can be seen in Figure 3.4, the UK is in the top three, slightly ahead of Melbourne (Australia) and behind the USA. Northern European countries are lower than the UK on obesity prevalence and higher on a measure of active travel.

The WHO (2007) report on obesity summarises international variation in obesity prevalence. The highest rates for primary schoolchildren were Portugal (32 per cent) and Spain (31 per cent). The lowest was Germany (13 per cent). The UK figure was 20 per cent. The International Obesity Task Force predicted (WHO, 2007) that about 38 per cent of school-age children in the WHO European region would be overweight by 2010 and that more than a quarter of these children would be obese.

Pucher *et al.* (2010a) carried out a detailed statistical analysis of walking, cycling and obesity rates in 14 countries, 50 US states and 47 of the 50 largest cities in the US and concluded: 'At all three geographical levels we found statistically significant negative relationships between active travel and physical activity and statistically significant negative relationships between active travel and diabetes.' The authors do not construct an explanation that suggests obesity is caused solely by lack of physical activity, and they acknowledge diet and other factors, but they raise the strong possibility that rates of obesity may vary in line with variation in walking and cycling levels, which is both important and recognised by the UK policy community (NICE, 2008) as something that should be addressed to create a physical environment that encourages walking and cycling.

In a wide-ranging study and literature review on car use, motorisation and obesity, Davis *et al.* (2007) unequivocally describe the rising prevalence of childhood

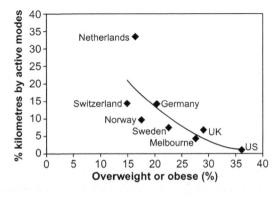

Figure 3.4 Children's active travel distance and overweight/obesity

and adult obesity (one leads to the other) as the mismatch between food intake and physical activity. Increasing levels of energy-rich food consumption, noted as especially concentrated amongst children, and declining levels of physical activity or so-called active transport have created the obesity epidemic, and it has been further fuelled by the dominance of the obesogenic environment. The environment in which we live and work and in which children operate and move around deters active travel and promotes sitting in cars: 'The obesity epidemic is paralleled across much of the developed world, a world in which the built environment has increasingly been designed to accommodate travel by car at the expense of walking and cycling.'

The authors also draw attention to the fact that food intake and energy intake may also have declined in the period 1996–2005 in the UK at the same time as obesity rates have increased, and they interpret this relationship as clear evidence that physical activity is of far more importance than previously realised. The increase in the prevalence of obesity can be explained by a decline of energy intake coinciding with a very steep decline in physical activity, and as we have noted in the discussion on children's independent mobility children are increasingly withdrawn from the world of active travel and taken to places by car.

Davis *et al.* (2007) quote Frank *et al.* (2004): 'Each additional kilometre walked per day is associated with a 4.8 per cent reduction in the likelihood of obesity, whereas each additional hour spent in a car per day was associated with a 6 per cent increase in the likelihood of obesity.'

The links with the way children travel to school in the UK and the decline of walking and cycling amongst children of school age are clear and provide an even clearer policy direction. There is a relationship between diet and physical activity in that an energy-rich diet consumed in a low-physical-activity lifestyle is clearly a 'double hit' requiring a number of highly coordinated policies to deal with interactions and induce lifestyle changes. The whole lifestyle-changing agenda is very important and will be returned to later when we discuss larger-scale interventions to bring about desirable changes in poverty, inequality and happiness.

There are also important links between poverty and obesity, and these are discussed in WHO (2007) and Hanlon *et al.* (2006).

Policy recommendations for childhood obesity

Implement recommendations from WHO (2007) about diet and creating a physical environment and urban design that specifically build in the concept of active children. Raising levels of physical activity in everyday behaviour is an essential part of an obesity strategy.

Implement the recommendations of the UK National Institute for Health and Clinical Excellence (NICE, 2008) on transport and the built environment to ensure that as many walk and cycle journeys as possible for children can be accomplished in a safe and trusted environment (NICE, 2008). These recommendations go into some detail on wider pavements, introducing cycle lanes, restricting motor vehicle access, creating safe routes to school and ensuring that open space and recreation space can be reached safely on foot and by bicycle.

Implement the recommendations in Davis *et al.* (2007) about the overriding importance of increasing walking and cycling levels and eliminating obesogenic environments.

Implement the recommendations of the Commission for Architecture and the Built Environment (CABE, 2009) on designing a built environment that will positively stimulate higher levels of physical activity.

Children's experiences: the last word

It is clear that children have experienced deterioration in what they can do and how much independent control they have over daily activities and how they spend their time. This has been documented in the work of Hillman (1993), Hillman *et al.* (1990) and Louv (2008).

The decline in child freedom and mobility has been summarised very clearly indeed in the case of Sheffield using personal histories spanning four generations (Derbyshire, 2007):

- Great-grandfather George aged eight was allowed to walk six miles to go fishing.
- Grandfather Jack aged eight in 1950 was allowed to travel one mile on his own to the woods.
- Mother Vicky aged eight in 1979 was allowed to go to the swimming pool alone half a mile away.
- Son Ed now aged eight is allowed to walk on his own only to the end of his street, a journey of 300 yards.

Children frequently express the desire to have more freedom and independent mobility.

Children in Glasgow (Whyte and Livingston, 2009) when asked how they would like to travel to school expressed a strong liking for cycling, revealing a large gap between the percentage actually cycling and those who would like to cycle. They also appear to dislike walking and bus use, and more of them would prefer to go by car. In spite of supporting policy statements from Glasgow City Council and the Scottish Government about the importance of cycling, conditions on the ground are poor, the city is dominated by car traffic and traffic danger, and cycling potential is not converted into actual behaviour. Figure 3.5 reveals the transport preferences of Glasgow's schoolchildren.

Children have no voice in the discussion around children and what kind of experiences, built environment or opportunities they should be allowed to enjoy. It is appropriate therefore to finish a chapter on children with a small number of quotations from primary schoolchildren in Lancaster (UK). This school is located

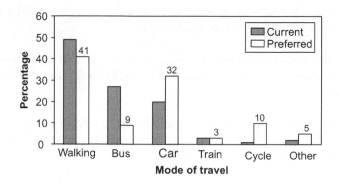

Figure 3.5 Current and preferred methods of travel to school by Glasgow children

on a very busy road in this small city with a large amount of fast-moving traffic and associated noise, danger and pollution. The routes to the school involving walking are along very narrow pedestrian pavements (sidewalks) and very close to fast-moving traffic. The children were given an opportunity to express their own feelings about this environment, and this is what they said:

- 'Every time I am on the pavement my hair swirls to the side.'
- 'I keep on thinking that there's going to be a car crash.'
- 'Cars might crash. . . . They must go slower. . . . We must stop them. . . . What shall we do? . . . Shall we make wheels shorter? . . . Shall we put them in the dustbin?'
- 'They are going so quickly when they pass. . . . It's like you cannot see them pass by. . . . It's not good at all.'
- 'I am starting to get worried about the traffic because the cars are on full speed. . . . One day someone will get run over.'
- 'It is like a race track on Derwent Road.'
- 'I don't like people getting killed by cars. . . . It makes me really sad there's less people on the island. . . . I hope cars don't go fast and kill people.'
- 'My mum and dad think it is dangerous to cross the road and when you are walking on the path.'
- 'We have a lollipop lady and I am scared that the lollipop lady might get hit, and she is very friendly.'
- 'My parents are worried about us. It is when the pavements are narrow. It is very dangerous. . . . I think it is very scary.'
- 'It's very busy and we want it to be safer. People are going quicker every day when I am going to school. I don't like it.'

Listening to children and developing the ability to shape the built environment and the opportunities it provides for children in a way that takes notice of what they say have a great deal to offer to designing and delivering better places and making sure that those better places are child-friendly. In turn child-friendly places are likely to be excellent places for all population groups. A significant amount of professional and expert information and evidence points to the direction of travel likely to improve things for children, but this evidence is still incomplete. Listening to children and taking their views seriously will complete the picture.

4 Older people

Introduction

In very much the same way that children can be regarded as an 'indicator species' for tracking overall societal performance and quality-of-life outcomes so it is also the case for older people. In the case of older people there is the added dimension that demographic change is leading to significant increases in the size of the over-65-years group, with policy implications for a large number of areas including health, transport, carbon reduction, housing and budgets.

Demographic change is now a major policy concern for those undertaking policy development work in care for older people, housing, health service provision and the built environment. Researchers have also identified the link between demographic change and climate change and the need to adopt age-group sensitivity to the reduction of greenhouse gas emissions. Haq *et al.* (2007) calculated that the carbon footprint of the 50- to 64-year-old age group was the highest of all age groups in the UK and that of the 65–74 group the second highest and emphasised the importance of working with these groups to mitigate carbon emissions against a background of the growing size of these groups:

> Older people are making up an increasing proportion of the UK population. Individuals aged 50 and over represent approximately 20 million people (33 per cent). They possess an estimated 80 per cent of the UK's private wealth, 60 per cent of its savings and 40 per cent of its disposable income. By 2031 over 50s are expected to represent approximately 40 per cent of the UK population (27.2 million).
>
> (Haq *et al.*, 2007)

Eurostat (2009) has estimated the relative size of the group aged over 65 as a percentage of the size of the group aged 15–64 in 2050. The EU average in 2050 will be 52.8 per cent. This conceals some large variations, with the UK at 45 per cent, Luxembourg at 36.1 per cent and Spain and Italy in the 66–67 per cent range.

Demographic change is a serious policy concern at regional and sub-regional levels and was identified as a public health issue in Scotland (Hanlon *et al.*, 2006). This study calculated that the number of older people will increase markedly in

Scotland and by 2024 there will be approximately 200,000 more in the 75-plus age group and 130,000 more in the 65–74 age group. This has major public health implications in Scotland related to the care of older people, dealing with chronic ailments and ensuring that service provision and budgets can deal with these demands. This may be especially difficult in Scotland given the concentrations of poverty in these age groups and the relative inability to pay the energy bills needed to maintain adequate warmth in winter months.

Life expectancy is also an important indicator of the success of overall policies that deal with the 65-plus age group. If life expectancy is declining or is considerably less in one part of the EU than in another then we can conclude that policies are not having the desired impact.

The consideration of life expectancy is complicated by very significant small area variation. In Glasgow at the small area level there is a 15-year difference in life expectancy for males (Hanlon *et al.*, 2006: 67):

> In Bridgeton & Dennistoun life expectancy for a man at birth was estimated to be less than 64 years (in 1998–2002). At the other end of the spectrum three communities in Greater Glasgow have the highest male life expectancy within the West of Scotland – Strathkelvin, Anniesland, Bearsden & Milngavie and Eastwood. The 15 year gap in male life expectancy between Bridgeton & Dennistoun and Anniesland, Bearsden & Milngavie highlights the differences in life circumstances, lifestyles and life chances that exist in the city.

Hanlon *et al.* (2006) give these data additional impact by presenting them in terms of the likelihood that a 15-year-old boy will reach his 65th birthday in different parts of Glasgow:

> From life expectancy data it is also possible to estimate the likelihood of a 15 year old boy reaching his 65th birthday. This is again an estimate with wide confidence intervals but re-emphasises the differences in health across Greater Glasgow. In Bridgeton & Dennistoun, it is estimated that just 53 per cent of 15 year old boys will reach their 65th birthday, while in Eastwood and Anniesland, Bearsden & Milngavie the estimates are that at least 87 per cent are likely to reach this age.

Clearly there is something wrong in Bridgeton and Dennistoun.

There is also evidence that things are getting worse (Hanlon *et al.*, 2006: 71): 'The gap in life expectancy for men in Greater Glasgow has widened from 6.9 years to 11.8 years. In other words, the gap in male life expectancy between the most and least affluent parts of Greater Glasgow has widened by five years over a twenty year period.'

In discussing international comparisons and differences in the characteristics of older age groups there is another strong link with the discussion about children. Unhealthy children do not suddenly become healthy adults and healthy older people. The conditions, exposures and experiences of children are, not surprisingly, good predictors of the health of older people (Glasgow Centre for Population Health, 2010):

- Childhood social circumstances are good predictors for adult mortality (Ben-Shlomo and Kuh, 2002).
- Chronic conditions experienced in later life reflect an 'accumulation over the life course' (Power *et al.*, 2007).
- Childhood conditions are important predictors of risk regardless of social class destination in adulthood (Lynch *et al.*, 2004).

This carry-over effect from childhood to adulthood and old age brings with it a dual policy responsibility. By improving the health of children as discussed in Chapter 3 there is likely to be a measurable improvement in health outcomes in later life. Similarly in discussing international variations in the experiences and quality of life of older people we need to bear in mind the possibility that interventions several decades earlier may be more effective than dealing with housing, traffic, air quality, physical activity and poverty in the older age groups in isolation. As always an integrated approach that sets out to promote healthy, active, engaged children, with all the advantages that brings for older age groups, should be reinforced by specific interventions required by older people. An example of a specific intervention in this context would be energy prices and the need to promote warm, well-ventilated, energy-efficient homes. Older people are unlikely to thrive in cold, damp, mouldy housing regardless of the excellent starting conditions they may have experienced as children (Hills, 2011).

International comparison of poverty amongst the 65-plus age group

Poverty amongst older people is a primary indicator of the condition of this group and a determinant of health outcomes (Hanlon *et al.*, 2006; Marmot, 2010). Eurostat (2009) has documented the variations in poverty by age group in the EU:

The risk of poverty faced by people aged 65 or more ranges from 5 per cent in the Czech Republic to 30 per cent in Lithuania and the United Kingdom, 33 per cent in Estonia and Latvia, and even reaches 51 per cent in Cyprus. These differences in the relative situation of older people depend on a number of factors including the adequacy of the pension systems for current pensioners and the age and gender structure of older people population, since elderly women and the very old tend to face much higher risks.

The UK performs badly on the measure used by Eurostat. The measure used is: 'At risk of poverty rate by age group in the EU, expressed as a percentage for those aged 65 and above in 2007'. The UK figure is 30 per cent, compared with an EU average figure of 19 per cent. Of the 29 countries represented in this analysis

25 do better than the UK, and the UK appears in the same group as Latvia (33 per cent), Lithuania (30 per cent) and Estonia (33 per cent). The best performers are the Czech Republic (5 per cent), Luxembourg (7 per cent), Hungary (6 per cent), the Netherlands (10 per cent), Poland (8 per cent) and Slovakia (8 per cent).

Social Trends (2010) tabulates expenditure on social protection as a percentage of GDP, and the UK is at position nine, with France, Sweden, Belgium, the Netherlands, Denmark, Germany, Austria and Italy spending a higher percentage of GDP on social protection than the UK. The better health outcomes for elderly citizens in other EU countries (ESAW, 2001) have a strong link with the higher levels of expenditure on the social conditions, income and welfare of older people, and there is a strong case for aligning the UK with those countries with higher levels of expenditure on social protection.

Clearly life is a great deal better for the over-65 age group in those countries that manage a poverty rate of one-third that of the UK (as the Netherlands does) or better.

Fuel poverty

Fuel poverty is defined in the UK as having to spend more than 10 per cent of household income on energy to maintain an 'adequate level of warmth' throughout the year and on other energy costs (Hills, 2011). On this definition Hills reports that there were 4 million households living in fuel poverty in England in 2009. Fuel poverty is a major issue in the EU and is experienced by a number of social and demographic groups, including single-parent families and those aged above 65 years (EPEE, n.d.a, n.d.b).

The EPEE study does not quantify the number of those aged 65-plus experiencing fuel poverty in either absolute or percentage terms but makes the link between fuel poverty and this age group. Hills (2011) identifies three groups as at risk from fuel poverty:

- elderly people;
- very young children;
- people with long-term sickness or disability.

Hills (2011) presents data to show that single-pensioner households account for the largest proportion of fuel-poor households in both 2004 and 2009, that there are 27,000 excess winter deaths and that, 'if only a tenth of them are due directly to fuel poverty, that means that 2,700 people in England and Wales are dying each year as a result – more than the number killed in traffic accidents'.

Fuel poverty has been linked to excess winter deaths (EWDs), and a particular source of concern is the elevated level of EWDs in the UK when compared with much colder countries, including Finland, Norway and Sweden. This is illustrated in Figure 4.1.

Hills notes that, if similar rates had been achieved in England as in neighbouring Northern European countries in the 1990s, EWDs in 2009–10 would have been reduced by 7,000–10,000 cases.

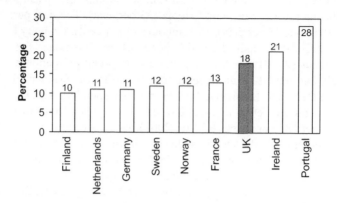

Figure 4.1 Average proportion of winter deaths that are excess, 1988–97, selected European countries

Source: Hills (2011).

The largest single group affected by EWDs are the over 65s (Figure 4.2), who have accounted for over 90 per cent of excess deaths in each of the last 20 years. The over 85s are worst affected, accounting for the largest proportion of EWDs regardless of the primary cause.

Healy (2003) describes 'the paradox of excess winter mortality' in that colder countries in Northern Europe have a lower excess mortality than warmer countries in Southern Europe. This is explained by reference to high standards of thermal efficiency in buildings in Scandinavia and the lack of thermal efficiency in Southern Europe.

The relatively poor performance of the UK when compared to countries like Germany, the Netherlands, Denmark and Finland, all of which have lower per capita GDP than the UK, demonstrates that the UK has considerable room for

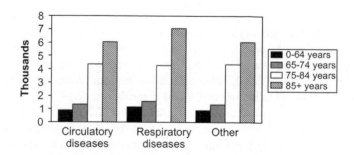

Figure 4.2 Number of excess winter deaths by cause and age group, 2008–09, England and Wales

Source: Hills (2011).

improvement on this measure and on the basis of Healy's analysis that progress is most likely to be found in dealing with housing quality and thermal efficiency. This is not the only characteristic of EU countries that is likely to feed into excess mortality. Healy (2003) shows that there is a link with inequality as measured by the Gini coefficient, and we have already shown that older people in the UK are poorer than in comparable countries. Measures to alleviate excess winter mortality will necessarily have to embrace increases in social protection expenditure (Eurostat, 2009) to protect older people from the consequences of poverty and the links between poverty, fuel poverty and poor housing quality and targeted programmes aimed at improving the housing quality of older people. There is much to be learnt in all these respects from Scandinavian, German and Dutch experience.

Health status of older people

Eurostat (2008) reports the incidence of self-reported health and poor health by age (Figure 4.3). In the age group 65-plus, 29 per cent of women report that their health is bad or very bad, and the figure for men is 23 per cent. With such high rates of self-reported poor health and forecasts of increased numbers of people in the over-65 age group it will become increasingly important to identify policy interventions that can improve the quality of life of this group and for these policies to range very widely indeed over the energy efficiency of their homes, their ability to afford warmth and good-quality housing, the degree to which the built environment is conducive to independent, sociable physical activity for this group, and environmental quality including air quality. We return to these quality-of-life attributes later.

Jagger *et al.* (2008) discuss the concept of healthy life years (HLYs) at the age of 50 and its variation across 25 EU countries in 2005. The increase in life expectancy over time is well documented, but it is clear that 'healthy life years' are also important. The extent to which older people can expect 10, 20

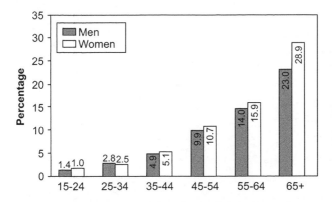

Figure 4.3 Percentage of the population whose perceived health is bad or very bad, by age and sex, EU-25, 2005

or 30 years of healthy lives after the age of 50 has important and rather obvious implications for quality-of-life measurement and public policy adjustments to the presence of larger numbers of older people. The results are reproduced in Figure 4.4.

The range in HLYs for men is from a high of 23.64 for Denmark to a low of 9.05 for Estonia. The range for women is very similar. Denmark is 24.12 and Estonia is 10.42. The UK is a relatively high performer on this measure at 19.74 for men and 20.78 for women. For men there are only five countries better than the UK, and these are Greece, Italy, Malta, the Netherlands and Sweden. For women only two are better, and these are Greece and Italy.

A study of six countries focusing on adults aged 50–90 and their self-reported health conditions (ESAW, 2001) produced a different assessment of the relative performance of the UK when compared to other countries. A comparison of the mean prevalence rates of the five most often reported diseases showed that Italy and the UK have the highest mean prevalence rates. Dutch and Swedish respondents reported the lowest impairment levels and described these two countries 'as having the best health' for this age group. The conclusion for the UK was: 'the UK sample is clearly characterised by the lowest ratings of general health'.

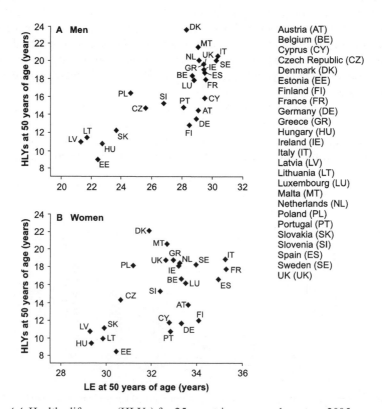

Figure 4.4 Healthy life years (HLYs) for 25 countries, men and women, 2005

The ESAW (2001) report makes a clear link between income and poor health outcomes, which as in the case of children points once again to the need for health and social policy in the UK to accord a much higher priority to ensuring that those over the age of 65 have enough income to eat well, pay for care services, provide comfortable and health-promoting temperatures in their homes and have access to local services and modest amounts of physical activity, mobility and social interaction in their own communities for as long as possible. This will also require attention to road safety, which has an especially damaging impact on older people.

Road safety

Deaths and serious injuries amongst older people are a serious problem for older people. Living Streets (2009) has emphasised the issue:

> More pedestrians over 70 are killed on the roads than any other age group. Given that the proportion of the population aged 75+ is projected to increase from seven per cent to over 13 per cent by 2018 to over 700,000 people . . . this has major implications on how we design and manage our streets.

Those aged over 65 are susceptible to death and injury because they are likely to spend more time in a road traffic environment, and they may also be experiencing a decline in the ability to see and hear vehicular traffic approaching them and to move out of the way quickly if the vehicle is threatening them (ESAW, 2001).

In the period June 2007 to March 2008 the city of Portsmouth introduced system-wide 20 mph speed limits on 94 per cent of its road lengths and was the first city in the UK to do this. The new speed limit was a reduction from 30 mph and was implemented with signage only and without the humps, bumps and chicanes normally associated with 20 mph zones. In a detailed comparison of before and after road traffic casualties (DfT, 2010) the report concluded: 'Comparing the 3 years before the system was implemented and the two years afterwards, the number of recorded road casualties has fallen by 22 per cent from 183 per year to 142 per year. During that period casualty numbers fell nationally by around 14 per cent in comparable areas.'

The DfT report did not contain a detailed analysis of statistical significance, and this has subsequently been carried out by Campbell (2011). Campbell concludes that the headline finding of a 22 per cent reduction in casualties is statistically significant at the $p = 0.0005$ level and 'that the change in the observed rate is very unlikely to be due to chance year-to-year variation and that there is strong evidence that the introduction of the 20mph limits is associated with a fall in the total risk of road casualties'.

A more detailed analysis of change over time in numbers killed or seriously injured (KSI) does not produce a statistically significant result. The change in KSI numbers is relatively small and falls within the year-to-year variation that can be expected in road safety statistics.

Garrard (2008) has identified road safety and speed issues as especially relevant to elderly groups. She presents evidence to show that older people are at greater risk of death and injury in the road traffic environment and discusses speed reduction programmes in Denmark and the impact of these projects on improving the quality of life of older people:

> Examples include an evaluation of speed reduction measures in Denmark which reported increased feelings of security and a reduced 'barrier effect', particularly for elderly pedestrians. Following the implementation of ten speed reduction schemes in Scotland, residents reported increased neighbourly interaction, improved perceptions of pedestrian safety, and improved neighbourhood appearance.
>
> Speed reduction interventions in three towns in Denmark led to similar improvements in safety perceptions. Intercept interviews with pedestrians and cyclists showed that feelings of security were improved considerably in the intervention towns. Perceptions of security improved for all age groups, but the greatest improvements were among older people. The authors concluded that the barrier effect (of high traffic speed) was reduced in the three pilot towns (Herrstedt 1992).

Clearly older people need special consideration in the design of the built environment and road traffic environment in which they live and access local shops and services including trips to the doctor, dentist, optician and other services used intensively by this age group. Current built environment priorities are not sensitive to older people. The mayor of London has been reported as shortening the green phase on traffic-light-controlled pedestrian crossings (the time allowed for a pedestrian to cross) in order to smooth the traffic flow and reduce congestion (*London Evening Standard*, 2008). This is a policy that damages the quality of life of older people. The organisation and management of time in an urban environment are crucial to the quality of life of older people (Whitelegg, 1993a). Whitelegg characterises the way time is managed in an urban environment as 'time theft'. Transport planning and practice based on encouraging motorisation and car-based trips achieve their success by stealing time from other groups, especially the elderly, who must now spend more time waiting to cross a road, being diverted through an unpleasant underpass, or having to negotiate ugly metal barriers that obstruct direct walking routes, or who find that local services they prefer to use have closed and they must now travel longer distances to shopping centres, hospitals or clinics because these have relocated to more inaccessible, pedestrian-unfriendly locations. All these tendencies bring about substantial time penalties that must be endured by the very young, older people, women and those on low incomes.

This has been recognised in a remarkably insightful visual image by Seifried (1990) (Figure 4.5). Clearly the city planners and traffic engineers in Kassel at the time these measurements were taken did not care very much for elderly residents, and their colleagues in Hamburg did show some consideration.

Where pedestrians are left waiting because of cars
How long is the red light for pedestrians?

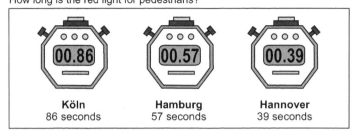

Köln	Hamburg	Hannover
86 seconds	57 seconds	39 seconds

Where grandmothers have to hurry
This is the speed pedestrians must cross the road when the light is green

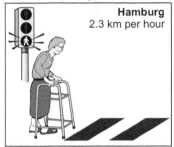

Figure 4.5 How fast can your grandmother run?

Source: Whitelegg (1993b).

Conclusions

Elderly UK citizens appear to be unhealthier than their peer group in other EU countries. They experience high rates of death and injury in the road traffic environment, more of them die in winter than would be the case if their income and housing quality matched Scandinavian, German and Dutch standards, they have difficulty in keeping their homes warm, and they are poor. It is unlikely that this situation is the result of explicit policy objectives so we can assume that it is (a) something we would wish to change for the better and (b) ripe for policy changes that learn from international comparisons and bring with them a good chance of success. On the basis of the evidence from other countries there are a small number of changes that could be made, and these are listed below.

Policy recommendations

Increase social protection expenditure (Eurostat, 2010) to bring UK expenditure into line with that of the Netherlands, Sweden, Germany, Austria and Denmark. Figure 4.6 illustrates national variations in member state social protection expenditure in the EU and the size of the spending gap that the UK should bridge.

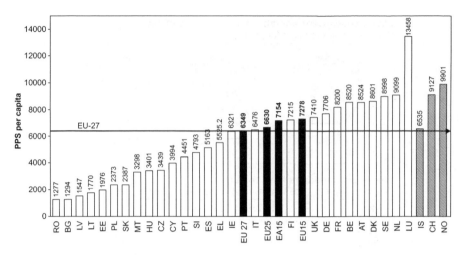

Figure 4.6 Expenditure on social protection in PPS per capita in 2006

Note: PPS is purchasing power standard (a unit independent of any national currency that removes the distortions due to price level differences).

Having regard to the special vulnerabilities of older people in using streets, cross-ing roads and accessing local facilities, the street environment should be designed with the needs of this group in mind. The design principles are covered in more detail in Chapter 5 and the policy recommendations at the end of that chapter, and can be found in ITDP *et al.* (2010). These same design principles will also deliver the child-friendly outcomes listed in Chapter 3.

Having regard to the special vulnerabilities of older people in their homes as a result of poor-quality housing, poor-quality energy efficiency and large energy bills it is essential that a large-scale retro-fit programme on all dwellings in the UK be funded and implemented, starting with older people and covering all privately owned, rented, council and housing association properties to deliver the German 'Passivhaus' standard of energy efficiency and low energy bills (Passivhaus Institut, 2011). The main characteristic of the 'Passivhaus' is that the energy required for space heating must not exceed 15 kWh per square metre. This is less than one-tenth of the average heating requirement of the existing housing stock. Further work needs to be done on the extent to which 'Passivhaus' standards can be achieved on existing UK dwellings, but Haines *et al.* (2009) have analysed the public health benefits of strategies to reduce greenhouse gas emissions and report that: 'A household energy efficiency programme in the UK, to achieve the exacting standards specified, would cost in the range $5000–50 000 per dwelling, resulting in reduced fuel bills by an average of around $500 a year at current prices, but much more as fossil-fuel and electricity prices increase.'

5 The built environment

In a remarkable and innovative manner Appleyard (1981) and Appleyard and Appleyard (forthcoming) have demonstrated the importance of streets as a locus for activity, sociability, place identity and community life. Appleyard's much-reproduced diagram is reproduced once again in Figure 5.1, which very neatly encapsulates a great deal of insight into the debate about public space, the street, people and social interaction. As traffic levels increase (proceeding from top to bottom in Figure 5.1), the use of the street by local residents decreases, the number of people on the street decreases and the number of friends and acquaintances reported by local residents decreases.

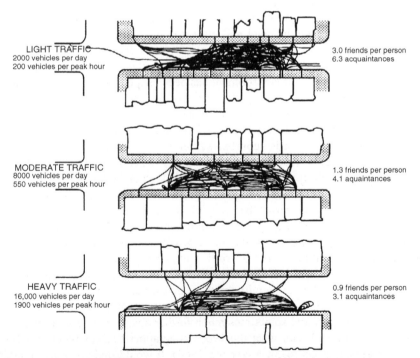

LIGHT TRAFFIC
2000 vehicles per day
200 vehicles per peak hour

3.0 friends per person
6.3 acquaintances

MODERATE TRAFFIC
8000 vehicles per day
550 vehicles per peak hour

1.3 friends per person
4.1 aquaintances

HEAVY TRAFFIC
16,000 vehicles per day
1900 vehicles per peak hour

0.9 friends per person
3.1 acquaintances

Figure 5.1 The influence of traffic volume on people and the number of acquaintances and friends of residents living in streets with different traffic volumes

The significance of Appleyard's work is clear. It says more about quality of life in general and in cities than many detailed quality-of-life publications. It has also been largely ignored by planners, traffic engineers, politicians and those responsible for quality of life in cities. For several decades streets in most European cities have been defined and designed as spaces that can facilitate the movement of motorised vehicles. Much of UK transport planning and traffic engineering is heavily loaded towards reducing congestion and improving journey time reliability. This is the same thing as ignoring people who live on streets in urban areas. It prioritises the car and the truck regardless of the impact that this prioritisation has on 'liveable streets' or on the elderly, children, active travel, air pollution or the sheer pleasure and delight of living in a high-quality urban environment that attaches importance to people and places and the enjoyment of places. German discussions of traffic, people and streets embrace the concept of *Aufenthaltszeit* (a stay or a sojourn) and the positive qualities associated with people spending time on the street and associating with other residents who live on the same street.

It is interesting that the English language is not very good at capturing the sense of *Aufenthaltszeit* and its positive connotations. The UK debate around people in public places is often characterised by discussion of how to prevent *Aufenthaltszeit*, and the language emphasises the negative, for example the use of 'lingering', 'loitering' and 'hanging about'. The language and the practice of transport planning are characterised by an emphasis on movement (good) and a lack of emphasis on not moving (bad).

The subtle but successful colonisation of the street so that it serves the purposes of circulation and through travel and does not assist the residents or the local community is part of a much bigger ideological and cultural shift towards car-dominated thinking and its prioritisation above any other kind of thinking (Sachs, 1992). In this way the built environment has been shaped to serve the interests of motorised transport and not the pedestrian, cyclist, child or elderly person who would like to 'linger' in a street environment and enjoy the public realm.

At larger scales than the street, though with direct consequences for the street, there are tendencies towards suburbanisation and the lengthening of journeys, which reshape cities so that they become heavily dependent on motorised transport and relatively cheap oil and exterminate walking and cycling trips (Newman *et al.*, 2009). In a closely related manner transport systems change to increase the speed of travel, with the result that people substitute the possibility for quicker journeys with longer journeys to maintain a constant travel time budget (Metz, 2008). Time savings are consumed as extra distance so that a constant travel time budget is maintained. Given the overriding importance of time savings in cost–benefit analysis and project evaluation the result of this bias towards 'further and faster' is to reshape the built environment so that we are all encouraged to travel to exciting opportunities for shopping, leisure, tourism and so on that are further away than in the past and sometimes much further away. The built environment then becomes aligned with what the 1960s geographer Melvin Webber defined as the 'non-place urban realm' (Webber, 1964). It would make a useful thought experiment to imagine what the built environment would look like if the concept of time savings having a monetary value were deleted and no longer formed a part of transport, spatial and land use planning and project evaluation. The law of constant time allocation (Metz, 2008) provides the intellectual basis for such a deletion, and the sustainable development and quality-of-life debate points to the need for rebalancing the built environment so that it favours locality, community and active travel. There is a very strong argument reflected in Michael Ende's novel *Momo* (Ende, 1984) that community vitality, quality of life, friendliness and other important characteristics of normal everyday life improve dramatically if we spend more time doing something rather than less. The urge to 'save' time has not been justified empirically, intellectually or conceptually and is a prime determinant of many larger-scale societal and environmental problems described by Whitelegg (1993a) as 'time pollution'.

The idea that speed is not intrinsically 'a good thing' is still a difficult concept for politicians and transport planners in spite of the very clear analysis by Metz (2008) showing that time savings are quite simply consumed by increased distances travelled. The cross-party support for high-speed rail in the UK (House of Commons, 2011a) indicates that speed still captures the imagination and dominates thinking about transport planning, regional planning and public spending.

Tranter (2010) and Tranter and Ker (2007) have thoroughly demolished accepted wisdom on the speed of vehicles and shown that public transport and bicycles are effectively faster (the concept of 'social speed') and at the same time nurturing of active travel and protective of ecology.

Redelmeier and Bayoumi (2010) have shown that increases in speed of car traffic are associated with increased probabilities of fatalities in the road traffic environment and have calculated that the time savings achieved through driving are more than offset by the loss of life through death on the roads. In a detailed statistical calculation they estimate that a 1 kph increase in speed for the average driver yielded a 26-second increase in total expected lost time, because the savings from reduced travel time were more than offset by the increased prospect of a crash. A 3 kph decrease in average driving speed yielded the least amount of total time lost. This speed yielded about 11,000 fewer crashes each day and saved 3.6 hours per year for the average driver. The authors concluded: 'As a nation drivers in the US travel slightly too fast and could improve overall life expectancy by decreasing their average speed slightly.'

Illich (1974) anticipated new ways of conceptualising mobility, time and time savings when he calculated that:

> The typical American male devotes more than 1600 hours a year to his car. He sits in it while it goes and while it stands idling. He parks it and searches for it. He earns the money to put down on it and to meet the monthly instalments. He works to pay for petrol, tolls, insurance, taxes and tickets. He spends four of his sixteen waking hours on the road or gathering resources for it. And this figure does not take into account the time consumed by other activities dictated by transport: time spent in hospitals, traffic courts and garages; time spent watching automobile commercials or attending consumer education

meetings to improve the quality of the next buy. The model American puts in 1600 hours to get 7500 miles; less than five miles per hour.

(Illich, 1974: 30–31)

The misrepresentation of time has shaped the built environment in a way that rewards those who want to go fast and punishes those for whom there are other values, for example safety and security, clean air, ambience, neighbourliness and attractive surroundings. Illich (1974) is very clear indeed: 'beyond a certain speed, motorised vehicles create remoteness which only they can shrink. They create distances for all and shrink them for only a few' (pp. 42–43). The persistence of flawed concepts and methods in the transport domain continues to shape the built environment in ways that detract from quality of life, damage ecology, make climate change interventions less effective than they might be and skew public spending so that it favours rich people travelling long distances in and on energy-greedy modes of transport. Whitelegg (2009b) has described the flaws in high-speed rail investment based on earlier work by Whitelegg and Holzapfel (1993) on the same subject.

Bristol (UK)

Appleyard's (1981) study has been replicated in Bristol in the UK by Hart and Parkhurst (2011), and the results confirm the effects of increasing traffic volume on numbers of friends and acquaintances. The Bristol and San Francisco study results are compared in Table 5.1.

Hart and Parkhurst (2011) comment on the significance of their findings in terms relevant to the design of built environments:

What are the mechanisms behind traffic's apparent erosion of social capital? First, activities that lend themselves to social interaction – such as gardening and sitting outside – are especially vulnerable to traffic-related environmental impacts, particularly noise and air pollution. Second, as traffic increases, so does the barrier effect between opposite sides of the street – residents on

Table 5.1 Comparison of research findings with original study by Donald Appleyard

Study	Light street		Medium street		Heavy street	
	San Francisco	*Bristol*	*San Francisco*	*Bristol*	*San Francisco*	*Bristol*
Traffic volume	2,000	140	8,000	8,420	16,000	21,130
Average number of friends	3	5.35	1.3	2.45	0.9	1.15
Average number of acquaintances	6.3	6.1	4.1	3.65	3.1	2.8

Source: Hart and Parkhurst (2011).

Note: San Francisco was the study area in Appleyard (1981).

heavy street often had to wait as long as 5 minutes just to cross to the other side. Finally, the threat of being hit and injured or killed by a car in the street environment not only discourages people from spending time there, but those who do may be more likely to be on the defensive, and less inclined to engage in a spontaneous chat with a stranger.

The impact of the built environment on social and community attributes are then summarised graphically by Hart and Parkhurst (2011), adopting the same style as the original Appleyard study in San Francisco (Figure 5.2).

Very clearly the street is a crucially important determinant of behaviour, sociability and interaction and hence has a direct impact on the amount of walking, cycling and use of that street. In turn this has a direct effect on the quality of life of

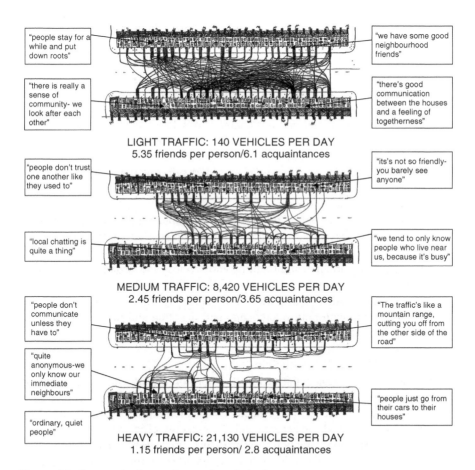

"people stay for a while and put down roots"

"we have some good neighbourhood friends"

"there is really a sense of community- we look after each other"

"there's good communication between the houses and a feeling of togetherness"

LIGHT TRAFFIC: 140 VEHICLES PER DAY
5.35 friends per person/6.1 acquaintances

"people don't trust one another like they used to"

"its's not so friendly- you barely see anyone"

"local chatting is quite a thing"

"we tend to only know people who live near us, because it's busy"

MEDIUM TRAFFIC: 8,420 VEHICLES PER DAY
2.45 friends per person/3.65 acquaintances

"people don't communicate unless they have to"

"The traffic's like a mountain range, cutting you off from the other side of the road"

"quite anonymous-we only know our immediate neighbours"

"people just go from their cars to their houses"

"ordinary, quiet people"

HEAVY TRAFFIC: 21,130 VEHICLES PER DAY
1.15 friends per person/ 2.8 acquaintances

Figure 5.2 Community interaction on three Bristol streets

Note: Lines represent friendships or acquaintances; dots represent where people are said to gather and chat.

children, the elderly, the mobility-challenged and those with caring responsibilities for the young or the old. The street also has an important role in influencing happiness (Layard, 2005) and health (British Medical Association, 1997). It is a remarkable legacy of twentieth-century and (so far) twenty-first-century public policy that something so important and so central to so many quality-of-life and community attributes has been left to wither on the vine.

Freiburg and the built environment

In Freiburg im Breisgau in southern Germany the street has been reclaimed for ordinary, everyday use by residents and all age groups. Freiburg has a very distinctive transport, public realm, spatial planning and green space policy that restores the role of the street in community life (Stadt Freiburg, 2010).

The elements that feed into a high-quality living environment with streets for people are clear, effective and transferable and include the following:

- There are general 30 kph/20 mph speed limits on all residential roads (the largest roads are excluded). Ninety per cent of Freiburg's 240,000 residents live on streets that are limited to 30 kph/20 mph.
- Cycling infrastructure and cycling promotion are high on the political agenda and have produced the environmental and safety/security conditions that encourage cycling, with the result that 26 per cent of all trips every day are by bike. The same can be said for walking, with a 23 per cent modal share. By 2020 Freiburg plans to increase cycling to 28 per cent and walking to 24 per cent modal shares and produce a 20 per cent share for public transport, leaving 28 per cent for the car.
- The spatial planning policy is organised to maintain and intensify the compact city idea (Newman *et al.*, 2009). The city resists attempts to expand the suburbs and blocks plans for out-of-town shopping centres and retail parks to maintain strong urban centre retailing and services and strong local shopping centres that can supply everyday needs (Salomon, 2010).
- There is high-quality public transport, especially trams and buses that are fully integrated with both interchange and ticketing and integrated with the development of new car-reduced areas in Vauban and Rieselfeld. The number of trips by public transport per annum in Freiburg has increased from 27.3 million in 1980 to 72.8 million in 2009.
- Vauban is a new residential area in Freiburg on the site of a former French barracks, with a population of 5,000, and Rieselfeld is a still-expanding new residential area with 10,500 residents (Stadt Freiburg, 2010). Both areas are served by tram, both have exceptionally high-energy-efficiency homes and photovoltaic installations, and both are car-reduced in the sense that car-free living is encouraged and *Aufenthaltsqualitaet in öffentlichen Raum* is a design principle that is actually implemented. The English translation of this concept is 'the quality of the public realm that encourages residents to spend time in that realm'. As noted earlier, the concept has very little resonance with thinking in the UK.

- The centre of Freiburg is almost totally car-free and in a way that is significantly different to the pedestrian areas of York, Lancaster or Oxford, where cars and lorries frequently invade the pedestrian areas and destroy the *Aufenthaltsqualitaet*.
- Freiburg attaches a very high importance to the quality of the public realm generally, including parks and green spaces, urban ecology, tree planting and the famous small streams that run through the city centre, the *Baechle* (Stadt Freiburg, 2009). Freiburg has planted 22,000 trees on streets and has 3,800 small garden allotments and 160 play areas.

Freiburg and the economy

Cities and regions throughout the world are concerned about their economies and the ways in which job creation and competitiveness can be advanced. There is a deeply embedded view that building new transport infrastructure, especially airport capacity, roads and high-speed rail links, will stimulate economic growth, create jobs and increase national and international competitiveness. This can be seen in most reports advocating new infrastructure (House of Commons, 2011a). These views have been challenged on many occasions (SACTRA, 1999; Whitelegg, 1994), but the challenges have had very little impact on the planning and policy process that supports new infrastructure.

Recent proposals for building new roads and bridges in the UK have all been supported by reference to the presumed positive impact of the new road on jobs and economic vitality. They include:

- the Westbury bypass in Wiltshire;
- the Heysham–M6 link, Lancaster;
- the Aberdeen western peripheral route;
- the M74 in Glasgow;
- the Thames Gateway Bridge, London.

Wherever these job creation estimates have been subjected to scrutiny the claims have been found to be flawed (Therivel and Whitelegg, 2005).

All of these road projects have a strongly negative impact on the built environment. They provide more road capacity to send strong signals to those making transport choices that the motorised option is better than others, they cause extra CO_2 emissions and air pollution, they create additional traffic which damages the daily lives of residents especially children and the elderly, they create barriers in and around cities which reduce the attractiveness of walking and cycling, and they destroy nature, habitat and biodiversity. They are also very popular with politicians and widely supported by local government in the UK.

All the local authorities promoting these road projects have policy commitments to create sustainable cities, regions and economies. All of them have responsibilities to improve air quality, reduce greenhouse gas emissions and improve levels of walking and cycling. The road projects are supported because the dominant ideology is an economic ideology, and job creation takes precedence over all other considerations even when evidence is available that more jobs can be created by spending on non-road projects, for example renewable energy and energy efficiency in homes linked to the elimination of fuel poverty.

Freiburg has achieved both economic and environmental success, and these closely interrelated policy strands are not seen as incompatible or contradictory (Stadt Freiburg, 2010). Approximately 10,000 jobs have been created in the city in solar and other environmental technology industries, and the city is the location for several research and development organisations working on environmental technology and sustainable development (Stadt Freiburg, 2009).

Freiburg is an example of 'decoupling' in practice.

Decoupling

Traditionally it has been assumed that the growth in demand for transport faithfully tracks economic growth measured in terms of growth in GDP. Closely related to this assumption is that 'improved' transport infrastructure will reduce transport costs, increase the attraction factor for inward investors and stimulate economic growth. There is now evidence of so-called 'decoupling', where economic growth is proceeding but transport growth is declining or static (OECD, 2006). This has very important policy implications. There is no conflict between policies that dampen down growth in demand for transport and those that stimulate economic growth. OECD (2006) discusses interventions and policy measures that can deliver decoupling.

Mingado *et al.* (2008) looked in detail at decoupling and the economies of Rotterdam, London, Goteborg and Hamburg:

> The main question addressed in this research is *how can a city increase its welfare and accessibility while reducing the negative environmental externalities of transport*? The main aim of the research is to develop a framework that can help cities to find the right balance among the development of transport, the improvement of the environment and economic growth. In other words, the purpose of this study is to provide a framework for decoupling the negative environmental effects of transport from economic activities at urban level.

The study's conclusions are of central importance to understanding the links between transport, the economy and the environment and then using this understanding to improve the quality of life and built environment of all those who live in Europe's towns and cities:

Decoupling (transport intensity from economic activities) must be considered as the ultimate goal of the policy. This can be mainly achieved in two ways: either by convincing people to travel with alternatives to car or by reducing people's need for travel. In this study we have focused mainly on the first. Nowadays, it's strategically wrong and not possible anymore to accommodate extra car traffic. Therefore cities face the challenge to reduce car use while maintaining economic growth. Unfortunately this aim is often difficult to realise because of huge political resistance. Restricting car use is not popular and politicians don't like to implement unpopular measures. Nevertheless, this is the only way that cities must follow. Cities that fail to reduce car use in the future might have negative consequences in terms of accessibility and quality of life. In the knowledge based economy, this could lead to dramatic consequences in terms of attractiveness both towards citizens and business.

European comparisons

The idea of comparing European cities on quality-of-life and built environment attributes is fraught with difficulty and is unlikely to pass a rigorous test of research design, data collection and inference. It is, nevertheless, an important part of the policy improvement cycle, and the absence of a serious policy-oriented discussion on such comparisons has undoubtedly contributed to the lack of learning, the lack of discussion of innovation and the existence of cities in the UK that show little sign of benchmarking, learning and innovation in key policy areas.

The European Commission has contributed to the high-quality evidence base on EU city comparisons and achievement through it annual Green Capital competition (European Commission, 2010a, 2010b, 2010c). This competition invites bids in an open competition from EU cities with a population greater than 200,000 and submits the bids to a rigorous evaluation by a panel of experts. The winners of the Green Capital competition since its inception in 2010 are Stockholm (2010), Hamburg (2011), Vitoria-Gasteiz (2012) and Nantes (2013). The winner undertakes to engage in the dissemination and collation of best practice so that all European cities can benefit.

The European Commission (2010a) defined the objectives of the Green Capital award as follows: 'The award will go to a city that consistently achieves high environmental standards, is committed to ongoing, ambitious goals for further environmental improvement and sustainable development and can serve as a role model for its peers.'

The Green Capital award is based on an evaluation of performance in 11 indicator areas. They are:

- local contribution to global climate change;
- local transport;
- green urban areas;
- sustainable land use;
- nature and biodiversity;
- quality of local ambient air;
- noise pollution;
- waste production and management;
- water consumption;
- waste water treatment;
- environmental management of the municipality.

In addition to the 11 environmental indicator areas, a twelfth indicator area is now included: the programme of communication actions aiming to disseminate experience and best practice on environmental matters (European Commission, 2010b). The 11 indicator areas are very closely aligned to the wider discussion and definition of built environment (Smith *et al.*, 1998) and provide a sound evidence base for policy formulation on how to improve the built environment.

Stockholm (population 820,000) won the competition for the 2010 Green Capital city on the basis of significant achievements and a documented commitment to do more in the future and to allocate budgets to the programme of continuous improvement. Its achievements included:

- 40 per cent of the land is in parks and recreation areas;
- seven nature reserves within the city limits;
- 12,000 trees in the city centre;
- a commitment to be fossil fuel free by 2050;
- 100 per cent of waste converted into heating and electricity;
- a commitment to reduce CO_2 emissions to 3 tonnes per resident by 2015;
- 68 per cent of all trips are by foot and bike;
- a London-style congestion charge has reduced traffic by 10–15 per cent;
- 760 kilometres of bike lanes have boosted bike use.

Hamburg (population 1.77 million) won the competition for the 2011 Green Capital city on the basis of significant achievements and a documented commitment to do more in the future and to allocate budgets to the programme of continuous improvement. Its achievements included:

- 1,700 hectares of Natura 2000 nature reserves;
- 25 hectares of a new green area to cover a motorway (the motorway continues to function underneath the green area);
- a commitment to reduce greenhouse gas emissions by 40 per cent by 2020;
- 11.75 per cent of its electricity consumption generated from renewables;
- strong local transport and land use planning to produce modal shares of 19 per cent (public transport), 47 per cent (car), 9 per cent (bike) and 25 per cent (pedestrian);

- 45 per cent of roads speed-limited to 30 kph/20 mph;
- 36,000 allotments;
- energy-efficient buildings.

Vitoria-Gasteiz in Spain (population 240,000) won the competition for the 2012 Green Capital city on the basis of significant achievements and a documented commitment to do more in the future and to allocate budgets to the programme of continuous improvement. Its achievements included:

- a commitment to go beyond the 20 per cent reduction in CO_2 by 2020;
- a modal split of 50 per cent walking, 26 per cent car, 8 per cent public transport and 4 per cent bike (does not add up to 100 per cent in original documentation);
- 97 kilometres of urban bike infrastructure;
- 1,091 hectares of public green areas (32.7 per cent of the total city area);
- 130,000 trees on city boulevards and 11,331 hectares of forest.

Nantes in France (population 285,000) won the competition for the 2013 Green Capital city on the basis of significant achievements and a documented commitment to do more in the future and to allocate budgets to the programme of continuous improvement. Its achievements included:

- 15,000 hectares of natural green areas;
- 60 per cent of the city area defined as agricultural, nature and green space;
- four Natura 2000 nature reserves;
- a commitment to reduce CO_2 emissions by 25 per cent by 2020 (on a 1990 baseline);
- modal split data showing 57 per cent of trips by car, 15 per cent by public transport, 24 per cent on foot, 2 per cent by bike and 2 per cent by motorbike.

The key elements of success in the bids from all four Green Capital cities are a strong evidence base in support of achievements in several main areas contributing to the quality of the built environment, including actual performance on:

- nature, green spaces and trees;
- modal split shifts in favour of walking and cycling;
- improvements in air quality;
- better-than-average performance on carbon reduction in a well-funded climate change plan;
- a strongly coordinated environmental management strategy with clear evidence of leadership and commitment from senior politicians.

Two bids have been submitted by UK cities, Bristol in the joint 2010–11 application round and Glasgow for the 2012 title. Both were unsuccessful, though Bristol made the list of eight finalists in its round.

The European Commission (2010c) evaluated the eight bids in the 2010–11 joint application round. The eight bids were from Bristol, Freiburg, Oslo, Stockholm, Copenhagen, Amsterdam, Muenster and Hamburg. In many respects Bristol performed badly when compared to others in this group.

Bristol was the only city in its evaluation group that could not supply CO_2 data (percentage from transport, and per capita emissions, 2005–06). Other aspects of the Bristol bid identified by the expert panel of assessors included:

- lowest level of kilometres of segregated cycle tracks;
- lowest level of kilometres of all bike and cycle paths;
- lowest percentage of population living less than 300 metres from a public transport stop;
- highest modal share for car and motorised transport;
- lowest modal share for bikes;
- no data on accessibility of public open spaces;
- highest percentage of population exposed to road noise.

And on policy: 'All the cities – with the exception of Bristol – aim to contain the car use' (European Commission, 2010c).

Bristol was commended for its environmental management systems, its information and communications systems for air quality monitoring, and its approach to spatial planning, especially the use of brownfield sites for new development and containing urban sprawl.

Australian cities

Australian cities would not normally figure in a discussion of the built environment and quality of life except as illustrative of an urbanism that has emphasised suburbanisation, high levels of car dependency and high per capita energy use (Newman and Kenworthy, 1989). Global comparisons of transport-related energy use (Figure 5.3) show that Australian cities are much more closely aligned with US cities than with European or densely populated Asian cities (Newman and Kenworthy, 1989).

Kenworthy (2008) has explored the relationship between density and car use and these results are shown in Figure 5.4.

Cities that are characterised by low-density developments are heavily dependent on fossil fuels and car-based mobility, and this produces a large number of problems associated with vulnerability to peak oil, air quality and equity. Dodson and Sipe (2008a) have summarised these problems and made a very strong link between fossil fuel use, density and the impact of the 'spread-out city' on the vulnerability of low- and middle-income groups to oil price increases and the combined effects of low income, car dependency and the necessity to make long-distance trips in a suburbanised city. The built environment in Australian cities (with some notable exceptions) has created very serious problems for low-income groups with high transport dependency.

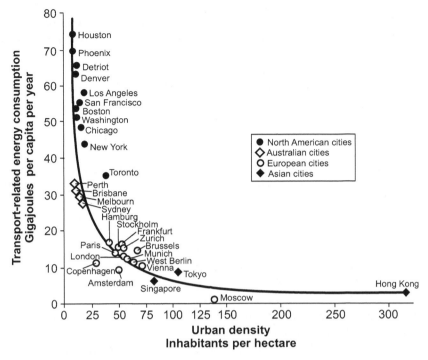

Figure 5.3 Urban density and transport-related energy consumption

Source: Newman and Kenworthy (1989).

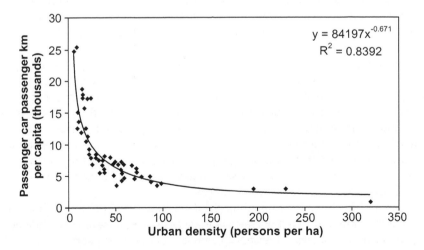

Figure 5.4 Relationship between passenger kilometres of car use per capita and urban density

Source: Kenworthy (2008).

This urban legacy makes recent developments in Australian cities all the more remarkable and significant. Australian cities are setting new standards in built environment and quality of life which accept the difficult starting point (lower density than a European city) but rapidly move in a direction that emphasises liveability, sustainability and quality of life and all linked to a strong emphasis on reshaping the built environment. All Australian cities are doing this to varying degrees, and best practice examples include:

- significant improvements to the public realm, for example South Bank in Brisbane and Federation Square in Melbourne;
- a major shift in the spatial development and structure of Perth in Western Australia stimulated by new electrified railway lines to Fremantle and the north;
- major changes in Sydney, including new trams and a traffic ban on the main north–south route through the central business district, George St (Zeibots, 2010);
- a comprehensive approach to the reshaping of Brisbane in its River City Blueprint (Brisbane City Council, 2010).

Australian cities, like British cities, are still heavily car-dependent and cycling- and walking-unfriendly and have a long way to go, but the groundswell of change in thinking about built environment and quality of life is clear and gathering momentum.

Mees (2010) is very critical of Australian land use and transport planning, especially the emphasis on densification, which he rejects as a central organising principle underpinning sustainable cities. A very different perspective is provided by Ewing *et al.* (2008), who analyse the links between urban density and transport and CO_2 reduction and show that densification can produce significant reductions in emissions.

Mees (2010) is still correct to emphasise highly connected public transport systems offering seamless modal transfer opportunities as a key element in any attempt to reshape Australian cities and, he argues, this is not happening. Australian cities, like British cities, have departed significantly from the German, Swiss and Austrian models, where high levels of integration delivered by strong regional transport authorities under democratic control are the norm. Mees quotes the Zurich model, which delivers a high-quality integrated public transport system that is heavily used and for much the same reasons as the Freiburg system is heavily used. Both are under democratic and public control.

Britain and Australia have opted for the deregulation and privatisation model, which in the form in which it operates in Manchester or Melbourne is fundamentally inimical to sustainable transport planning working to support a sustainable built environment and vice versa.

Policy interventions to promote high quality in the built environment

Policies and interventions that can deliver a high-quality built environment are well documented in best practice summaries and surveys (European Commission, 2010b; EEA, 2009). Freiburg is particularly well documented. The Freiburg approach to transport, spatial planning, housing quality, new residential areas and renewable energy delivered consistently over a 30-year period has achieved a widely recognised high quality of life and high quality of the built environment for its 240,000 residents. The reality is there to see and experience, and the experiential domain is of greater significance than a policy document or a design guide. The UK has a plethora of high-quality design guides (e.g. DfT, 2008) but very little application of those guides on the ground to produce demonstrably superior built environments.

The Freiburg approach to high-quality integrated urban design and environmental management has been developed at a larger urban scale by the Wuppertal Institute (2009) in the case of Munich (population 1.3 million).

Best practice: Munich

The transformation of transport systems to meet multiple economic, social, environmental and greenhouse gas reduction policies requires a highly integrated scenario-based approach. The Wuppertal Institute in Germany has conducted such a study for the southern German city of Munich. The study was commissioned by Siemens, which is based in Munich, and brings together the key components of integrated scenario building across all sectors of the Munich economy with the intention of describing in detail the interactions and synergies between sectors and policy instruments.

The study concludes that Munich can achieve a 90 per cent reduction in greenhouse gases by the 900th anniversary of the city in 2058. This 90 per cent reduction is from a 1990 baseline and will reduce the per capita per annum emissions of Munich citizens to 750 kilograms, which is well below the often-quoted global share target of 2 tonnes.

The study examines in detail all aspects of Munich's energy and transport system, including:

- electricity use by buildings;
- 'Passivhaus' concepts (homes that reach only 10 per cent of current best practice energy use);
- heating requirement of buildings;
- electricity use and role of electric vehicles;
- developing higher levels of use of walking, cycling and public transport modes;
- developing a 'compact settlement' approach to shorten travel distances and encourage walking and cycling;

- renewable power generation through wind and PVs;
- smart grid and load management.

The study concludes that the 'nearly carbon-free urban centre' is achievable and 'in order to succeed the goal of becoming carbon-free must be assigned a high priority in the overall development of the urban infrastructure'. The study also concludes that this approach has relevance to the EU as a whole, since 80 per cent of its citizens live in cities and this approach can be developed intensively in these locations to achieve overall 90 per cent reductions in greenhouse gas emissions in a coordinated manner across all energy and transport sectors and sub-sectors.

The Munich study is not yet a city council adopted plan, but it shows very clearly indeed that it is possible to design ambitious and dramatic improvements in quality of life, economic sectors and the built environment in a highly integrated way to achieve what Freiburg has already achieved but at a larger scale and in a way that can be applied to all Europe's towns and cities for the benefit of approximately 400 million citizens.

The Freiburg reality and the Munich plan are also reflected in the work of one of the world's leading architects and urbanists, Jan Gehl. Gehl runs his own architectural consultancy in Denmark and has carried out consultancy studies for Brisbane, London, Melbourne and other cities around the world, all of which focus on the failures of car-dominated cities to deliver quality outcomes and how cities can be 'reconquered' to produce high-quality living environments.

Gehl's report on Brisbane (Gehl Architects, 2008) is illustrative of his approach. The key elements of the approach are those already contained in Chapter 3 (on children) and Chapter 4 (on older people). A liveable city that can lay claim to an attractive built environment and democratic quality of life (everyone benefits and no one group is sacrificed to favour another group) will put people first. Gehl takes up this point very early in his report for Brisbane City Council:

Putting people first

If Brisbane is to remain livable and keep up with international standards, a new approach is needed. This implies acknowledging the economic, social and environmental benefits of a new sensitivity towards the public realm and the promotion of proximity as an urban ideal.

Gehl also adopts a comparative approach. In his work on Brisbane and more generally, he makes explicit comparison with Melbourne, Adelaide, Perth, Copenhagen and Stockholm. Gehl adopts the same overall strategy as we do in this book by interrogating international best practice to provide real-world insights into the possibilities for improvement in selected cities and regions. In this book we rely heavily on Freiburg im Breisgau, but find much of value in Copenhagen, Stockholm and Swiss cities.

Gehl identifies Brisbane as a city with many desirable qualities and potential, but one that is organised around the car and creates an environment that fails the elderly and children. In his report for Brisbane City Council he delivers an assessment of that city that is rather uncompromising and specifically identifies problems of 'disconnected neighbourhoods', problems for children and older people, and damage to social networks because of heavy traffic.

Gehl recommends corrective measures to create or restore high-quality city living and effectively recommends 'doing a Freiburg':

> Acknowledging the importance of an inviting public realm, gradually reconquering the public spaces taken over by cars in the past 5 decades has become a key priority in cities throughout the world. Reconquering means gradually shifting portions of the surface space currently used for cars to people activities. This shift should go together with a greater awareness of the public realm and its importance for the social fabric of the citizens. Reconquered cities apply a holistic approach to their public realm in which the total experience of being present in and moving through public space is cared for with a new sensitivity.

Gehl coins the terms 'reconquering cities' and 'reconquered cities' to describe the process and the desirable end point of policies that improve the built environment, restore quality places and celebrate people rather than cars. He lists 11 cities that are being 'reconquered':

- Portland, USA;
- Curitiba, Brazil;
- Copenhagen, Denmark;
- Lyon, France;
- Melbourne, Australia;
- Bogota, Colombia;
- Strasbourg, France;
- Saint-Denis, France;
- Barcelona, Spain;
- Freiburg, Germany;
- Cordoba, Spain.

None are in the UK.

Policy recommendations

It is desirable that all UK cities should offer the same high-quality built environment and high quality of life as that provided for Freiburg's citizens. With its 27 per cent of all journeys every day by bike, its integrated public transport and spatial planning, and its high-quality, energy-efficient housing and emphasis on renewable energy, Freiburg represents an achievable target for all cities. Each of these areas and the wider policy context that ensures delivery of results is described in Stadt Freiburg (2010).

Implement the recommendations suggested by 19 public health experts in the *Lancet* (Woodcock *et al.*, 2009):

- creation of safe urban environments for mass active travel and the prioritisation of the needs of pedestrians and cyclists over those of motorists;
- diverting of resources from roads for motorists towards provision of infrastructure for pedestrians and cyclists;
- substantial investment in the design of infrastructure for pedestrians and cyclists to reshape the streetscape and public realm;
- carbon rationing;
- geographically expanded road pricing;
- traffic demand management;
- restrictions on car parking and access;
- reduced speed limits;
- behavioural change approaches, including raised awareness and travel planning.

The key elements and principles that underpin what needs to be done to achieve the dramatic improvements to be found in Freiburg have been detailed in the Green Capital assessments described in this chapter and in the Gehl work on many cities around the world. ITDP *et al.* (2010) have published a further guide to the creation of high-quality environments summarised in 10 principles. These are:

1   Walk the walk: focusing on slower vehicle speeds, direct pedestrian access to destinations, and improved design of streets.
2   Powered by people: focusing on measures to improve cycling rates.
3   Get on the bus: focusing on bus rapid transit (BRT).
4   Cruise control: focusing on traffic reduction policies, including parking charges and congestion charging.
5   Deliver the goods: focusing on 'smart urban logistics' to reduce the numbers of lorries in cities and the German lorry taxation regime.
6   Mix it up: focusing on mixed uses in urban areas (work, retail and leisure can all happily coexist and can reduce vehicle kilometres per person by 30 per cent).
7   Fill it in: focusing on 'densification' around transport nodes according to pedestrian and cycling 10-minute catchment areas. A pedestrian can walk 800 metres in 10 minutes, and a cyclist can cover 3 kilometres.
8   Get real: focusing on preserving and enhancing local cultural, social and historical assets.
9   Connect the blocks: shaping the city so that there are many short streets and many intersections per unit of area. This enhances pedestrian permeability and is less attractive to cars.
10   Make it last: by always using design methods and materials that are memorable, malleable, good-quality and well maintained.

Summary

- Adopt and implement the 10 principles in ITDP *et al.* (2010) in all UK cities.
- Learn from Freiburg and adopt as many of the key elements of implemented policy in that city as possible (Stadt Freiburg, 2010).
- Reconquer cities in the way described by Gehl Architects (2008).
- Implement the recommendations made by 19 public health experts (Woodcock *et al.*, 2009).

6 Air pollution

It is estimated that around 4,000 people died as a result of the Great Smog of London in 1952. That led to the introduction of the Clean Air Act in 1956. In 2008, 4,000 people died in London from air pollution and 30,000 died across the whole of the UK. The Government needs to act now, as Government did in the 1950s, to save the health of the nation.

(House of Commons, 2011b)

Urban air pollution is a serious problem. Four thousand deaths per annum in London alone are a significant public health problem that ordinarily would trigger a major response to eliminate such large-scale loss of life. It is also a problem more generally in the European Union, and this has a direct impact on the 80 per cent of the EU population who live in cities (European Commission, 1999). The same period has also seen improvements in vehicle efficiency, exhaust systems, particulate traps and fuel quality that could be expected to contribute to the improvement of air quality but have not delivered a significant improvement in air quality (House of Commons, 2011b). The problem of poor air quality persists.

The European Environment Agency (EEA, 2009) commented on the air pollution problem as follows:

The EU estimates that human exposure to fine particulate matter ($PM_{2.5}$) causes about 350 000 premature deaths each year. In other words, at these exposure levels the average life expectancy is reduced by almost a year – almost two years in the most affected urban areas of Belgium, the Netherlands, Northern Italy and parts of Poland and Hungary. The major air pollutants in urban areas are particulate matter, ozone and nitrogen oxides (NO_x). These pollutants pose serious threats to human health, as they can cause respiratory disorders, aggravate asthma, and impair development of lung function in children. Measurements of air quality show that almost 90 per cent of the inhabitants of European cities where PM_{10} concentrations are measured are exposed to concentrations that exceed the WHO air quality guideline level of 20 micrograms per cubic metre.

The health impacts of one of the more serious pollutants (PM_{10}) have been summarised by Aphekom (2011), and this is reproduced in Figure 6.1.

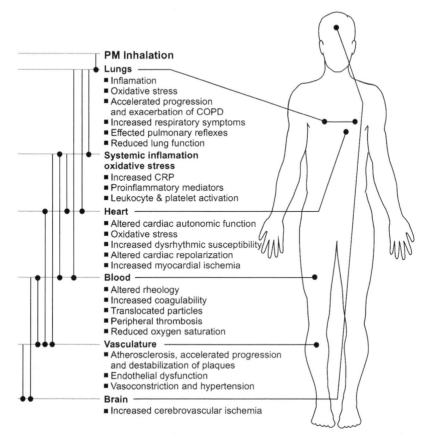

Figure 6.1 Health effects of particulate matter 10 microns or less in diameter (PM₁₀)

Air pollution is damaging to the health of children and older people (Aphekom, 2011): 'Living near busy roads could be responsible for some 15–30 per cent of all new cases of asthma in children; and of chronic obstructive pulmonary disease and coronary heart disease in adults 65 years of age and older.'

Clean Air in London has estimated that there are 1,148 schools within 150 metres of London roads carrying over 10,000 vehicles per day (Clean Air in London, 2011). This exposes several tens of thousands of children to unacceptably high health hazards and does not yet form any part of UK air quality policy, health policy or policy aimed at protecting children.

We have already discussed many of the factors that cause health and quality-of-life problems for children (Chapter 3) and older people (Chapter 4). Air pollution is yet another factor that is present and preventable and attracts a very poor-quality public policy response. The 2010 State of the Environment Report (EEA, 2010) shows that urban air quality (particulate emissions and ozone) is not on track to achieve its target, which is defined as 'to attain levels of air quality that do not give rise to negative health impacts'. The same report (EEA, 2010) assesses the air quality situation in European countries:

> In Europe, there have been successful reductions in the levels of sulphur dioxide (SO_2) and carbon monoxide (CO) in ambient air, as well as marked reductions in NO_x. Also, lead concentrations have declined considerably with the introduction of unleaded petrol. However, exposure to particulate matter (PM) and ozone (O_3) remain of major environment-related health concern, linked to a loss of life expectancy, acute and chronic respiratory and cardio-vascular effects, impaired lung development in children, and reduced birth weight.
>
> In the period 1997 to 2008, 13 to 62 per cent of Europe's urban population was potentially exposed to ambient air concentrations of fine and coarse particulate matter (PM_{10}) in excess of the EU limit value set for the protection of human health. However, particulate matter has no threshold concentration, thus adverse health effects can also occur below the limit values.

Air pollution in European cities

Air pollution in urban areas is a general EU problem, and comparisons are difficult because of variation in the pollutants measured, measurement in background situations compared with street-level measurements, and the exact measure used (e.g. number of days in a year when the air quality standard is breached). In addition to these considerations there are geographical differences, especially with respect to ozone pollution, which are likely to lead to higher concentrations and exceedances in sunnier parts of Europe such as southern Germany and Italy.

A recent ranking of European cities on best practice for clean air (BUND and European Environment Bureau, 2011) ranked 17 cities in terms of their performance and adoption of measures that can actually improve air quality. Each city was scored on a variety of criteria, and an overall grading on its performance was calculated on an A-to-F scale. No city got an A-grade. Five cities got a B-grade: Berlin came out best in class, followed by Stockholm, Copenhagen, Vienna and Zurich. Seven cities got an F-grade, including London. They were (in descending order of performance, so Brussels is better than London and so on): Brussels, London, Madrid, Stuttgart, Duesseldorf, Milan and Rome. Each city is evaluated on the strength of its interventions to improve air quality. London is a poor performer on this criterion. Its failings are:

- Its air quality data are not accurate, because London has changed the configuration of the measurement stations.
- Postponing phase 3 of the low emission zone (LEZ) was a backward step.
- Scaling back plans for all buses to be hybrid by 2012 was a backward step.
- Halving the congestion charge zone in January 2011 was a backward step.
- Sharp increases in public transport fares are not helpful when dealing with air pollution.

- The new mayor champions car use.
- There are no meaningful measures to increase the amount of walking.

(BUND and European Environment Bureau, 2011)

Italy has a serious air pollution problem. BUND and European Environment Bureau (2011) puts Milan and Rome at the bottom of its ranking. The Italian National Institute of Statistics (ISTAT, 2010) lists the 30 most polluted cities in Europe, and 17 of them are in Italy.

A large-scale WHO database (WHO, 2011a) has compiled air pollution data for 1,100 cities across 91 countries, including capital cities and cities with more than 100,000 residents. The WHO guideline value for PM_{10} is 20 micrograms per cubic metre as an annual average that should not be exceeded (WHO, 2011b). Average PM_{10} levels in European cities lie in the range 29–42 ug/m^3. The world average is 71 ug/m^3. World values range from 5–9 in some Texas and Californian urban areas, to Delhi (198), Peshawar (219) and Ahwaz in Iran (372).

European city variations are not large, as can be seen in a small selection in Table 6.1.

The WHO (2011a) database lists PM_{10} values for 28 UK cities. Thirteen of these cities are at or above the 20 ug/m^3 guideline level, and all of them lie in the range 15–29. This is not noticeably out of line with other large countries, while the PM_{10} levels in Liverpool and Manchester compare favourably with some best practice examples, for example Zurich in Switzerland. There are 58 cities listed in Germany, and of these 54 are in exceedance of the 20 ug/m^3 value. The UK performance is much better than Germany, with Liverpool and Manchester better than Stockholm and Copenhagen.

Air quality in the UK

The air quality situation in the UK has been summarised by the Department of Environment, Food and Rural Affairs (DEFRA, 2011), and this information is reproduced in Table 6.2.

Table 6.1 Selected European city PM_{10} concentrations

	PM_{10} ug/m^3
Edinburgh	15
Liverpool	16
Malmo	18
Manchester	20
Zurich	21
Hamburg	23
Kassel	24
Vienna	25
Copenhagen	26
Stockholm	28
London	29

Source: Extracted from WHO (2011a).

Table 6.2 Current UK-wide status of air quality management areas (AQMAs) and appraised action plans (as of September 2011)

Region	Total number of local authorities	Number of LAs with AQMAs	AQMAs for NO$_2$ (as of December 2010)	AQMAs for PM$_{10}$ (as of December 2010)	AQMAs for SO$_2$ (as of December 2010)	LAs with action plans submitted	LAs with action plans awaited
England (excluding London)	292	188	457	53	8	144	47
London	33	33	36	32	0	33	0
Scotland	32	13	14	12	1	9	5
Wales	22	8	29	1	0	5	3
Northern Ireland	26	12	13	7	1	10	0
Total	405	256	549	105	10	203	55

Source: DEFRA (2011, table 2.2, p. 7).

Air quality in UK urban areas is poor (DEFRA, 2010) and has not improved very much at all after 15 years of operation of an air quality management regime (DEFRA, 2011). A high level of awareness of air quality problems associated with a high-quality scientific analysis has not produced action on the ground to improve air quality, and this points to failures in the policy process and governance. Government, both central and local, has chosen not to implement policies and interventions that are able to deliver improvements in air quality. This is not a specifically UK problem, as the 350,000 excess deaths in Europe reported above (EEA, 2009) demonstrate. Nevertheless there is clear evidence that air quality is an area of policy failure. Air quality problems are still the norm rather than the exception and persist within a clear regulatory regime. The regulatory regime is very clear:

> Local authorities in the UK have statutory duties for managing local air quality under Part IV of the Environment Act 1995 and in Northern Ireland, Part III of the Environment (Northern Ireland) Order 2002.
> They are required to carry out regular reviews and assessments of air quality in their area against standards and objectives prescribed in regulations for the purpose of local air quality management (LAQM) before undertaking Action Planning if air quality is found to breach the regulations.
>
> (DEFRA, 2009)

A DEFRA review of local air quality management (DEFRA, 2010) concluded:

> The EU has set mandatory air quality targets for certain pollutants. The UK is at present failing to meet EU targets for ambient concentrations of particulate matter (PM$_{10}$) and nitrogen dioxide (NO$_2$).
> Road transport is the largest single source of air pollution, accounting for 33 per cent of emissions in the case of NO$_x$ and 21 per cent in the case of

PM_{10}. Transport is identified as the main source of pollution in 92 per cent of all AQMAs.

Local authority review and assessment has revealed continuing air pollution problems on a far wider scale than anticipated, with 58 per cent of all authorities declaring AQMAs, many of which cover the whole area of the authority. Measures put in place locally through LAQM action planning have had very limited impact, and few AQMAs have been revoked following the successful implementation of pollution reduction measures. Pollution levels which exceed EU limit values are far more widespread than a few hotspots, and LAQM is contributing little to reducing them.

Local authorities in the UK have a number of complicated duties related to Air Quality Management (AQM), the designation of areas with poor air quality, Air Quality Management Areas (AQMA) and the preparation of Air Quality Action Plans (AQAP) which have the purpose of implementing measures to deal with exceedances and deliver compliance with statutory guidelines and standards on all the major categories of pollution. The air quality standards that should not be exceeded are listed in DEFRA (2010).

This complicated process has failed. Since the 1995 Act, 223 local authorities have declared AQMAs, 178 local authorities have adopted AQAPs and 37 AQMAs have been revoked either because air quality has improved or for other reasons (DEFRA, 2011). The reasons for failure include:

- Lack of willingness on the part of local authorities to take air quality seriously and implement AQAPs that contain measures that will improve air quality. An example of this lack of willingness to deal effectively with air quality problems can be found in Lancaster (UK). Brooks (2009) carried out a review of the Lancaster City Council air quality action plan and concluded:

    The Lancaster City Council 2007 AQAP section 5.4 lists 19 options for actions to take forward for improving air quality within the Lancaster AQMA. Eleven of these are stated as originating from the Vision Board transport strategy workshop but not a single one offers the prospect of a concrete improvement. Most of them are simple re-iterations of various guidelines and advice for reviewing air quality management issues such as intentions to perform reviews, explore potentials, identify opportunities etc.

- Active complicity on the part of local authorities to make things worse through the promotion of road building, large new car parks, business and science parks, traffic generation and the extra pollution caused by higher levels of kilometres driven. The support given by Lancaster City Council for new road building (Whitelegg, 2007a) and a new edge of city centre retail development (Brooks, 2009) shows this complicity in action. Whitelegg (2007a) presents evidence on the impact of bypasses on generating new traffic and worsening air quality. Lancaster City Council is the statutory body for delivering improvements in air quality and at the same time actively promotes developments that will worsen air quality. This is a general problem which to varying degrees is characteristic of all local authorities with air quality responsibilities. Lancaster City Council is not unusual in this respect.

• Lack of support from central government to ensure that the whole air quality management process delivers results both through the allocation of funding to deliver air quality improvements and through direction to those local authorities that are not doing enough to improve. Local authorities are not funded specifically to implement air quality policies, and it is not surprising therefore that interventions with a price tag are not pursued as often as they might be.

Notwithstanding this lukewarm approach to a serious public health problem there is an international evidence base on measures and interventions that are associated with demonstrable air quality improvements, and these are discussed under 'Policy recommendations' below.

Policy recommendations for improving air quality

Actively interrogate the full menu of possibilities that can be employed to improve air quality. A starting point is Citeair (n.d.). Interrogation should then be followed by implementation, with the objective of improving air quality so that it meets EU standards.

Adopt policies that will deliver the Freiburg modal split (a city with 30 per cent of all trips by car will have cleaner air than a city with 60 per cent of trips by car).

Replace all diesel buses and taxis with alternatively fuelled vehicles. Nantes in France has replaced 80 per cent of its bus fleet with CNG-fuelled buses (Civitas, 2009). Graz in Austria has a 100 per cent bio-diesel bus fleet 'fed' by waste oil from catering establishments (Civitas, 2008). Civitas (2010) contains more information on similar work undertaken in Bremen.

Create low emission zones (LEZs) that will allow only the cleanest cars into the city and eventually will allow only zero-pollution cars into the city. The London LEZ was expected to reduce particulate emission by 6.6 per cent by 2012 (TfL, 2008).

Adopt a German-style LEZ policy. Forty-seven cities in Germany have implemented the LEZ approach, with the specific intention of improving air quality. There are none in the UK outside of London. (The German cities are listed at http://www.lowemissionzones.eu/countries-mainmenu-147/germany-mainmenu-61.)

Suspend traffic when there is a danger of EU limit values being exceeded. The city of Milan was totally car-free for 10 hours on 9 October 2011 because pollution had exceeded permitted levels for 12 consecutive days (Transport and Environment, 2011). This policy suggestion originated with the European Commission in

1999 but has not been actioned in the UK: 'An important option offered to city authorities by the framework directive is the right to suspend activities, including motor-vehicle traffic when there is a risk of limit values being exceeded' (European Commission, 1999).

Implement urban logistics projects to intercept trucks on the edge of cities and trans-ship the freight on to smaller and less polluting vehicles for final delivery. Urban logistics already exists in a number of German cities and is implemented in the Broadmeads shopping centre in Bristol and at Heathrow Airport. Urban logistic solutions are defined and evaluated in BESTUFS (2007). In the Tenjin Joint Distribution System in Fukuoka in Japan there was a decrease of 65 per cent in the number of lorries entering the area served and a decrease of 28 per cent in total distance travelled. This has a direct effect on improving air quality.

Implement large-scale car share/car club schemes (Glotz-Richter, 2010). The detailed monitoring of car share schemes in Bremen shows that one car share car can replace 9.5 individually owned vehicles (Civitas, 2010). Based on the proportion of the Swiss population who car-share (100,000 out of 8 million) the potential car sharer population of the EU-27 is 6 million (Momo, 2010). Car sharers have much reduced car ownership levels, a shared car emits 15–25 per cent less CO_2 per kilometre driven, and car share club members make much heavier use of bus, train, bike and foot, contributing to reductions in greenhouse gas emissions and air pollution.

Implement large-scale new residential developments to cope with any growth in housing demand on the model of Vauban and Rieselfeld in Freiburg. These new residential areas have very low car ownership and use rates (Stadt Freiburg, 2010).

Implement congestion charging/road pricing schemes along the lines of the London and Stockholm schemes (VTPI, 2011) and scale up the geographical extent of the charging area so that in the case of London (but generalisable to all metropolitan regions in the EU-27) the charging area would extend to the whole of the administrative area of London, with a population of 7 million (Whitelegg, 2011b).

Allocate a high political importance to improving air quality and put this into practice in all land use, spatial planning, housing, economic development and regeneration strategies and policies. Developments must pass the air pollution test. If they add to air pollution then they cannot go ahead. If they are designed in line with a decoupling agenda (OECD, 2006) and with best practice on traffic reduction, demand management and the absolute prioritisation of walking, cycling and public transport, they can go ahead.

Introduce new planning legislation along the lines suggested by the Campaign for Clean Air in London (House of Commons, 2011b): 'The Campaign for Clean Air in London (CAL) urges the Environmental Audit Committee to recommend a requirement under UK planning law to protect sensitive populations (e.g. children and the elderly) from air pollution. This should build upon standards applied to school siting in California.'

Summary

Air pollution is a serious problem in the UK that leads to loss of life, illnesses, hospitalisation and substantial economic costs. The problem is especially damaging to the quality of life of children and older people. It is a problem that persists because of its relatively low prioritisation amongst politicians and decision makers at all levels. It is possible to improve air quality dramatically, and there is no shortage of practical and tangible interventions that can deliver these improvements. A continuing refusal to implement these interventions is a policy commitment to maintain 30,000 premature deaths every year in the UK when they could be largely eliminated.

7   Renewable energy

The UK has some of the richest renewable resources in Europe – particularly in terms of our wind and marine (wave and tidal stream) resources. If they can be captured effectively they can make a significant contribution to our long term energy goals relating to climate change and security of supply.

(DTI, 2007)

Renewable energy sources will have to play a central role in moving the world onto a more secure, reliable and sustainable energy path.

(IEA, 2010)

Renewable energy is energy produced from non-fossil fuel and non-nuclear sources and does not have characteristics associated with depletion of natural resources. Normally this means electricity generated by wind, wave, tidal, geothermal, hydro and photovoltaic technologies but can also refer to heat supplied directly to users from geothermal, ground and water sources. Energy production from crops or crop residues is not included in this discussion, though it does figure in European and UK discussions of renewables. There are a number of serious concerns about the use of biomass and fuel crops, principally around the whole-life-cycle carbon emissions, impacts of land use change on carbon emissions, and impacts on food availability for human consumption (Al-Riffai *et al.*, 2010; Bringezu *et al.*, 2009; De Santi *et al.*, 2008; Edwards *et al.*, 2010; EEA, 2008a; Gallagher, 2008; Howarth and Bringezu, 2009; Melillo *et al.*, 2009; Ros *et al.*, 2010; Schubert *et al.*, 2010; Searchinger *et al.*, 2008). The weight of scientific and policy analysis currently suggests that biomass and fuel crops should be excluded from efforts to increase the proportion of renewable energy feeding into the energy mix.

The discussion about renewable energy needs to take account of the relative demands of different sectors for final energy consumption. The breakdown of final energy consumption is shown in Figure 7.1. Households are responsible for 37.1 per cent of final energy consumption, transport 32.6 per cent and industry 27.9 per cent.

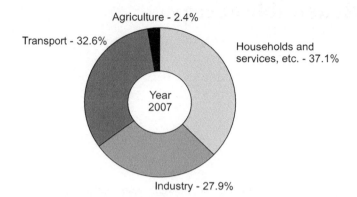

Figure 7.1 Final energy consumption by sector (Mtoe)

Source: European Commission (2010d).
Note: Mtoe = million tonnes of oil equivalent.

Renewable energy (RE) applications and installations have a great deal to contribute to the household sector through microgeneration (wind and PV) to produce electricity and district heating schemes to produce heat. In the same way, industry can substitute RE for traditional fossil-fuel-based sources of electricity and heat, for example the Ganter brewery in Freiburg (Stadt Freiburg, 2005).

Transport is a heavy user of energy and in particular energy derived from oil. We have already discussed in Chapter 5 the degree to which transport systems can adjust to decreased reliance on fossil fuel mobility and increased reliance on walking, cycling and public transport. Increased accessibility, much improved spatial planning and the detailed implementation of policies and investments that promote walking and cycling can produce significant reductions in transport's energy use. These modal shifts have the same role in a renewable energy debate as reducing energy use in buildings. Transport is perfectly capable of reducing its energy use, and this in turn produces a more manageable task in converting the remaining demand for what was motorised transport away from fossil fuel and towards electricity. Gilbert and Perl (2008) have shown that transport systems globally can move substantially away from oil dependence and embrace electricity produced from renewable sources.

We have already noted that transport is responsible for 32.6 per cent of EU-27 final energy demand. Reducing this level and switching residual demand to modes of transport that are much more energy efficient or effectively zero-energy (the bicycle) have a large role to play in overall energy policy and in any discussion of reducing demand and achieving a 20 per cent renewable energy target in the European Union (Whitelegg *et al.*, 2010). The European debate on the role of renewables in transport and the importance of demand management in achieving climate change and energy policy objectives has not captured the significance of this area of policy. When renewables and energy policies are discussed in transport (European Commission, 2011) the discussion is dominated by biofuels, electric vehicles and the need to reduce grams of CO_2 emissions per kilometre of passenger car travel. The White Paper on Transport (European Commission, 2011) establishes a 'goal for a resource-efficient transport system' that halves the use of conventionally fuelled cars in urban transport by 2030 and phases them out in cities by 2050. It does not embrace serious land use planning, demand management and modal shift policy of the kind developed in Freiburg. This is not likely to be enough to ensure the achievement of high-level strategic objectives in climate change and energy policy.

Heaps *et al.* (2009) describe a business-as-usual scenario for EU transport and its energy use. The authors of this report show that, in the absence of significant interventions to change the growth trend in transport energy demand to the year 2050, demand will increase by 16 per cent compared to 2010 levels. This growth in energy demand is driven by increases in air travel and road freight and takes place in spite of improvements in fuel efficiency.

The study then goes on to construct a mitigation scenario in which total transport demand is reduced. The importance of the mitigation scenario cannot be overstated. It demonstrates that existing trend forecasts can be breached. Transport energy demand can be reduced in ways that not only support a healthy economy and society but also bring about a number of co-benefits, for example the reduction in air pollution and noise. The reductions in energy demand are brought about by a reduction in overall activity, a shift to less energy-intensive modes (rail over road and air travel) and the introduction of much more energy-efficient and much less carbon-intensive technologies such as electric vehicles and fully electric rail travel. The mitigation scenario assumes no growth in the use of biofuels.

The concept of avoided transport is of central importance and relates to the consequences of spatial planning to reduce distances travelled and other policies, for example ICT substitution for physical travel (videoconferencing, teleconferencing and so on). This is exactly the same methodology used by Whitelegg *et al.* (2010) in the zero-carbon transport study for UK 2050. Both the Heaps and the Whitelegg scenario-based approaches to mitigation emphasise the importance of urban planning, land use standards, and bicycle- and pedestrian-friendly community development. They also emphasise the importance of removing subsidies for air transport.

Heaps *et al.* (2009) predict a significant shift to hybrid and electric cars as soon as they become available, 'so that by 2050 virtually all cars on the road are fully electrified'.

Kampman *et al.* (2010) developed several scenarios for the market penetration of electric vehicles (EVs) and plug-in hybrid electric vehicles (PHEVs) showing a range of values for the number of vehicles in 2030 in the European Union ranging from 10 million to 170 million. This is reproduced in Figure 7.2. Kampman (2011) has commented that she regards the fast and the ultra-fast uptake scenarios illustrated in Figure 7.2 'to be very ambitious . . . and will not realize without a great deal of effort'.

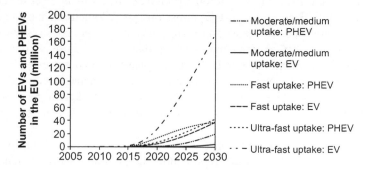

Figure 7.2 Total number of EVs and PHEVs in the EU car fleet in the three scenarios for the period up to 2030

Source: Kampman *et al.* (2010).

Renewable energy brings significant benefits in terms of reduced use of fossil fuels, meeting climate change carbon reduction targets, improved air quality, reductions in waste, increased energy security, and job creation, for example wind turbine manufacturing in Denmark and PV manufacturing in Germany. Renewables also represent a significant increase in efficiency. Traditional thermal electricity generating stations average around 45 per cent efficiency, where efficiency is defined as output divided by total fuel input to public conventional thermal plants (EEA, 2008b: 52).

The benefits of a large-scale shift to renewable energy

Renewables are a key component in climate change strategies:

> Renewable energy is an integral part of the Government's strategy for reducing carbon emissions as renewable energy resources produce very little carbon or other greenhouse gases. For every 1GW of fossil fuel fired electricity generation capacity displaced by an equivalent amount of renewable electricity, carbon emissions would be around 0.7 MtC to 1.5 MtC lower.
>
> (DTI, 2007, para. 5.3.3)

Reducing the demand for energy and switching residual demand away from fossil fuel sources and towards renewable energy are correlated in the sense that both must be progressed at the same time and with some vigour (Ecofys and Fraunhofer ISI, 2010):

> Energy savings are fundamental to increasing the share of renewable energy supply (RES) at affordable prices. A binding energy savings target would make a major contribution to the achievement of the 2020 RES target. As overall demand growth slows or decreases, the more achievable the 20 per cent supply and higher RES targets becomes.
>
> (Ecofys and Fraunhofer ISI, 2010: 19)

Ecofys and Fraunhofer ISI (2010) summarise the outcomes associated with a 20 per cent reduction in energy demand:

- EU annual energy consumption will decline from 1800 Mtoe in 2005 to 1600 Mtoe in 2020.
- Annual energy bills will fall by €78 billion by 2020.
- CO_2 emissions will decline by 560 million tonnes by 2020.
- One million jobs will be created in the EU in the energy industry.

The European Renewable Energy Directive (European Commission, 2009) explicitly links demand reduction and achieving the 20 per cent renewable energy target by specifying that reducing energy demand will be one of the most effective strategies that can ensure the 20 per cent renewable share is achieved.

The proportion of total energy sourced from renewables is an excellent indicator of a wider shift in society as a whole away from polluting and damaging technologies that are dependent on imports and subject to geopolitical volatility towards diversified, resilient, zero- or very low-polluting technologies that use indigenous resources and do not depend on imports from unstable regions of the world.

The wider shift in societal perspectives and values is also characterised by demand management and demand reduction so that renewables can play a larger part in electricity supply because demand has reduced. Demand reduction already plays a large part in transport policy, for example Freiburg's transport policy with the majority of trips accomplished by walking, bicycle and public transport resulting in much reduced use of the car and consequential reductions in the consumption of petrol and diesel fuels (Stadt Freiburg, 2010). Demand reduction also has a large part to play in the use of energy in buildings, especially domestic properties. The German 'Passivhaus' design concept based on actual construction and use data (Passivhaus Institut, 2010) shows that considerable reductions in household energy use can be achieved (Figure 7.3).

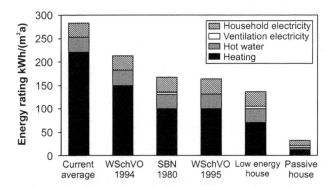

Figure 7.3 Household energy use in Germany: current average compared with other types and with the 'Passivhaus'

Reductions in energy demand in the home are clearly of considerable benefit to consumers, who are then able to reduce expenditure on energy and maintain levels of heating that ensure health and comfort and avoid the consequences of so-called 'fuel poverty' (discussed in Chapter 4).

Renewable energy becomes a far more significant source of supply for meeting energy demand when the demand itself has been reduced to the level shown in the far right column of Figure 7.3. The view of the Passivhaus Institut is that all the energy demands of the house can be met from renewable sources. This becomes even more important at the city region level, when as in the case of Freiburg significant progress with reducing energy demand in transport is matched by a similar level of achievement in reducing the energy demand of buildings and by Germany's largest application of renewable energy technology in the form of PVs on public buildings and private homes. Freiburg is very well placed indeed to deal with a large number of shocks that may be associated with peak oil and oil price increases predicted to rise to $113 per barrel by 2035 (IEA, 2010).

Freiburg is a resilient city and well placed to survive shocks of the kind described by Dodson and Sipe (2008a). UK cities are not at all resilient, and life in Liverpool or Manchester will be especially difficult on current trends when 60–70 per cent of all trips every day are by car and the price of oil rises in line with IEA predictions. In addition many UK homes are poorly constructed and are not energy efficient, and the percentage of energy demand met by renewables is less than 1 per cent.

Freiburg's successes in renewable energy applications (Stadt Freiburg, 2005) have set a high standard for all European cities to follow:

* Out of the 70 municipal schools, 35 have installed PV systems, and some have also installed solar thermal water heating.
* Freiburg has the world's first football stadium with solar equipment. The stadium has installed a large solar PV array on its roof, generating a total of 290 kW, and has some 60 square metres of thermal collectors for showers.
* An office block adjacent to Freiburg's central station has a solar PV façade that is 19 floors tall, with 240 solar modules.
* The university hospital cafeteria has a 272 square metre solar thermal equipment installation for its kitchen and dishwashing.
* The Exhibition and Trade Fair, which has hosted Europe's largest solar trade fair, Intersolar, over the last few years, has a 440 kW solar panel on its roof and an extra 254 kWp on the recent extension of the exhibition halls.

Renewable energy in the European Union

Renewable energy in the EU, particularly the generation of electricity from non-nuclear and non-fossil-fuel sources, is recognised as an important component of EU energy policy (European Commission, 2010e). EU energy policy has three main objectives:

Figure 7.4 Solar roof of the Freiburg Trade Fair Centre, Freiburg im Breisgau

- to reduce greenhouse gases by 20 per cent by 2020 (binding target);
- to increase energy efficiency/reduce energy use by 20 per cent by 2020 (non-binding target);
- to increase the share of renewables to 20 per cent by 2020 (binding target).

These objectives have been adopted against a background of rapid change in the energy mix and the development of renewables:

- The share of renewable energy in final energy consumption has increased steadily since 1990 and reached 8.6 per cent in 2005.
- The percentage of renewables in the final energy consumption total varied between countries from almost 40 per cent in the case of Sweden to almost zero at the bottom end of the scale.
- Large hydropower (over 10 MW) continues to dominate renewable electricity production, accounting in 2005 for two-thirds of the total across the EU (compared to 17 per cent from biomass and waste, 15 per cent from wind, 1.2 per cent from geothermal and 0.3 per cent from solar (EEA, 2008b).
- Growth in most forms of renewable energy accelerated after 2000, with large growth in PVs in Germany.

The current status of renewable energy sources (RES) compared to non-renewable sources is shown graphically in Figure 7.5.

The performance of EU-27 countries on renewable energy production is shown in Figure 7.6, and the UK is third from the bottom.

The very poor performance of the UK in this ranking is remarkable when compared with the very high potential in the UK for wind, wave and tidal energy contributions to the renewable total. The UK-based Carbon Trust (Carbon Trust, 2006) estimates that wave and tidal stream energy around the UK can supply 15–20 per cent of total UK electricity demand.

Heaps *et al.* (2009) have collated data from the European Environment Agency and other sources to show the potential of each of the 27 EU member states for

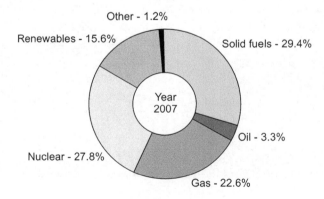

Figure 7.5 EU-27 net installed electricity production capacity of renewable energy

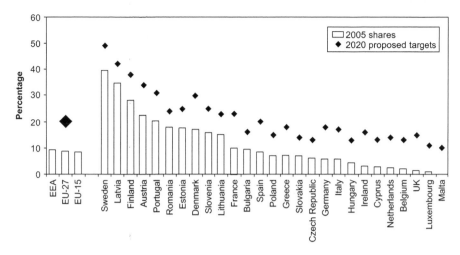

Figure 7.6 Renewables as a percentage of final energy consumption by member states (2005 data)

producing renewable energy compared to the total for the EU. This is summarised for the UK in Table 7.1.

The enormous potential of renewables in the UK (16 per cent of the total EU potential and 50 per cent of the total EU wave and tidal potential) when seen in the context of the very poor levels of exploitation (Figure 7.6) demonstrates a significant failure of UK public policy in an area of direct relevance to energy security, efficiency, resource use and climate change.

Renewable energy in the UK

The Sustainable Development Commission (SDC, 2006) reviews a number of studies about the potential of renewable energy to supply energy demand in the

Table 7.1 Renewable energy potential in the EU and the UK by 2030

	EU (TWh/yr)	UK (TWh/yr)	UK as percentage of EU
Hydro	477.8	8	1.67
Geothermal	180.3	0.3	0.16
Biomass	3,297.6	284.9	8.63
Solar PV	130.8	7.8	5.96
Solar thermal	1,453		
Wind on-shore	25,102	4,409	17.56
Wind off-shore	3,400	750.7	22.07
Wave and tidal	118.7	60	50.54
Total	34,160	5,520.8	16.16

UK and estimates that renewables can supply 85 per cent of current electricity production.

The government's renewable energy strategy (DECC, 2009) reports that the renewable share of UK energy supply in 2008 was 2.25 per cent and commits the UK to increase this to 15 per cent by 2020. The strategy defines renewable energy as including electricity generated from renewables (including biomass), heat generated from renewables (including biomass and biogas) and transport energy from renewables. The increase in the size of the renewable energy sector is illustrated in Figure 7.7.

The advantages of pursuing the strategy are listed as including:

- reducing the UK's CO_2 emissions by 750 million tonnes by 2030;
- increasing energy security;
- reducing fossil fuel use by 10 per cent;
- reducing gas imports by 20–30 per cent;
- creating half a million jobs.

Whilst it may be too early to pass judgements on the success of the strategy and the degree of implementation the signs in 2011 are not good. There are still large numbers of wind turbines rejected by the planning system. Wave and tidal energy is still at the research and prototype stage, and there are no significant installations contributing to electricity supply. Microgeneration by wind turbine and PV on domestic properties and public buildings is still very poorly developed, and the UK government on 31 October 2011 announced a 50 per cent cut in the feed-in tariff (FIT) for domestic PV installations of up to 4 kW in size. Governmental activity has been dominated by encouraging nuclear new-build on existing sites in spite of clear evidence that the nuclear option is bad value for money and will damage progress with developing renewable capacity (SDC, 2006).

The future

Heaps *et al.* (2009) have carried out an analysis of electricity generation in the European Union to the year 2050 and how it could be organised to deliver sufficient

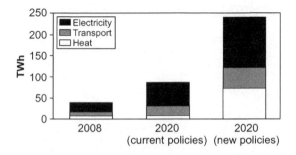

Figure 7.7 The size of the challenge: a potential scenario to reach 15 per cent renewable energy by 2020

electricity to end users and greenhouse gas reductions that are enough to protect the climate and recognise the development rights of less developed nations. The electricity generation mix shifts dramatically as coal and nuclear plants are rapidly decommissioned and large amounts of renewables are introduced. In the scenario, all coal is retired by 2035 and all nuclear by 2050. Wind increases its share of the generating mix from only 3.3 per cent in 2010 to 22 per cent in 2020 and 55 per cent in 2050. Solar (including imported solar) increases its share from close to zero in 2010 to 2.5 per cent in 2020 and 15 per cent in 2050. The share of electricity from combined heat and power (CHP) decreases from 19 per cent in 2010 to 14 per cent in 2020 and 11 per cent in 2050. However by 2050 CHP is fully biomass based.

In the UK the Sustainable Development Commission (SDC, 2006) has produced scenarios for electricity production up to the year 2050 and in its non-nuclear scenario shows a significant role for renewables (Figure 7.8).

The weight of scientific and policy evidence points unequivocally to a much increased role for renewables in the EU and the UK to 2050, and the challenge is to move from scenario and analysis to delivery and implementation.

Policy recommendations

The starting point for a serious renewable energy strategy at city, regional or national level is a significant increase in energy efficiency in all new buildings, retro-fit in existing buildings and a strategy that embraces serious demand reduction in the firm, household, school, clinic and public building (IEA, 2009). The technology and the case studies already exist and are in use in Freiburg and in many other cities around the world. The deficit is implementation of existing knowledge and not the need for new knowledge.

All new houses should achieve the German 'Passivhaus' standard of 15 kWh/m²/yr. This regulation was introduced in Freiburg in January 2009.

The reduction in demand for energy should be implemented in all relevant sectors, especially buildings, transport and appliances (Heaps *et al.*, 2009), and with a strong sense of urgency and political will.

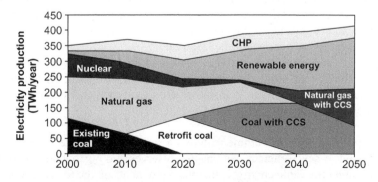

Figure 7.8 Non-nuclear scenario for electricity production in the UK to 2050

In the transport sector the policy recommendation in Chapter 5 around the form and structure of the built environment and a significant element of demand reduction through spatial planning and increased uptake of walking, cycling and public transport should be implemented.

Implement the recommendations in Whitelegg *et al.* (2010) in transport, especially those related to increases in fuel taxation, reducing subsidies to environmentally damaging transport modes, congestion charging, increased parking fees, and significant improvements in public transport so that it is at least as good as that of Freiburg, Zurich and Basel.

Adopt fiscal, taxation and funding reforms modelled on the German FIT (Stern Review, 2006). Stern discusses the German FIT as part of that country's ambitions to achieve renewable energy goals of 12.5 per cent of gross electricity consumption by 2010 and 20 per cent by 2020. The payments vary by technology, with PV receiving €0.457–0.624 per kWh and wind €0.055–0.091 per kWh. The rate is guaranteed for 20 years, but the level of support for deployment in subsequent years declines. In 2005, 10.2 per cent of electricity came from renewables (70 per cent supported by the FIT), saving 52 million tonnes of CO_2 in 2010. The total level of subsidy was €2.4 billion in 2005, at a cost shared by all consumers of €0.0056 per kWh (3 per cent of household electricity costs). Germany's strong support for renewables has produced valuable economic spin-offs, with an estimated 170,000 people working in the renewable sector and an industry turnover of €8.7 billion. Germany's achievements in PV manufacturing and installation are world-class. Germany in 2005 had 39 per cent of the installed global PV capacity and 23 per cent of global production.

Adopt the policies and strategies pioneered by Woking Borough Council (Stern Review, 2006), which is at the forefront of UK local authority efforts to tackle climate change. Between 1991 and 2005 the Council reduced energy consumption by approximately 50 per cent and carbon emission by 79 per cent across its own buildings. In 1999 the Council established an energy services company, Thamesway Energy Ltd, to finance sustainable and renewable energy projects. Its projects include a town centre CHP station which provides heat and power to civic offices, the Holiday Inn Hotel and a number of other town centre customers. Its PV installations account for 10 per cent of the UK total.

Adopt the policies and strategies pioneered by Kirklees Council, especially interest-free loans to householders to install small-scale renewable energy technologies on domestic properties (Kirklees Council, 2010).

Shift central and local government thinking into spend-to-save mode (CABE, 2007). Spend-to-save schemes can channel reserves and borrowings into energy efficiency and renewable energy so that the repayments on the loan are more than covered by the reductions in energy bills over the life of the installation.

Renewable energy (RE) is by definition available in many forms, and a thorough assessment of RE potential city by city and region by region is essential to identify an appropriate mix of sources for each locality (IEA, 2009). This evaluation and assessment can be informed by case study material on successful RE applications, for example Freiburg in Germany, Guessing in Austria and Samso in Denmark (IEA, 2009). These are amongst 13 case studies of successful RE applications reviewed by the IEA. The Austrian and Danish case studies have reported 100 per cent fossil-fuel-free status and are self-sufficient in electricity generated from RE.

8   Resilience

Atlanta needs 782 gallons of gasoline per person each year for its urban system to work, but in Barcelona it is just 64 gallons. With oil supply cuts and carbon taxes the decline in availability of oil will seriously confront Atlanta, yet Barcelona is likely to cope with ease. Both cities still need to have plans in place that help their citizenry to cope with such a disturbance.

(Newman *et al.*, 2009: 7)

Altered frequencies and intensities of extreme weather, together with sea level rise, are expected to have mostly adverse effects on natural and human systems.

(IPCC, 2007)

Introduction

There is a growing realisation that quality of life, well-being and the effective delivery of key public and private services, including health, welfare, education, food and access to everyday destinations, is not as dependable and reliable as might be assumed. The combination of climate change impacts, especially severe weather events such as floods, storms, droughts and heatwaves (IPCC, 2007; Munich RE, 2012), oil price volatility, energy security and peak oil (Heinberg, 2003), require a very different approach to governance, public services, logistics and the prudent management and spending of tax dollars than at any time in the past. There is now a real need for risk management in Europe (EEA, 2011) as a result of the rising scale of disasters and economic damage, including the 70,000 excess deaths in the 2003 heatwave and the economic losses associated with floods (€52 billion) and storms (€44 billion) in the time period 1998–2009 (EEA, 2011). These considerations have fuelled the development of analyses and policies that are aimed at increasing the resilience of cities, regions and nations (Newman *et al.*, 2009).

Resilience can be seen as a new focus for public policy, but in essence it is little different from policies and accepted practices that may have created resilience long before the word itself came to be applied in discussions of city, regional and national planning and organisation. Examples of resilience that would be understood by the majority of citizens include:

- Large percentages of the workforce in hospitals or schools living within easy commuting distances by foot, bike and public transport. This has the effect of ensuring the continuation of those services should fuel shortages or severe weather disrupt the road system.
- A large percentage of food consumed locally being grown locally. This has the effect of insulating (making more resilient) the residents of any locality from events that disrupt logistic chains or long supply chains for food. This is now recognised in public policy (City of Oakland, 2008; Whitelegg, 2005).
- Electricity supply that has moved away from large thermal power stations fed by gas, coal or oil to those supplied by wind, wave, PV and other technologies that are supplied in the locality and do not depend on large, centralised national grids or long transmission lines (e.g. gas pipelines and electricity transmission systems).
- Cities with high levels of bike use, for example Freiburg with 27 per cent of trips every day by bike, are in a much better situation to 'weather the storm' of oil shocks, including rapid price rises, shortages or civil unrest blocking oil depots and fuel supply systems. Manchester, with its 0.9 per cent of all trips each day by bike (Pinfield, 2010), is extremely vulnerable to these shocks (it has very little resilience).
- Those cities that rely heavily on electricity for public transport systems (e.g. trams) have high levels of resilience. The electricity can be generated from many different sources, and public transport can cope with oil shocks (Gilbert and Perl, 2008).
- Cities that are compact or can be transformed into cities 'of short distances' (Holzapfel, 2012).

Climate change and resilience

The documentation and debate on climate change is very large and will not be repeated here. Serious scientific analysis and policy debate (Ekman *et al.*, 2009) are clear that: (a) climate change is real and poses very serious threats to human and ecological systems; (b) business as usual is not an option; and (c) intensified efforts to deal with mitigation (reducing greenhouse gases, GHGs) are urgently needed. Ekman *et al.* (2009) recommend a global 90 per cent reduction in GHGs from a 1990 base by 2050 and a 100 per cent reduction in domestic emissions from so-called 'Annexe 1 countries' (including the UK) 'to be achieved entirely by domestic at-source reductions in order to ensure the transition to a carbon-free energy path'. The State of Baden-Wuerttemberg in southern Germany has adopted a 90 per cent reduction target in GHGs, demonstrating that scientific analysis can be translated into determined public policy implementation.

Rockstrom *et al.* (2009) identify nine 'planetary boundaries' within which humanity can safely operate. Three of these have already been transgressed:

- climate change;
- loss of biodiversity;
- changes to the global nitrogen cycle.

Rockstrom *et al.* (2009) are very clear about the seriousness of the situation facing humanity and the interrelatedness of many of the large-scale ecological and environmental crises facing humanity. Ekman *et al.* (2009) are equally clear about the need for urgent action and changes in governance to increase the chances that actions will be taken. Both contributions are scientifically robust and policy-relevant but fail to locate the need for change and action firmly within the contemporary political discourse in the EU, Sweden or the UK. Any UK discussion of climate change actions that will actually reduce real emissions in real places rapidly founders on the political prioritisation of economic growth, international competiveness, the need to create jobs and the unquestioning commitment to higher and higher levels of mobility. It is a very rare local authority in the UK that is not actively pursuing higher levels of GHG emissions through one or more of the following:

*   support for the expansion of airports, runways and terminals;
*   support for new road building, with clear implications for newly generated traffic and higher CO_2 emissions;
*   support for new shopping centres with very large car parks.

These largely unquestioned policy objectives reduce the resilience of nations, regions and cities (Newman *et al.*, 2009) and have not produced the gains in quality of life and welfare that we discussed in Chapter 1 of this book. In the case of road building as a regeneration and economic strategy to create jobs, there is strong evidence that investing in transport infrastructure to create jobs in a local economy simply does not deliver the jobs (Whitelegg, 1994).

In the UK, the governmental commitment to tripling the volume of flying and expanding road capacity more than cancels out any reductions in CO_2 from renewable energy developments and improvements in the energy efficiency of buildings. Unger *et al.* (2010) confirm that climate change policies aimed at reducing the severity of the impacts require exploitation of 'effective opportunities' that lie in 'reducing emissions from the on-road transportation, household biofuel and animal husbandry sectors'. Currently member state policy in the EU, including the UK, is not exploiting these 'effective opportunities' as they apply to on-road transportation.

Newman *et al.* (2009) give detailed attention to resilience and climate change, with an emphasis on buildings and transport. We have already discussed how the built environment can change and adapt so that it provides a high quality of life, reduces demand for transport and contributes to a low-carbon future (Chapter 5) and how buildings can make their own contribution through renewable energy and energy efficiency (Chapter 7). Newman *et al.* (2009) bring all these points together in a detailed assessment of what needs to be done to create a resilient city. They summarise the key elements of a strategy to create the resilient city in the form of three acronyms, TODs, PODs and GODs:

*   Transit-oriented developments (TODs) combine density and mass transit to reduce vehicle use significantly. Families currently living in TODs drive 50 per cent less and own fewer cars, saving 20 per cent of their income every year.

- Pedestrian-oriented developments (PODs) and bike-oriented developments (BODs) improve walkability, reduce air pollution, and encourage citizens to live healthier lifestyles.
- Green-oriented developments (GODs) ensure that every new building and development meets strict sustainability criteria. These buildings recycle water, lower energy use and GHG emissions, and reduce the effects of the urban heat island.

Governmental response to climate change problems

Climate change policy at the EU and UK levels is characterised by a large amount of rhetoric and aspirational language but a very small amount of determined action to reduce GHGs. Jordan *et al.* (2010) discuss climate change policy initiated by the EU and conclude that 'it is not delivering emission reductions of the scale or at the speed demanded by scientists'.

The European Environment Agency's *European Environment: State and Outlook 2010* report (EEA, 2010) is upbeat about the EU achieving its target to reduce GHG emissions by 20 per cent by 2020 but also warns that this may not be enough to avoid serious climate change consequences and increases in global temperatures beyond the critical 2 degrees C. The same report identifies the transport sector as 'problematic' in that GHG emissions increased by 24 per cent in the period 1990–2008 in the EU-27, excluding emissions from international aviation and maritime transport. In addition rail freight and inland waterways declined in market share and the number of cars increased by 22 per cent or 52 million between 1995 and 2006.

Data on GHG emissions within the EU territory underestimates 'real' GHG emissions. The rapid development of world trade, globalisation and the dependence of Europe on imports from China are associated with additional carbon burdens that are embedded within the goods and services that are imported. Including the carbon content of imports from goods and services in national CO_2 accounts would increase carbon emissions allocated to the EU by approximately 30 per cent (Davis and Caldeira, 2010). The top four importers of carbon emissions were the USA (1), Japan (2), the UK (3) and Germany (4).

Wiedman *et al.* (2008) carried out a detailed study of embedded carbon in imports into the UK and concluded that the carbon emissions added an extra 37 per cent to the UK inventory when compared to national data reported to the United Nations Framework Convention on Climate Change (UNFCCC).

The incompleteness of EU and UK GHG emissions data arising from the exclusion of international aviation, maritime emissions and embedded carbon, in addition to the very poor performance on renewable energy, leads inexorably to the conclusion that the results of climate change policy are inadequate to deliver the objectives of keeping temperature increases below 2 degrees C and reducing atmospheric concentrations of CO_2 to no more than 350 ppm.

The European Environment Agency (EEA, 2010) has documented per capita CO_2 equivalent emissions by each of the 27 EU member states. The UK appears almost exactly in the middle of this distribution. There are 14 countries with emissions that are greater than those of the UK and 12 with emissions that are lower than those of the UK.

National-level comparisons tell only part of the story. Some of the most impressive climate change strategies are being designed and implemented at the city region level. We have already discussed Freiburg and its achievements across a wide range of policy areas, all of which contribute to GHG reduction. These include car-reduced residential areas with a population of approximately 17,000, renewable energy funding and installation (especially PVs) and building standards to reduce energy use. These form part of a coordinated effort to reduce CO_2 equivalent emissions by 40 per cent by 2030 on a 1992 base, with an intermediate target of a 29 per cent reduction by 2020 (Stadt Freiburg, 2007). The reductions in key sectors of the economy of Freiburg are illustrated in Figure 8.1.

Local government at city and regional levels is performing better than many national governments (Arikan *et al.*, 2011):

> 75 per cent of community GHG commitments aim for GHG reductions of more than one per cent per annum which exceeds the reductions commitments of most national governments under the Kyoto protocol, as well as recommendations of the IPCC for the post-2012 period . . . national and global goals for reducing GHG emissions can significantly be leveraged if commitments of local governments are better integrated and enabling environments for rapid investment and suitable financing opportunities are created.

Arikan *et al.* (2011) also highlight the City of Copenhagen's commitment to be the world's first carbon-neutral capital by 2025 and the commitments by Palmerston North (New Zealand) and Calgary (Canada) to eliminate fossil fuels in their energy supply by 2012–15.

Vaxjo in Sweden (population 79,000) is another exemplar of local government action to deal with climate change. In 1996 it adopted a target to become fossil fuel free (Vaxjo Kommun, 2011):

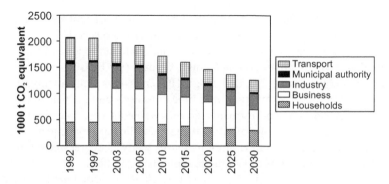

Figure 8.1 Freiburg's climate protection policy

As early as 1996 the city of Vaxjo unanimously decided to become a fossil fuel free city. Since then, a great deal has happened. The goal up to 2015 from 1993 is to reduce CO_2 emissions by 55 per cent per inhabitant and to become completely fossil fuel free by the year 2030. The results in 2009 show that carbon dioxide emissions have reduced by 34%. At the same time economic growth has been excellent – 70% up to 2007.

A detailed study of several UK city regions (Echenique *et al.*, 2010) concluded that total CO_2 emissions could increase by 34 per cent in south-east England and 10 per cent in Tyne and Wear. The report casts doubt on the ability of the UK to meet its CO_2 reduction targets, citing the continuation of existing social and economic trends such as new housing, suburbanisation and increased car use as major factors in this increase.

Peak oil and resilience

The Oil Depletion Analysis Centre (ODAC, 2008) provides a useful definition of 'peak oil':

> People often ask when the world's oil is going to 'run out', but this is the wrong question. 'Peak Oil' refers to the moment at which global oil production will reach its maximum level and then go into sustained decline. This is expected to happen at the mid-point of depletion – when roughly half the oil that has ever been produced will have been consumed, and the other half is still underground. This is a pattern which has already been observed in over sixty of the world's 98 oil producing countries. British oil production peaked in 1999 and daily output has already fallen by well over half. Britain became a net oil importer of oil in 2006.

Gilbert and Perl (2008) describe the peak oil problem as a combination of significant increases in the demand for oil and a serious shortfall in the supply of oil and/or a decrease in the number of discoveries of new oil fields to replace those that are running out and in the final stages of exhaustion. Peak oil is a controversial subject, with a great deal of disagreement around the 'tipping point', that is, what is the year when peak oil arrives and production after that point goes into decline? There is even more disagreement on the role of prices and technology in ensuring that the planet will continue to have sufficient oil or oil-based products to keep up with demand. The Dutch-based Peak Oil Centre (2011) summarises the collision of increased demand and falling production in Figure 8.2.

Gilbert and Perl (2008) illustrate the peak oil problem with a diagram showing actual and estimated production of petroleum liquids by region, 1930–2050 (Figure 8.3).

The United Kingdom Energy Research Centre (UKERC, 2009) has carried out a large-scale systematic survey and analysis of the peak oil problem and concluded:

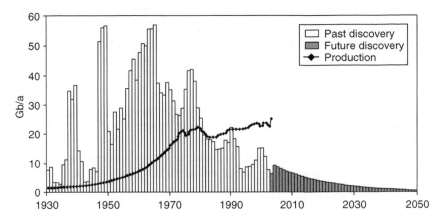

Figure 8.2 Comparison of oil availability (discovery) and consumption, 1930–2050

Source: Peak Oil Centre (2011).

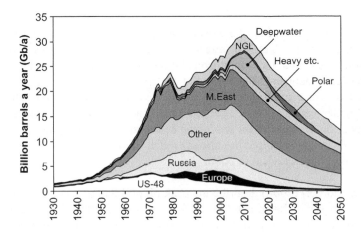

Figure 8.3 Actual and estimated production of petroleum liquids by region, 1930–2050

On the basis of current evidence we suggest that a peak of conventional oil production before 2030 appears likely and there is a significant risk of a peak before 2020. Given the lead times required to both develop substitute fuels and improve energy efficiency, this risk needs to be given serious consideration.

In essence the peak oil problem is a subset of the long-running precautionarity debate. The consequences of high levels of oil dependency in all our global supply and logistic systems, should oil supplies falter or prices rise dramatically, are so serious that actions to remove this threat would be very sensible indeed. This is the same thing as increasing resilience. When linked to the debate about co-benefits, including dealing with climate change, energy security, food security and reducing air pollution, the precautionarity strategy rapidly becomes an optimum strategy. It would be perverse not to transform our economies and societies so that we could avoid major threats over the next two to three decades arising from climate change and peak oil.

Governmental responses to the peak oil problem

The Local Government Association (LGA) in England and Wales represents 400 local authorities and in 2008 produced a report on peak oil and how local government could deal with the problem (LGA, 2008a). The LGA accepted that peak oil is a problem that should be prepared for and dealt with:

> Peak oil theory would suggest that oil prices will continue to rise, with recent estimates of an average of US$150 a barrel by 2010 and over US$200 a barrel by 2012. The theory is controversial, but regardless of the arguments, all will agree that oil is a finite resource and will become a declining resource at some point.

The LGA recommends that local authorities should:

- encourage, lead and motivate the transition towards a much reduced fossil fuel future;
- promote smarter choices (a package of measures to persuade residents to use cars less and increase the use of walking, cycling and public transport);
- green the transport fleet (much improved fuel efficiency);
- introduce urban logistics, for example the Bristol freight consolidation scheme, which reduces lorry numbers and miles;
- use the planning system to reduce the need to travel.

To help it to do these things the LGA requests central government to assist in the following ways:

- Change the funding models for transport to emphasise smarter choices and demand management.
- Give powers to local authorities to improve bus services.

The LGA report avoids the rather obvious conclusion that most local authorities are making things worse through the planning system, for example the decisions of Lancaster City Council to support a new bypass that will generate extra traffic and an extra 23,000 tonnes of CO_2 per annum (Whitelegg, 2007b) and a decision by the same planning authority to support an increase of 500 car parking spaces in the city centre to support a new shopping development (Whitelegg and Pye, 2009). Most local authorities are actively reducing existing levels of resilience by encouraging higher levels of car-based mobility and higher levels of fossil fuel dependency. This encouragement is mainly through the planning system and its ideological bias in favour of any new development and any new investment that might bring the possibility of jobs and prosperity.

At the time of writing there is no UK government national peak oil strategy.

The ODAC (2008) report is aimed at local authorities and provides a detailed checklist of practical policy initiatives that can be taken at local level to address the problem. These are summarised in the 'Policy recommendations' section at the end of this chapter.

The Swedish government has examined the evidence for peak oil and produced a strategy to deal with the problem (Swedish Government, 2006). The Swedish strategy is more ambitious than EU or local authority strategies and is an authoritative position produced by the Commission on Oil Independence chaired by the prime minister. It sets out a number of ambitions to be achieved by 2020, including:

- forest growth to be increased by 15–20 per cent by 2020 to increase the supply of fuel for bioenergy;
- increased production of domestic renewable energy, for example an extra 10 TWh of wind energy and 25 TWh of district-heating-based electricity;
- no use of oil for heating purposes;
- improved energy efficiency in buildings and in industry;
- reduced oil use in transport of 40–50 per cent by 2020.

The transport ambitions will be achieved by:

- increases in fuel efficiency in petrol and diesel vehicles;
- the encouragement of hybrid and electric vehicles;
- the use of biofuels in transport;
- public transport being made cheaper and more attractive;
- trains being made more attractive for longer-distance journeys;
- the use of ICT as a substitute for physical travel.

It is significant that, as in the case of climate change policies, several local administrations have taken up the challenge of peak oil and produced strategies to deal with the problem. These strategies are implicitly resilience strategies in that they prepare and plan for a future that will be able to cope with interruptions in oil supply from whatever causes. The local administrations in Maribyrnong (Melbourne), Oakland (California), Bristol (UK) and Portland (Oregon) have produced peak oil strategies.

The Maribyrnong strategy document (Fishman, 2009) contains 32 recommendations to the local authority, which concentrate on transport, planning and food supply. They include changing the mix of travel choices for staff who work for the council to increase walking, cycling and public transport and reduce car use. Other recommendations cover physical planning to encourage more mixed-use developments, shorter distances and the encouragement of walking and cycling.

The Oakland peak oil strategy (City of Oakland, 2008) made a number of recommendations, including:

- Drive less.
- Redesign the city so that residents can reduce automobile dependency.
- Develop transportation alternatives so that when residents do need to travel they have options other than driving private automobiles.

The recommendations are linked to their 'key initiatives':

- Adopt the Oil Depletion Protocol.
- Redesign the city into numerous 'urban villages' where jobs, services and shopping are conveniently located so that walking, biking and electric vehicle use can increase.
- Encourage more use of public transit.

The City of Portland strategy (City of Portland, 2007) calls for:

- a reduction in oil and gas consumption of 50 per cent over the next 25 years;
- changes to urban design to facilitate walking and cycling and improved access to services and transportation systems;
- the encouragement of energy efficiency in transport;
- the encouragement of energy efficiency in all new and existing structures;
- improved methods of communication to inform and engage citizens.

The peak oil strategy prepared for Bristol (Bristol City Council, 2009) is more specific and wide-ranging than the three examples quoted above. It has a large number of recommendations, including:

- a 50 per cent reduction in oil consumption by 2020;
- adding stringent walking and cycling accessibility targets to new housing planning requirements;
- implementing maximum parking standards for new dwellings of one space per dwelling;
- promoting walking, cycling and public transport options by progressively increasing the budgets devoted to these modes;
- implementing wide area 20 mph speed limits;
- reducing road transport for goods by 50 per cent by 2020 based on the success of existing urban logistics in Bristol;
- 50 per cent of all public sector food sourcing should be local by 2012;
- exploring the possibility of implementing a local currency;
- implementing renewable energy loan schemes to encourage householders to install renewables;
- cutting car use by 50 per cent by 2015.

All four local authority strategies focus on transport and oil dependency but also include local food production and energy efficiency. All accept that there will be serious problems in the future arising from peak oil and that it would be prudent to prepare contingency plans, reduce oil dependency and minimise as far as possible the disruption and economic dislocation that would result from interruptions in oil supply. The peak oil problem is considered as an important issue in its own right, but it also has links with climate change and the need to address both with some vigour.

The proliferation of city region peak oil strategies demonstrates a growing sense of awareness of the importance of dealing with this set of issues and a growing sense that a fundamental responsibility of local government is to anticipate problems that may happen at some time in the future and put in place plans to mitigate the impact. This is also about building resilience and making connections between employment, social cohesion, public services, mobility and climate change and providing the right mix of infrastructure and incentives to maximise resilience. In the next section we discuss the transition town and city movement as a strong civil society contribution to increasing resilience in cities and regions.

Transition towns and cities

The transition town and city movement is a well-established feature of many localities across the globe. It is by definition a broadly based, highly integrated citizen initiative designed to build solutions to many of the problems that flow from fossil fuel dependency, climate change and the food and transport systems they have spawned (Hopkins, 2008; Transition Network, 2011). Transition initiatives (as they are more generally known) are shaped by the people who live in the communities, who come together to operate collectively in an optimistic, solution-building mode of thinking and doing. They frequently involve 'energy descent plans', sustainable transport initiatives (walking, cycling, car-share and public transport), local food initiatives and local currencies and markets.

In 2011 there were 348 transition initiatives labelled as 'official', 186 of which were in the UK, and 341 'mulling' initiatives (not yet fully developed). They exist in 31 countries (Transition Network, 2011).

Transition town initiatives (TTIs) are centrally concerned with building resilience. Building resilience 'increases the capacity of our businesses, communities and settlements to deal as well as possible with shock' (Transition Network, 2011).

TTIs take many forms, and all are intended to build strong, resilient communities with the capacity and resources to move decisively towards a clear vision of a low-carbon, fossil-fuel-free, strong local economy. Some of the best known initiatives include the Totnes energy descent action plan (Transition Town Totnes, 2010) and the Lewes local currency. Both these projects and dozens of others bring together local people, clear thinking, an overall goal of becoming more resilient and a real effort on the part of citizens to become more self-sufficient and reduce dependence on oil, large external corporations and long-distance food supply chains.

Figure 8.4 The Lewes pound

The Lewes local currency, pictured in Figure 8.4, has been a great success and can be used in most local shops and businesses. Its objective is to retain as much of the money spent in the local economy actually in the local economy rather than siphoned off through large supermarket chains or internet purchases. This then acts as a stimulus to local entrepreneurship and a very practical boost to resilience. The existence of the local currency and the network of traders who accept it and consumers who spend it effectively give Lewes a stronger and more resilient economic foundation that is better able to weather shocks (Lewes Pound Group, 2011).

TTIs are not part of the governmental undergrowth and are not bogged down in council bureaucracy. They are genuine citizen initiatives based on the principle that actually doing something is an important part of sorting out quality of life and sustainability, resilience and peak oil concerns. There is enthusiasm to cooperate with councils and government agencies but an overriding desire to demonstrate that local action works and change can be 'bottom-up'.

Measuring vulnerability and resilience

Dodson and Sipe (2008a) have constructed a numerical index of vulnerability in Australian cities, VAMPIRE (Vulnerability Assessment for Mortgage, Petroleum and Inflation Risks and Expenditure). VAMPIRE measures the degree of exposure of households in Australian cities to financial problems related to the costs of oil and also rising interest rates which feed through to the rising costs of servicing mortgages. The purpose of VAMPIRE is as follows:

> To understand household vulnerability to socio-economic stressors we created the 'Vulnerability Assessment for Mortgage, Petrol and Inflation Risks and Expenditure', known as the VAMPIRE. This is an index which calculates the level of household vulnerability at the local level and is based on Australian Census data. It combines information on car dependence, mortgage and incomes at the Collection District (CD) level (about 200 households).

The VAMPIRE analysis shows that Australian cities have developed a spatial structure and an exposure to fuel cost increases which is regressive (it penalises lower-income residents more than higher-income residents). Lower-income groups tend to live in relatively remote suburbs (e.g. in Western Sydney) with a higher degree of dependence on long-distance commutes by car than their relatively wealthy neighbours who live in central Sydney or equivalent areas in Melbourne and Brisbane. The problems of vulnerability to rising oil and fuel prices are compounded by the relatively poor quality of public transport services in the more distant suburbs of Australian cities. Dodson and Sipe are describing the lack of resilience of these suburban communities and the changes over time that make them less resilient. They also map the numerical indicator for all Australian cities. The maps clearly identify the geographical areas in these cities that have very high vulnerability. The western suburbs of Sydney are highly vulnerable, with concentrations of relatively low-income groups, high levels of car dependency and vulnerability to fuel price increases, and low availability of means of transport that can provide alternatives to the car.

The historical development of Australian cities has been driven by the availability of cheap oil and an ideology of home ownership, low densities, the car, and long distances separating origins and destinations. This has produced a regressive city. The impacts of peak oil are already being felt in these cities, but they are being felt unfairly and regressively. Lower-income groups are already making changes that include forgoing holidays and cutting back on food to ensure that enough disposable income is left over to feed the car.

This conclusion leads to very clear policy recommendations which are directed at 'rescuing the suburbs' and using VAMPIRE to target those suburbs with high vulnerability when it comes to the design, funding and implementation of new transport infrastructure. This is especially relevant to the distant suburbs of Australian cities but would also be a valuable tool in targeting public transport improvement around all UK cities.

The Australian city analysis should be compared with the reality of Freiburg in southern Germany discussed in earlier chapters. Freiburg is a compact city with a dense and interconnected network of public transport services and cycling infrastructure that renders car use unnecessary for many journeys. Whilst no city on the planet is immune from oil shocks and other major disruptions to systems that have developed in a more relaxed period of generous supplies of cheap oil it is incontrovertible that the citizens of Freiburg are in a luxurious position when compared to the citizens of Western Sydney, especially those living in Cabramatta, Parramatta, Hebersham and Fairfield East. The citizens of these western suburbs have poor-quality public transport and inadequate cycling facilities and are heavily dependent on car use and the drain on household finances imposed by car dependency. Freiburg is at the opposite end of the spectrum, and there is an urgent governmental and public policy task to be done in changing the geography of Australian cities so that they move towards the Freiburg model. In Freiburg people do not need to own a car to carry out their daily activities. In Australian city suburbs as currently organised they do need to own a car. This embedded need is storing up problems for the future and is a denial of resilience.

Localisation

One of the key concepts in the transition town movement is localisation (sometimes referred to as relocalisation). Localisation is central to the delivery of resilience because it effectively substitutes shorter supply lines for longer supply lines and in so doing reduces vehicle kilometres of freight and passenger travel, GHG emissions and pollution. Localisation goes much further than spatial relationships, important as they are. Cato (2009) discusses relocalisation in some detail around a political agenda of reducing the dominance of large multinational corporations, 'maximum self-sufficiency' (p. 143) and rewriting the EU treaty and the rules of the World Trade Organization. Localisation is a difficult concept for a world that has promoted globalisation as a panacea for all manner of human development and economic objectives and developed sophisticated logistics and supply chain technologies to deliver a globalised world. At the national level, complex patterns of commuting and widely distributed activity patterns in space and time have been welcomed as progressive and supported by cheap oil and the declining cost in real terms of owning and running a car. Longer distances and increased complexity are initially seductive and susceptible to claims that we are in some way better off or liberated but rapidly become problematic when peak oil issues come to the fore and fiscal realities kick in (Dodson and Sipe, 2008b). At the level of a city, region or nation this love affair with modernity (Sachs, 1992) severely hinders and fetters our ability to manage and intervene in ways that can deliver lower-energy and zero-carbon scenarios.

Localisation envisages a rebalancing of activities, structures and distances so that a given region or locality can sustain its flows of goods and people, with more work being done within the locality than over long national and international distances. It does not seek to establish a closed system with no interaction across a boundary, but it does seek to maximise internal flows and minimise external flows.

The concept of localisation is not new. Keynes (1933) anticipated this twenty-first-century interest in localisation almost 80 years ago:

> I sympathise with those who would minimise, rather than with those who would maximise economic entanglements among nations. Ideas, knowledge, science, hospitality, travel – these are the things which should of their nature be international. But let goods be homespun whenever it is reasonably and conveniently possible and, above all, let finance be primarily national.

More recently Douthwaite (1996) has presented a powerful case for localisation as an economic strategy with significant potential to deal with a large number of problems associated with peak oil, climate change, energy security and resilience. Douthwaite argues that there are four basic steps that are necessary for greater self-reliance. They are:

- setting up an independent currency system;
- setting up an independent banking system;

- the production of enough energy to meet local needs;
- meeting people's needs for food and clothing from within the local economy.

Localisation strategies can be highly effective as contributions to increasing resilience, reducing oil dependency and reducing GHG emissions. Holzapfel (1995) analyses road freight activity in Germany and quantifies the gains from a localisation strategy. He calculates that a 'regional co-operation model' for road freight which involves developing sources of supply that are nearer the points that need to utilise these goods has the potential to reduce the kilometres driven by lorries by 67 per cent. This brings a number of benefits, including significant reductions in GHGs from one of the fastest-growing and most intractable sources of GHG in Germany and an increase in local self-sufficiency and resilience.

The potential of this approach is significantly greater than a static comparison might reveal. German freight regionalisation is a localisation strategy and can contribute to a significant reduction in miles of lorry travel, but the trends at the moment (Boege, 1995) clearly indicate that the logic of supply chains has become starkly illogical when the basic ingredients of a pot of yoghurt are travelling thousands of kilometres across Europe before being assembled into the product a consumer would buy in a supermarket. Figure 8.5 summarises the Boege analysis.

The Boege analysis shows very clearly the coexistence of a very sophisticated supply chain system with a fundamentally wasteful and inefficient concept of production. The ingredients of yoghurt are widely available, and there is ample opportunity for substituting local milk and fruit products for more distant sources. The onset of peak oil and climate change challenges requires the rapid development of regional production systems and the implementation of localisation strategies.

In a similar vein Demmeler (2004) has shown that regional sourcing systems for food products can produce significant reductions in GHG emissions and a number of other desirable co-benefits, including reductions in acidification, energy use, noise, photochemical smog and land lost to development. The main results are shown in Figure 8.6.

Demmeler (2009) quantifies the GHG emissions for apples, asparagus and beef from three sources (overseas, national or EU, and the local region) and shows that local sourcing produces significant reductions in GHGs. This is shown in Figure 8.7.

Demmeler concludes that three-quarters of the food purchased by a German consumer can be sourced within a radius of 100 kilometres of his or her home address.

Conclusions

The concept of resilience is now well established in thinking about cities and the challenges that they have to face in the very near future. The concept is equally relevant to rural areas, regions that are bigger than city regions, and the nation state. It brings together many of the policy considerations that are raised by discussions around peak oil and climate change but in a way that is positive, optimistic and

Transportation Relations

Strawberry Yoghurt 150 g

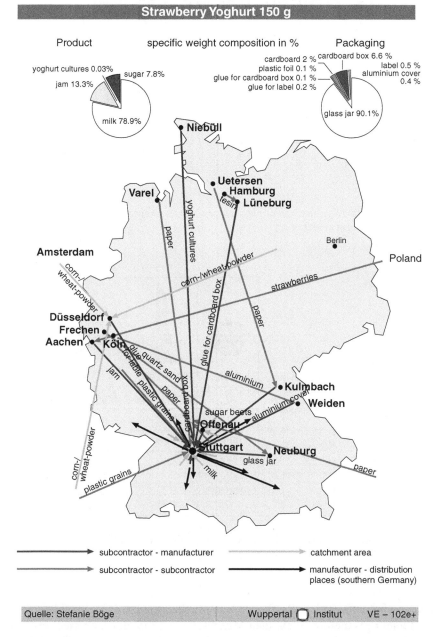

Figure 8.5 The origins and supply chains associated with yoghurt production in Stuttgart, Germany

Source: Boege (1995).

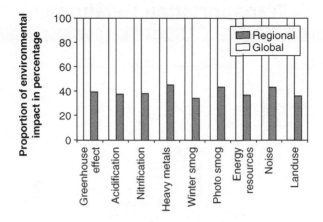

Figure 8.6 A life cycle analysis of national or global sourcing strategies with a regional sourcing model

Source: Demmeler (2004).

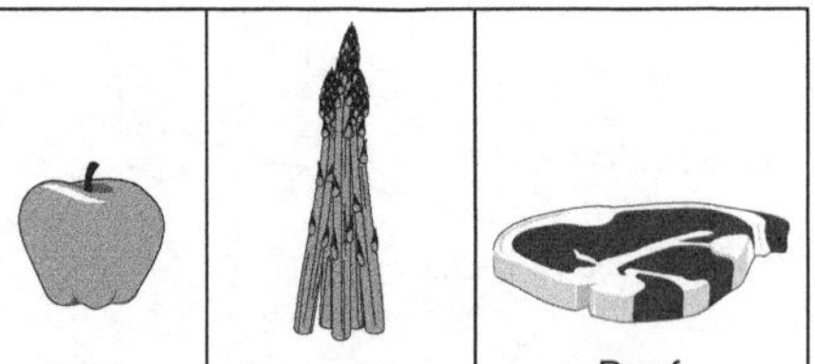

		Apple	Asparagus	Beef
Overseas	Ship/plane	New Zealand, Ship	Chile, plane	Argentina, ship
		513	16,894	349
Europe, Germany	Truck	Italy	Spain	Denmark
		219	359	179
Local	Truck	Lake Constance	Schrobenhausen	Oberallgäu
		76	60	61

Figure 8.7 Greenhouse gas emissions for three products from three origins consumed in Munich g/CO_2 equivalent/kg

Source: Demmeler (2009).

linked to implementation. Resilience is not rocket science. It is palpably obvious that Freiburg is more resilient than Manchester and that this increased resilience is associated with a much higher quality of life for the citizens of Freiburg than is available to the citizens of Manchester. Australian cities are now well aware that they are not resilient and that this lack of resilience is associated with severely regressive consequences that will bear down heavily on low-paid workers living in distant suburbs. Sorting out resilience in an Australian city context is the same thing as sorting out quality of life for several million Australians, delivering significant reductions in GHGs and insulating Australian citizens from the risks associated with oil dependency and lack of food security. The same point applies to European cities, which are in the main more resilient than their Australian comparators because of the historical legacy of nineteenth-century development, which was intrinsically more resilient than twentieth-century automobile based suburbanisation.

It is not too late to recognise the problem of lack of resilience and to implement changes in planning, urban design, fiscal restructuring and the dramatic improvement in sustainable transport options to deal with the problem. This will entail a very close fit with the conclusions and policy recommendations of earlier chapters in this book, especially those on the built environment (Chapter 5) and renewable energy (Chapter 7). Resilient cities, rural areas and regions will in turn deliver the long-overdue changes that are needed to deal with specific issues faced by children (Chapter 3) and the elderly (Chapter 4). There are no credible reasons for not making these changes and making them now, and the basic things that have to change are summarised below in the 'Policy recommendations'.

Policy recommendations

Implement the recommendations in Dodson and Sipe (2008b):

- shifting infrastructure spending towards sustainable transport options and away from road construction, or halting major road construction generally;
- not approving new fringe developments that lack viable alternatives to private motor vehicle travel;
- increasing space for walking and cycling within road reservations;
- reducing car parking requirements for new developments;
- designing new developments to minimise car use by providing local centres or villages;
- encouraging local food production by providing community gardens and farmers' markets;
- planning for renewable energy recharge requirements for electric vehicles;
- encouraging state governments (important in the Australian context) to improve public transport provision.

Implement in full the recommendations in the ODAC (2008) report on peak oil:

- Conduct a detailed energy audit of all council activities and buildings.
- Develop an emergency energy supply plan.
- Introduce rigorous energy-efficiency and conservation programmes.
- Encourage a major shift away from private to public transport, cycling and walking.

- Expand existing programmes such as cycle lanes and road pricing.
- Reduce overall transport demand by using planning powers to shape the built environment.
- Promote the use of locally produced, non-fossil transport fuels such as biogas and renewable electricity in both council operations and public transport.
- Launch a major public energy awareness campaign.
- Find ways to encourage local food production and processing and facilitate reduction of energy used in refrigeration and transport of food.
- Set up a joint peak oil task force with other councils and partner closely with existing community-led initiatives.
- Coordinate policy on peak oil and climate change.
- Adopt the Oil Depletion Protocol and then 'do it'. (The protocol can be seen at www.oildepletionprotocol.org.)

Implement the spatial and structural changes suggested by Holzapfel (2012) to create the city of short distances and the improvements in quality of life that flow from spatial propinquity and high-quality accessibility for all social groups, ages and genders.

Implement the recommendations in Totnes and District 2030: An Energy Descent Action Plan (Transition Town Totnes, 2010). This plan contains a detailed account of what can be achieved by way of reducing energy use, supplying energy needs through renewables, improving the building stock, increasing the supply of local food and delivering a sustainable, healthy transport system. It is a practical DIY manual for sorting out a locality.

9 What do they do that we don't do? The role of age and gender in political representation and budgets

After eight chapters of discussion on the performance of the UK it is clear that the UK performs less well than some other EU countries on a number of important indicators of social and economic welfare, quality of life and environment. Some of these measures are very significant indeed and describe the ways in which children (Chapter 3) and the elderly (Chapter 4) are experiencing a greater level of difficulty or hardship in the UK than in other EU countries. This requires an explanation. Why does the UK underperform when compared with some other countries? Explanation can then inform resolution. What can or should we do to upgrade the UK so that it relocates into the high-performing group?

A starting point for discussing explanation and the problems associated with explanation can be found in the work of Layard (2005) and Wilkinson and Pickett (2009). Layard discusses the concept of happiness and ranks Britain as unhappier than Indonesia, Mexico, New Zealand, Singapore, Sweden, Ireland, Austria, the Netherlands, Denmark, Finland, Canada, Switzerland, Norway and the USA (p. 32). He explains variations in happiness as a function of six 'key factors' (p. 226):

- the proportion of people who say that other people can be trusted;
- the proportion who belong to social organisations;
- the divorce rate;
- the unemployment rate;
- the quality of government;
- religious belief.

Interestingly Layard concludes: 'Unhappily over the last 40 years levels of trust have fallen drastically in Britain and America, though not in continental Europe.' This comment chimes perfectly with much of the content of this book in that Britain emerges as a country that has moved a lot closer to the USA and has increasingly less in common with its mainland EU neighbours. Chapter 3 in particular shows that Britain and the USA are very close to each other on child poverty and child welfare and Scandinavian countries are at the other end of the spectrum with relatively little child poverty. This 'less in common' characteristic is particularly evident on the general welfare of children and the elderly and the quality and quantity of public transport and cycling provision.

Layard's explanation of differences in happiness is not entirely convincing, not-withstanding the fact that his contribution to our understanding of economics and human welfare is very significant indeed. Layard shows unequivocally that happi-ness is about far more than increases in GDP or income and wealth and that public policy is losing its focus as it pursues economic growth rather than increases in happiness. Layard's six 'key factors' are themselves dimensions of unhappiness, and there is an element of non-explanation in relying on subsets of a problem to try to explain the problem. Explaining variations in happiness by reference to variations in divorce and unemployment merely redefines the problem so that we now need to explain variations in divorce and unemployment. The original subject of the explanation has been transferred to a new subject. This is not very satisfactory.

More recent work (NEF, 2009) has ranked 143 countries on a 'Happy Planet Index'. The UK comes out at 74 out of 143 countries, and most EU members states are ranked above the UK. The NEF report does not attempt any kind of explana-tion. Why is the Netherlands a relatively happy place at number 43 and the UK a relatively unhappy place at number 74?

Wilkinson and Pickett (2009) have made a dramatic impact on the way social scientists explain differences in well-being and health and the ways that many social problems (e.g. teenage pregnancy, violence and mental illness) follow a clear pattern with respect to inequalities. The greater the level of inequality in a given society (either nations or the 50 states of the USA) the greater are the social and health problems. This is clearly illustrated in Figure 9.1.

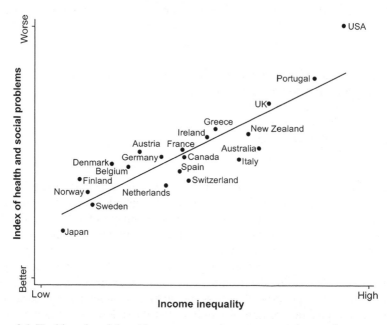

Figure 9.1 Health and social problems are worse in more unequal countries

Wilkinson and Pickett (2009) have dealt with explanation by making clear links between inequality and the degree to which countries experience dysfunctionality. They argue that there is a 'tendency for some countries to do well on just about everything and others to do badly'. The UK is in the 'do badly' group. They argue from an extensive evidence base that 'inequality seems to make countries socially dysfunctional across a wide range of outcomes'. In the context of the first eight chapters of this book it is very interesting indeed that they conclude: 'Internationally at the healthy end of the distribution we always seem to find the Scandinavian countries and Japan. At the opposite end, suffering high rates of most of the health and social problems, are usually the USA, Portugal and the UK.'

The explanation of inequality itself would take us considerably beyond the remit of this book and is not considered in Wilkinson and Pickett, but clearly there is a strong suggestion that countries based on collective, socially progressive and redistributive policies (e.g. Scandinavia) are performing better on inequality (i.e. they are more equal) than countries pursuing individualistic, low-taxation, privatised models of economic and social life, for example the USA and Britain. The same countries that fall in the 'more equal' part of the spectrum identified by Wilkinson and Pickett are the same countries that have been repeatedly identified as high performers in this book. More equal societies have better outcomes for children, the elderly, renewable energy, sustainable mobility (e.g. high-quality public transport and cycling), and built environments that support high rates of cycling and public transport use.

The emphasis and primary thesis of this book do not depend on the identification of wider social, economic and political drivers in the countries we have examined. The primary focus has been on identifying 'good' performers and 'bad' performers and locating the UK on this spectrum, and the result is that the UK is in the majority of cases 'bad'. We then show how it is possible to improve 'bad' to make it considerably 'better', and the transformative steps that must be taken are practical, pragmatic, achievable and doable on a short time scale.

Wilkinson and Pickett's analysis is still relevant in that there is a strong case for transformative steps that are based on reducing inequalities and through that reduction and its social and economic impact bring about a more fundamental change in the choices that we all make and the options that local and central government pursue to improve the quality of life of all citizens. We concur with the Wilkinson and Pickett thesis and take the view that all the topics reviewed so far in this book have the potential to develop in ways that produce much improved outcomes if we can achieve a more equal society. Indeed it may be the case that long-lasting transformative change may be achievable only through this more fundamental process and that this more fundamental change should underpin the detailed practical recommendations we make in earlier chapters.

The Wilkinson and Pickett thesis is taken up in a more overtly political manner by Hutton (2010). Hutton describes the way in which Britain has become more unequal in the era covered by prime ministers Thatcher and Blair: 'Britain moved from being one of Europe's most equal societies to one of its least equal within the space of 20 years. The Institute for Fiscal Studies reckons that 40 per cent of this transformation was due to the tax and benefit changes' (pp. 275–276).

The importance of this finding cannot be exaggerated. A shift to greater inequality was created by changes in the taxation and benefits system and this, whilst regrettable, means that the same process can be thrown into reverse and Britain made more equal. This would have the impact of shifting Britain towards the bottom left in Figure 9.1 and make Britain more like Sweden and Norway. This in turn would deliver the many benefits noted by Wilkinson and Pickett and would underpin the more pragmatic recommendations in this book about creating a smarter, more resilient society and giving communities a much improved quality of life and built environment to go along with a more equal society.

Hutton (2010: 297) then explains what must be done:

> This logjam must be broken. Essentially the political task is to construct a cross-class coalition that will accept the case for at least maintained if not higher social spending, funded by taxation. It must also create a cultural climate in which it is much harder to argue that the 'undeserving' poor do not merit the support of the 'deserving' better-off. To achieve that, social spending must be seen to be working, it must be fit for contemporary purposes and it must address the risks everyone is facing. . . . Britain has to rediscover the merits of acting together to mitigate common risk.

Hutton (2010) concludes his detailed political and social analysis of what is going on in Britain with a rallying call for action: 'We are starting to understand the link between fairness, prosperity and the good life. Now we just have to deliver it. After all, we deserve better' (p. 395).

Hutton's concluding comment is an admirable summary of what this book is about. An even shorter summary would be 'Just do it.' We have seen that UK performance leaves lots of scope for an upgrade in our performance and that the bigger-picture analyses of Layard, Wilkinson and Pickett, and Hutton show that there are clear policy deficits in the UK that can be remedied. Interestingly none of these three analyses is totally convincing on explanation. Layard dodges explanation by shifting ground on what is to be explained. Wilkinson and Pickett identify the links between inequalities and negative outcomes, suggesting that if we become more equal we eliminate the negatives. Hutton identifies political failures and the need to increase social spending to remedy the deficiencies. The central message of this current book is that these sources of explanation have value in understanding where we went wrong and what needs to be done to put things right but the main task still remains one of what Hutton calls 'delivery'. We should just get on with whatever needs to be done to deliver the upgrade. We now turn to the task of creating fertile ground for the task of doing it.

The practicalities

We have now seen many examples of best practice in Germany, Switzerland, the Netherlands, Sweden and Denmark and clear evidence that the UK is not doing very well. The existence of differences of this kind between the UK and comparator countries raises the possibility that things could be improved in the UK so that our performance is up there with the best performers. We have taken the view that each thematic area, for example children, older people, air quality and resilience, can be improved by reference to clear thinking, analysis of best practice in other countries, and rational decision making that accepts that we can do better; we just need to do it. If this model of analysis and decision taking were accurate then we would not be in the laggard class to begin with, so a wider and deeper set of changes must be initiated to create the fertile conditions that are a prerequisite for rationality to kick in and upgrade to be implemented. Crompton (2010) has reinforced this view by explicitly rejecting the rationality paradigm and suggesting other ways in which virtuous change and continuous improvement can be released into the UK body politic. Crompton could not be clearer:

> Our dominant model of human decision-making needs updating. . . .
>
> There is mounting evidence from a range of studies in cognitive science that the dominant 'Enlightenment model' of human decision-making is extremely incomplete. According to this model we imagine ourselves, when faced with a decision, to be capable of dispassionately assessing the facts, foreseeing probable outcomes of different responses, and then selecting and pursuing an optimal course of action. As a result many approaches to campaigning on bigger-than-self problems still adhere to the conviction that 'if only people knew' the true nature or full scale of the problems which we confront, then they would be galvanised into demanding more proportionate action in response.
>
> But this understanding of how people reach decisions is very incomplete. There is mounting evidence that facts play only a partial role in shaping people's judgement. Emotion is often far more important. It is increasingly apparent that our collective decisions are based importantly upon a set of factors that often lie beyond conscious awareness, and which are informed in important part by emotion – in particular, dominant cultural values, which are tied to emotion.

Whilst accepting Crompton's views about values, emotions and empathy and working on these dimensions as part of social change, we take the view that there are three practical areas where changes can be made and that if these three sets of changes could be fostered then the wider virtuous changes we recommend would be far more likely to happen. For upgrade to happen it is not enough to say that 'emotion is far more important' and leave it at that. It is necessary to explore ways in which these emotions, perceptions, values and preferences can change in response to other things that we can change, and there are at least three sets of factors we can change:

• Getting greater diversity and representativeness amongst politicians so that the age and gender of political representatives match those of the total population in any jurisdiction and introduce different values and emotions into the debates and policy choices.

- Reallocating budgets so that more money is spent on things that matter and things that reduce the need for 'picking up the pieces', for example dealing with obesity and respiratory diseases caused by poor air quality. Success with managing budgets differently and seeing demonstrably better outcomes can change expectations and aspirations and support emotions linked to the concept of 'Just do it' rather than listing all the reasons why we can't do it.
- Constitutional changes to give local authorities more power and independence and in turn encourage greater levels of political involvement in those citizens who want to make these changes. More powers and more influence will bring the double dividend of doing more things with better outcomes and attracting more vigorous councillors into the system in the first place.

In the next part of this chapter we examine diversity in political representation and budgets, and in Chapter 10 we explore the nature of central–local government relationships and the case for constitutional change to give UK local authorities much more power and responsibility than is currently the case.

Diversity in political representation

English councillors have been described as 'male, pale and stale' (*First*, 2008). A survey of 19,617 councillors in England (NFER, 2009) reported that 68.4 per cent are male, 96.6 per cent are described as 'white' (i.e. pale) and 86.8 per cent are over the age of 55 (i.e. 'stale'). This book does not in any way subscribe to the pejorative use of any of these descriptors, but it is clear that English councillors are not representative of the communities over which they exercise powers of budget setting, priority setting and place shaping. It is also clear that in debates about policies, priorities and budgets they cannot bring the clear insights that come from the personal experiences of those categories of councillor who are under-represented. Under-representation of younger people, women or those from a variety of non-white ethnic groups is a cause for concern. It means that the age, gender and ethnic origin perspectives are not directly fed into the debate and decision taking, and this can have the effect of skewing outcomes. Young people will have very clear views about the importance of youth facilities, young women with children will similarly have strong views about play areas, road safety and schools, and the direct articulation of these perspectives can bring diversity and clarity into debates about priorities and budgets that might otherwise be absent.

Wilson and Game (2006) are very clear about the importance of gender, ethnicity and age when discussing councillors and local government in the UK. On gender imbalance they say:

> Does such gender distortion matter? Inevitably, yes. Councils on which 75 per cent of members are men simply do not pursue the same priorities and arrive in the same way at the same decision as would councils with even 40 per cent let alone 75 per cent of women members . . . women are the main users of council services, they make three quarters of all calls to council

departments. They are the majority of tenants, the family members who make most use of swimming pools and libraries, who are most likely to put bins out for collection and who are most affected by the quality of the local environment – inadequate street cleansing, poor lighting, dog fouling, pot holed roads and pavements, inadequate public transport and street crime. They are likely to have distinctive priorities and agendas.

(Wilson and Game, 2006: 255)

Paxton and Hughes (2007) explore the links between rates of female representation in politics and the degree to which this produces outcomes that are unlikely to be present in male-dominated discourse:

In general, male lawmakers are less likely to initiate and pass laws that serve women's and children's interests. They less often think about rape, domestic violence, women's health and child care. But in democracies, the points of view of all groups need to be taken into account. Therefore, the views and opinions of women as well as men must be incorporated into political decision making.

(Paxton and Hughes, 2007: 4)

And:

Without women's full participation in politics, political decision making will be of lower quality than it could or should be. The quality of political decision making should also increase with greater inclusion of women because including women increases the overall diversity of ideas, values, priorities and political styles. Introducing women to the political realm should introduce new ideas because women have different interests.

The authors of these quotes draw an analogy with ecological diversity that is very relevant to the discussion around resilience in Chapter 8 of this book:

Diversity is certainly good in and of itself but it should also make political decision making more flexible and capable of change . . . biologists know that ecological niches dominated by a single species are more vulnerable to changes in the environment than niches with a diversity of species. In a similar manner, having only the ideas and perspectives of men represented in a country's policy could make a country less flexible to changes in its internal or international environment.

Whilst we do not argue that a large number of women in politics or a perfect proportional match between councillors and the population they represent will unequivocally produce the improvements and upgrades we are arguing for, the evidence is convincing that more women in politics is a good thing and is likely to improve matters. It is a necessary but not a sufficient pre-condition for an upgrade.

Shears (2008) has analysed female participation rates in national parliaments and finds that the UK is ranked at 53 jointly with the Dominican Republic. Denmark, Sweden, Norway, Finland, the Netherlands, Spain and Belgium are in the top 10 and Germany at 14.

> In many countries around the world women have increased their presence as elected representatives. Despite these advancements, the overall percentage of women elected to national parliaments remains at 18 per cent. There are considerable variations between countries. The Inter-Parliamentary Union has compiled a table ranking 190 countries in descending order according to the percentage of women in their lower or single house of parliament. Rwanda has the highest, 48.8 per cent, the UK is joint 53rd with Dominican Republic, and currently 19.7 per cent of MPs elected to the House of Commons are women.
>
> (Shears, 2008)

A comparison of the age distribution of councillors in the UK, Germany, Denmark and Sweden shows that there are some important differences (Table 9.1). There are no national statistics in Germany on the age distribution of councillors (Mitglieder des Rates). Two German cities are included in this table to give an indication of the German age distribution. Bochum is a city in the Ruhr region of the state of North Rhine-Westphalia, and Darmstadt is south of Frankfurt in the state of Hessen.

Table 9.1 Age and gender comparison between German, English, Danish and Swedish local councillors

	Germany	England	Denmark	Sweden	Bochum	Darmstadt
Councillors	45,652	19,617	2,468	12,969	83	66
Percentage retired		43.5				
Average age		58.8	50.2			
Percentage female	25	30.8	31.8	43	27.7	43
Age distribution		%	%			
Under 25		0.6	2.3		—	—
25–29		1.6	3.2		3.6	9
30–34		2.1	5.5		4.8	9
35–39		3.4	6.9		2.4	10.6
40–44		5.4	9.9		8.4	9
45–49		7.3	15.4		10.8	19.6
50–54		9.3	17.3		7.2	16.6
55–59		14.0	16.1		21.6	9
60–64		21.9	14.5		25.3	6
Over 64		34.3	8.5		14.5	10.6

Sources: England data from NFER (2009); German data on gender from Deutscher Staedtetag (2011); Danish data on gender (2009) from http://www.statistikbanken.dk/statbank5a/default.asp?w=1440 (accessed 14 January 2012); Danish data on age distribution (2009 local elections) from Danmarks Statistik (2010); Swedish data on gender from Statistics Sweden (2011).

Swedish national statistics on the age distribution of local councillors use age bands that are not directly comparable with UK and Danish data. There are four age bands, and these are shown in Table 9.2.

Sweden

In Chapters 3 and 4 we discussed policy outcomes for children and the elderly and noted that Sweden performs very well in these policy areas in international rankings. Child poverty and the likelihood that older people will experience poverty are both at the successful end of the spectrum in Sweden. Sweden performs very well in its highly egalitarian social and economic structures and low level of inequality (Wilkinson and Pickett, 2009). Sweden also performs very well on the degree to which women participate in politics (International Idea, n.d.). Forty-five per cent of its MPs are female, and Waengnerud (n.d.) asserts the qualitative impact of high rates of female representation. She associates the success of the Swedish social model, including health care, care for the elderly, and generous parental leave to facilitate male and female participation in the workforce, with the degree of female representation.

Waengnerud illustrates her point with empirical evidences on the attitudes and interests of male and female MPs. Figure 9.2 shows the number of male and female MPs who in interviews mentioned social policy, family policy, care for the elderly or health care as an area of personal interest in 1985, 1994 and 2002. Waengnerud argues that 'these four items can be seen as a broad way of conceptualising women's interests'.

Figure 9.2 clearly shows a strong bias in the issues that women bring into play as Swedish parliamentarians. They are more aware of these issues than are men and inject different perspectives. Waengnerud argues that this injection of perspective and emphasis is important in itself but has the additional benefit of pushing these issues higher up the political prioritisation list. Women are effective shapers of socially inclusive outcomes in Sweden and are well represented at all three levels of government (Table 9.3). It is also clear that these policy emphases contribute significantly to reducing inequalities in Swedish society and that more equal societies (Wilkinson and Pickett, 2009) are associated with better performance on health, income, poverty and other indicators of quality of life. Women politicians are also evident at local level in Sweden.

Table 9.2 The age distribution of local councillors in Sweden

Age band in years	Percentage (Sweden)	Percentage (England)
18–29	7	2.2
30–49	34	18.2
50–64	42	45.2
65 and over	17	34.3

Sources: England data from NFER (2009); Swedish data on gender from Statistics Sweden (2011); Swedish data on age distribution from http://www.scb.se/Pages/TableAndChart____160752.aspx (accessed 14 January 2012).

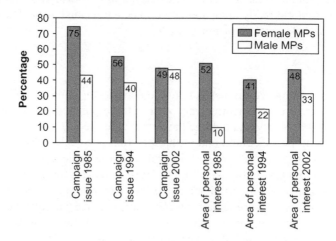

Figure 9.2 Gender differences amongst Swedish MPs on social, family, health care and the elderly, 1985–2002

Table 9.3 Women in local and national politics in Sweden (2010 data)

	Number of women	Number of men	Total	Percentage of elected politicians who are female (2010)
National elections	157	192	349	45
Regional elections	786	876	1,662	47.3
Local elections	5,582	7,387	12,969	43.0

Source: Statistics Sweden (2011).

In Sweden, 43 per cent of local councillors were women, which compares with the 31 per cent for England noted in Table 9.1. The high rate of female participation at each of the three levels of government in Sweden undoubtedly contributes to a strong sense of social and environmental purpose in Swedish politics. If we want to change the tempo and culture of British politics to increase the probabilities that the upgrade discussed in detail in this book will actually happen then it is clear that much higher numbers of women in politics at local and national level will help. If women are not present in much larger numbers there is no reason to expect that current ideology, paradigms, emphases and cultures will change enough to see the value and possibilities associated with upgrade.

Swedish Vision Zero

Sweden has led the world with a radical and dramatic transformation of a policy area that is of huge significance to all sections of community. Road safety provides a window into the general arguments made by Paxton and Hughes (2007) and the specific social policy points made by Waengnerud (n.d.). Vision Zero is the Swedish national road safety policy that asserts the ethical content of road safety perspectives and says that it is not acceptable that anyone should die as a result of a road crash incident. Vision Zero sets out a policy objective of zero deaths and zero serious injuries in the road traffic environment (Whitelegg and Haq, 2006). Vision Zero is based on the ethical imperative expressed by Tingvall and Haworth (1999): 'It can never be ethically acceptable that people are killed or seriously injured when moving within the road system.'

A key figure in the debate around Vision Zero and its eventual adoption by the Swedish Parliament in 1997 was Ines Uusmann, the minister of transport at that time. She took the view that road safety policy should not be based on economics or trade-offs between mobility and risk and that it was a fundamental ethical and moral issue to be resolved by an absolute commitment to zero deaths and zero serious injuries. Whilst this book is not in any way attempting to prove a general thesis on the foundation of one policy advocated and delivered by one woman it is nevertheless the case that such a radical and dramatic deviation from many decades of thinking on road safety was more likely to emerge from the diversity supplied by female politicians. The eventual implementation of the Vision Zero policy in Sweden owed a great deal to the (male) director of the National Roads Administration, Claes Tingvall.

The age distribution across the four countries in Tables 9.1 and Table 9.2 reveals larger differences between England and the three other countries than does gender. England has far more older councillors than the other three countries. If we pick out the over-64/65 age group we find England at 34.3 per cent, Sweden at 17 per cent and Denmark at 8.5 per cent. In the absence of German national data we looked at two German cities, and in Darmstadt the percentage of councillors over the age of 65 was 10.6 (Stadt Darmstadt, 2011). In Bochum the percentage was 14.5 (Stadt Bochum, 2011).

It is not possible or even desirable to construct a cause–effect relationship between the age distribution of councillors and the quality of outcomes flowing from debates in councils and parliaments around Europe, though the more general point that lack of diversity in councillor values and priorities can skew outcomes is still correct. Figures 9.3 and 9.4 show that views and perspectives do vary by gender and age, and it follows that an under-representation of younger councillors or female councillors (for example) will skew outcomes in the directions illustrated in these two figures.

It is also clear from political analysis and debate in Sweden that a high proportion of female politicians at local and national levels is having a desirable and positive effect on the selection of priorities and policies in that country (e.g. Vision Zero) and that increasing the participation rate of women politicians is part of the process of improving debate, delivery, priority and outcomes at all levels of government in those countries like the UK with low levels of female participation.

An example of the different perspectives of males and females can be seen in attitudes to nuclear power in the UK (Ipsos MORI, 2009), illustrated in Figure 9.3.

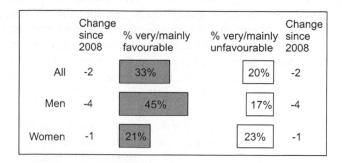

Figure 9.3 Gender differences in opinions and impressions of the nuclear power industry

There is a strong gender bias in attitudes towards the nuclear energy industry. While 45 per cent of men are very or mainly favourable to the nuclear industry, this falls to 21 per cent for women. A debate on energy, risk and the environment will take on a very different character in a scenario with high levels of female representation than it would with lower levels.

Similar points can be made about the age distribution of politicians and the nature of political outcomes. This does not mean subscribing to the view that younger or older councillors are better or worse (however defined) in getting to grips with policies, budgets and outcomes. As in the case of gender it is about what goes on the agenda and what is emphasised in debate and how experiences and expectations are fed into the political prioritisation process. The absence of younger councillors in England compared to the other countries in Table 9.1 deprives these debates of the perspectives provided by those in full-time work, dealing with complex time budgeting, balancing mortgages against other outgoings, worrying about educational provision for children and so on. Older councillors are not likely to bring these considerations into play but are likely to bring into play issues and considerations relevant to their long experience and their retired status. Those aged 65-plus in England report less awareness and concern about climate change (Haq *et al.*, 2008), and this inevitably filters into council debates (where this same age group is large) in terms of resistance to policies, strategies and thinking that promote low-carbon scenarios in transport, energy generation and buildings. They are not convinced that climate change is a problem, so they are not likely to favour climate change policies that set out to change behaviour in ways that reduce carbon emissions.

The percentage of older people supporting new nuclear power station building is higher in the over-55 and over-65 age group than in any other age group (Ipsos MORI, 2009). This is illustrated in Figure 9.4.

While 53 per cent of those over 65 years old support the building of new nuclear power stations, the figure falls to 30 per cent for those in the 16–24 age group. Age has a strong influence on attitude, and attitudes have a strong influence on outcomes when put into play in the debating chamber.

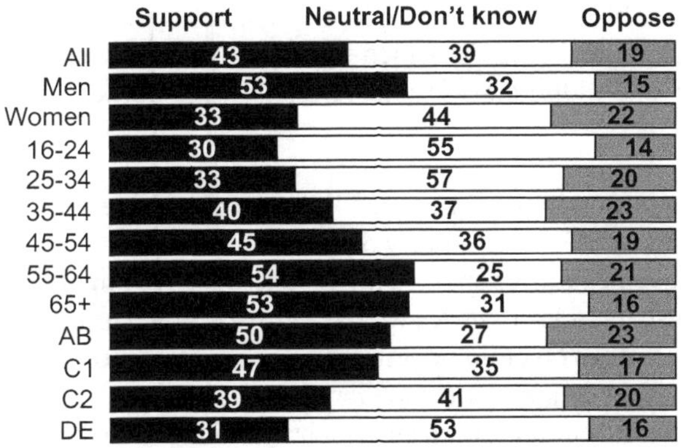

	Support	Neutral/Don't know	Oppose
All	43	39	19
Men	53	32	15
Women	33	44	22
16-24	30	55	14
25-34	33	57	20
35-44	40	37	23
45-54	45	36	19
55-64	54	25	21
65+	53	31	16
AB	50	27	23
C1	47	35	17
C2	39	41	20
DE	31	53	16

Figure 9.4 Age differences in the degree of support for replacement or new-build of nuclear power stations in Britain

Our conclusion is very simple. If we want to improve outcomes in a large number of detailed policy areas examined in this book we have to go much further than explaining how to increase rates of cycling or improve air quality or reduce child poverty or increase the amount of electricity generated from renewable sources (i.e. non-fossil fuel and non-nuclear). We have to change underlying factors that are producing decisions that are suboptimal with respect to international benchmarking. These underlying factors include the age and gender of our politicians, and it is imperative that UK local and national government moves as quickly as possible to getting the female participation rate up to 50 per cent and the age participation rate to the level that is representative of citizens as a whole. Not to do this will contribute to the continuation of the same debates and decision making that produce a general acceptance of poor-quality outcomes in UK cities, regions and places.

Budgets

Public expenditure on activities and facilities that improve the welfare and health of children and the elderly and create high-quality built environments and transport systems makes a substantial contribution to quality of life. Whilst it is very difficult to evaluate whether or not public funds have been spent wisely and effectively and have added to quality of life it is also the case that higher levels of expenditure are more likely to be associated with quality-of-life improvements than not. One useful indicator of the extent to which public expenditure supports quality-of-life outcomes is 'social protection expenditure'. This is defined by Eurostat (2010) :

Social protection encompasses all interventions from public or private bodies intended to relieve households and individuals of the burden of a defined set of risks or needs, associated with old age, sickness and/or healthcare, child-bearing and family, disability, unemployment, etc. Expenditure on social protection includes social benefits which consist of transfers in cash or in kind, to households and individuals to relieve them of the burden of a defined set of risks or needs.

Social expenditure data in the European Union reveal a wide variation in levels of expenditure (Figure 9.5). In Figure 9.5 the UK is ranked at 12 out of 27 EU member states. Eleven countries spend a higher percentage of their GDP on social protection, and these include countries we have already noted as being more equal or having better outcomes on child poverty and quality of life for older people, for example Denmark, Sweden, Austria and Germany.

Lower government spending on social protection and welfare has been justified in the past on the basis that this will increase economic efficiency and promote economic growth, especially as measured though growth in GDP (Lindert, 2007). This is a tacit acceptance of a transfer of wealth from the poor to the rich and of inequality (Wilkinson and Pickett, 2009). Lindert (2007) has carried out an empirical analysis of the relationship between government expenditure on social protection and growth in GDP and concludes that there is no relationship between these two variables. Higher social spending is not associated with lower rates of growth:

> This paper's claims that the welfare state is not the problem, and will not be the problem even in an older society, may seem at odds with two common assertions about a trade-off between how Americans and Europeans have accepted, or must accept, a trade-off between equity and efficiency. One

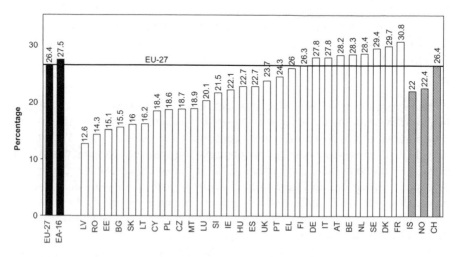

Figure 9.5 Expenditure on social protection as a percentage of GDP, 2008

Source: Eurostat (2011).

common assertion is correct: In practice, the American political balance has accepted more inequality, more poverty, and lower wages as a price to be paid for higher GDP. That is how political tastes have differed across the Atlantic, and nothing in this paper overturns such a conclusion.

(Lindert, 2007)

Lindert is very clear that the evidence he has reviewed supports the rejection of a 'common assertion'. The common assertion is 'that policy makers must trade some equality to get more efficiency'. This is incorrect. The Lindert conclusion is that we can have our cake and eat it. Hutton (2010) takes this point into a strong policy recommendation when he says: 'The move from the have-what-I-hold-society to a more fluid society requires substantial and sustained social invest-ment. There is no way round this necessity' (p. 280). Hutton's position has been strongly influenced by Lindert (2004), which establishes 'that those countries with the highest social spending as a share of national output achieve the highest and most sustained economic growth' and that this 'holds true even in those states where taxation is relatively high as a share of national output'.

Higher levels of government spending can produce much improved outcomes in terms of equality, quality of life and strong economies. This spending should be targeted at clearly defined population groups, for example children and the elderly, and at clearly defined tangible purposes that benefit the totality of popula-tion groups and eliminate regressive expenditure. Spending to eliminate poor air quality (Chapter 6) and to improve the built environment (Chapter 5) will ben-efit everyone and will deliver these benefits in a measurable way to low-income and disadvantaged or socially excluded groups. Spending on high-speed trains (Whitelegg, 2009b, 2011c) delivers over £30 billion of public money to the top 25 per cent of the population measured by income when similar amounts spent on walking, cycling and Freiburg or Zurich public transport systems will benefit everyone. The choice is simple, and on current evidence the decisions being made are wrong.

In earlier chapters we made frequent reference to Freiburg in southern Germany as an example of best practice and high quality-of-life outcomes. One possible reason for Freiburg's success as an exemplar of best practice in a large number of economic, social, climate change and environmental subject areas is that it spends more money on these things. We will now compare York in the UK with Freiburg to establish whether or not there are spending variations that could explain differ-ent outcomes.

Freiburg is a city with an acknowledged record of success in many policy areas, an outstandingly attractive urban environment, a totally integrated transport sys-tem with high-quality buses, trams and cycling hub, and a population of 240,000. York has a strong reputation as a very attractive tourist destination, an outstanding architectural and historical heritage, a fragmented transport system largely based on buses and with no tram system, and a pioneer in walking and cycling strategies that put it amongst the best in the UK. It has a population of 198,000. Both cities have highly regarded universities and a strong scientific resource base in terms of personnel and sites for cutting-edge technologies and spin-off job creation from the universities and the knowledge economy.

Table 9.4 summarises the key variables we use in this comparison. The per capita spend in York is 73.5 per cent of the per capita spend in Freiburg when uncorrected for educational spending. When education expenditure is deducted from York to provide a like-for-like comparison with Freiburg the percentage falls to 58.8. If York were funded at the same per capita level as Freiburg it would have available an annual budget of just under £600 million (£599.53 million) compared to the actual budget (2009–10) of £441 million.

Given this rather large differential in funding it is not surprising that Freiburg can achieve far more than York in terms of a high-quality public realm, attractive energy-efficient homes, high-quality walking, cycling and public transport offers,

Table 9.4 Freiburg and York compared

	Freiburg	*York*
Population	240,000	198,000
Total spend in 2009–10[a]	€823 million (£726.7 million)	£441.1 million
Per capita spend in 2009–10	£3,027.92	£2,227.78
Total spend excluding education[b]	€823 million (£726.7 million)	£352.8 million
Per capita spend in 2009–10 excluding education spending in York	£3,027.92	£1,781.82
Percentage of trips every day by mode[c]		
Car	28	Not available
Bike	28	Not available
Foot	24	Not available
Public transport	20	Not available
University staff	4,578	3,300
University students	21,622	12,000
World ranking of university, where 1 is the top rank[d]	132	81

Notes

a York's total spend is taken from the 2009–10 statement of accounts, http://www.york.gov.uk/content/finance/185102/Statement_of_Accounts_2009–10.pdf (accessed 14 January 2012). Freiburg's total spend is taken from the City of Freiburg Haushaltsplan 2009–10.

b York's budget includes spending on education and represents a large percentage of total spend. The dedicated schools grant in 2009–10 totalled £88.3 million: http://www.york.gov.uk/content/finance/185102/Statement_of_Accounts_2009–10.pdf, p. ix (accessed 14 January 2012). This amount has been deducted from the total expenditure of the City of York Council to give a like-for-like comparison with Freiburg. Teachers' salaries and other educational expenditure in Freiburg, in common with the remainder of Germany, are paid for by the Land government (the state of Baden-Württemberg in the case of Freiburg), and they are not a charge on the city budget.

c Freiburg modal split is taken from Stadt Freiburg (2010: 19). The City of York Council does not have information on modal split (York City Council, 2011).

d World ranking of universities carried out by the *Times Higher Education Supplement* (UK), http://www.timeshighereducation.co.uk/world-university-rankings/2010-2011/top-200.html (accessed 14 January 2012).

and low emission zones to improve air quality. The higher spend in Freiburg cannot be regarded as conclusive proof that this is the reason for better-quality outcomes, but it would be perverse to dismiss this factor as irrelevant. Many UK local authorities do not have the resources to devote to projects that can increase public realm and quality-of-life outcomes. A recent House of Lords report identified a significant funding gap in the resources available for transport in UK cities:

> An emphasis on promoting and enabling choice also confirms the importance of having an infrastructure which provides a broader range of cheap and efficient public transport services. We were told that European cities with low levels of car use have consistently spent far more per person on infrastructure. Cycling England said in relation to cycling, for example: 'levels of expenditure on cycling in successful European towns and cities . . . were at least £10 per head of population per year. By contrast analysis of Local Transport Plan outturn expenditure data for English local authorities, carried out at our request by the DfT calculated that the average level of spend by English local authorities was less than £1 per head of population per year'. In our seminar on reducing car use, it was noted that spend per person in Copenhagen was around £40 per head of population per year.
>
> (House of Lords, 2011, para. 7.37)

One of the most striking differences between York and Freiburg is the quality, network density and integration of the public transport offers. The same can be said of Manchester and Berlin, Sheffield and Bochum, Leeds and Dortmund, and any UK city compared with Stockholm, Copenhagen, Zurich, Amsterdam or Vienna. The UK has a fragmented, poorly integrated system of public transport offers which is partly but not entirely the result of bus and rail privatisation. Mainland European cities tend to have public transport operations that are still under direct political control with a strong emphasis on integration, links with spatial planning, and network density.

These large differentials in the quality, integration and availability of public transport options when UK cities are compared with mainland European cities are associated with the UK's high ranking on indicators of congestion (Inrix, 2011):

> U.K. drivers spend more time in traffic compared to drivers in Belgium, France, Germany, Luxembourg and the Netherlands. London ranks second after Paris as the most traffic clogged city among the 6 countries analyzed. The fallout from heavy traffic congestion hits the U.K. economy hard on several different levels. With many drivers paying over 117.1p at petrol stations and roads clogged with traffic congestion on average 35 hours a week across the country's 25 worst bottlenecks, traffic continues to have a major impact on consumers, the U.K. economy and the environment.

One measure of the difference between UK public transport operations and their mainland European comparators is the level of public funding of the city region transport systems. Kenworthy and Laube (2001) have assembled data on 84 cities and 200 indicators relevant to sustainable transport. The data are now quite old but still provide a clear indication of relativities in spending on public transport between city administrations in different countries. Table 9.5 compares the transport spend of UK cities with some of the best practice cities identified in the database.

Transport spending in the UK outside of London is amongst the lowest of all cities in developed countries in the world. It is far below that of Bangkok. Newcastle and Glasgow are in the same league as Beijing and Shanghai, and Manchester is at the same level as Houston in Texas, one of the most car-oriented cities on the planet. Interestingly Manchester is also close to Tunis on this indicator.

Figure 9.6 graphs the per capita spending using the complete data set in descending order of per capita spend. Figure 9.6 identifies London as a relatively high spender on transport but this falls away rapidly for Newcastle, Glasgow and Manchester. These three cities exhibit levels of spending considerably below those of comparable cities (e.g. Brussels and Berlin) and are amongst the lowest-funding-level group of all cities in developed countries.

More recent data on spending comparisons support the Kenworthy and Laube (2001) rankings. National expenditure on public transport support in Germany in 2008 was approximately €25 billion per annum (FES, 2010). This is compared with England, Sweden and Denmark in Table 9.6.

The per capita spending gap revealed in Table 9.6 shows that both Germany and Denmark spend more than twice as much per capita per annum on public transport support as England. This is a significant gap and explains the major part of the quality gap between the public transport systems in these two countries.

There are also significant variations at city region level when German and other EU cities are compared with English ones. Data availability at city region level across several countries is problematic, but data collected in 2011 and reported in Table 9.7 provide a snapshot that can be used to illustrate variations at the sub-national level.

Table 9.5 Public transport investment per capita per annum

	Per capita spend ($US)
London	271.33
Manchester	27.92
Glasgow	19.77
Newcastle	11.15
Vienna	407.18
Amsterdam	392.79
Stuttgart	298.95
Zurich	279.21
Berlin	183.16
Bangkok	100.28

Source: Kenworthy and Laube (2001).

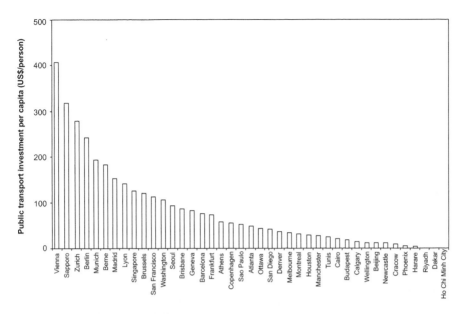

Figure 9.6 Public transport investment

Table 9.6 Public expenditure on public transport subsidy, Germany, England, Denmark and Sweden

	Annual subsidy total in national currency	Annual subsidy total	Population	Per capita subsidy
Germany[a]	€25 billion	£22,065,898,630	81,835,000	£269.63
England[b]		£5,880,000,000	52,234,000	£112.57
Denmark[c]	13.311 billion Danish kroner	£1,584,001,431	5,534,738	£286.19
Sweden[d]	15 billion Swedish kronor	£1.4 billion	9,471,174	£147.81

Notes

a German data is taken from FES (2010).

b England data is taken from DfT statistics, table BUS0502a for the year 2009–10, which is £2.472 billion for bus. Rail subsidy data are not available for England, so the national figure for Great Britain of £3.96 billion is factored by the percentage of England's population compared to that of Great Britain (excluding Northern Ireland), which is 86 per cent; 86 per cent of £3.96 billion is £3.4 billion. The public transport subsidy for England is £2.472 billion (bus) plus £3.4 billion (rail) = £5.88 billion.

c Danish data provided on 29 August 11 by Lone Schlüter, Statistics Denmark Library and Information, European Statistical Data Support, Statistics Denmark, http://www.statbank.dk/OFF17 (accessed 14 January 2012).

d Swedish data is from 'Local and regional public transport, 2010', Trafikanalys, Stockholm, www. trafa.se (accessed 14 January 2012).

Table 9.7 compares public transport 'subsidy', which is the direct transfer payment from the public sector (city, regional, state and national administrations) to public transport operators to make up the difference between revenue from

Table 9.7 Public transport subsidy in English and mainland European cities

	Local currency/ £ sterling	Population	Per capita spend
Canton of Zurich[a]	967 million Swiss francs/ £76,363,041	1,351,297	£56.51
Greater Copenhagen[b]	5.072 billion Danish kroner	1,800,000	£333.77
Skåne, including Lund, southern Sweden[c]	1,193 million Swedish kronor/ £113,441,448	1,243,329	£91.24
Liverpool city region[d]	£155,200,000	1,350,000	£114.96
York (UK)[e]	£4,127,000	198,000	£20.84
Stuttgart, Germany (VSS area)[f]	€260,100,000/ £226,829,905	2,419,694	£93.74
Bremen[g]	€54,400,000/ £48,232,682	547,000	£88.18
Vienna[h]	€270 million/ £231,975,887	1,680,000	£138.08

Notes

a Statistisches Jahrbuch des Kantons Zurich, http://www.statistik.zh.ch/internet/justiz_inneres/statistik/de/statistiken/veroeffentlichungen/zhiz.html (accessed 14 January 2012).

b Data are taken from three sources covering the City of Copenhagen: i) Bus: http://www.moviatrafik.dk/omos/bagomos/nogletalbus/okonomi/Documents/selvfinansieringsgrad.pdf (accessed 14 January 2012); http://www.moviatrafik.dk/omos/bagomos/okonomi/aarsregnskab09/Documents/AArsregnskab%202009.pdf (accessed 14 January 2012). ii) Metro: The Metro company is responsible for the Metro. The 2008 annual report including accounts is available in English at: http://intl.m.dk/About+the+Metro/~/media/Metro/PDF/PDF%202009/Metro-Annual-report-08-web.ashx (accessed 14 January 2012); iii) Trains (S-tog): The 2010 annual report of DSB S-Trains is available (in Danish) at: http://www.dsb.dk/Global/PDF/Årsrapport/Årsregnskabsmeddelese%202010.pdf (accessed 14 January 2012).

c Data on subsidy are taken from Trafikforsorjningsplan 2011, https://www.skanetrafiken.se/upload/Dokumentbank/Styrdokument/Trafikförsörjningsplan/Trafikförsörjningsplan_2011.pdf, p. 24 (accessed 14 January 2012).

d Liverpool city region includes the city of Liverpool and the local authorities of Knowsley, Wirral, Sefton and St Helens. Data were supplied by the director of resources (Jim Barclay) by e-mail on 17 August 2011. The rail total for Merseyrail services is £86.5 million, and local bus support is £17.4 million. The total for bus and rail is £155.2 million. This total includes £51.3 million in 2010–11 concessionary travel costs.

e York data were supplied by York City Council in an e-mail from Councillor Dave Merrett on 27 August 2011. York subsidy data include concessionary travel valued at £3.6 million of the total £4.127 million.

f Stuttgart data were extracted from 'Zahlen, Daten, Fakten', Verkehrs- und Tarifverbund Stuttgart (VSS), http://www.vvs.de/download/ZahlenDatenFaktenVB09_webansicht.pdf (accessed 14 January 2012).

g Bremen data were supplied by Michael Glotz-Richter, Freie Hansestadt Bremen, Der Senator für Umwelt, Bau, Verkehr und Europa, Referent 'nachhaltige Mobilität', Bremen.

h Vienna data were supplied by Anton Geyer, Technopolis, Vienna.

passengers and the total cost of operating the system. It is based on a very small sample but provides supporting evidence for the relativities noted by Kenworthy and Laube (2001). UK spending is still very much below that of its mainland comparator cities. Liverpool's annual per capita spend approaches the level of mainland

European best practice cities, for example Vienna, but is heavily influenced by over £50 million in concessionary travel payments which do not impact directly on the quality and quantity of public transport offers. The York figure is pitifully small and reflects the general reality of public transport support outside of London.

The picture presented by Table 9.7, which describes operating subsidies for public transport in a small selection of EU cities and regions, is complex. The complexity arises from a number of data and interpretation problems that are difficult to resolve. These are:

1   Lack of published English data on city region public transport subsidy. There is no standardised statistical source for this information, and this presents problems of comparison between English city regions and between these city regions and mainland European comparators.
2   Rail and bus subsidies are completely separate systems, and public transport companies in Germany reporting levels of subsidy to local transport do not include rail subsidies. In the UK rail subsidies are available for the national rail network and per passenger kilometres for individual train operating companies (TOCs), but there is no way of identifying rail subsidies for local transport in Leeds or Manchester (for example).
3   Concessionary travel in England is effectively a personal mobility subsidy for bus travel. It amounted to £971 million in 2009–10. It allows all those over the age of 60 to travel free of charge by local bus in England. It is a subsidy, but it is not a subsidy aimed at nurturing an integrated system of public transport choices in a city region and supporting services seven days a week and 20 hours a day as is normal in Switzerland. It is 'an inefficient and high-cost way of delivering public policy objectives' (Oxera, 2009).

The whole public transport operating subsidy in the European Union is unnecessarily complex, opaque and unhelpful and does not permit a reliable analysis of value for money.

It is still the case that where comparisons can be made (Table 9.7) there is evidence that more public money is going into the support of public transport services in Germany, Sweden, Denmark and Switzerland than in the UK. The low level of funding in the UK (excluding concessionary payments) is linked to the low level of use of public transport and the low level of quality of public transport offerings identified by many analysts. In a study of European comparisons on a number of transport parameters the UK was found to be 'below the European Peer Group' (CfIT, 2010). These parameters included our use of bus and coach, walking and cycling. The CfIT report observed:

It is clear that the UK does not use public transport to the same extent as other European nations. Whilst we have made more efficient use of our cars, we could do better at providing alternative modes of transport. As we currently have one of the worst obesity rates in Europe, there could be significant health benefits for the UK in better promotion of walking and cycling.

This is not a particularly surprising conclusion given the funding disparities and the glaringly obvious quality gap clearly visible to any user of public transport in the UK when he or she uses equivalent systems in Copenhagen, Stockholm, Bremen, Vienna, Frankfurt and Freiburg and many other cities in France and the Netherlands.

The public transport funding situation in England and Wales is also worsening (House of Commons, 2011c):

> The Coalition Government's Spending Review in October 2010 included three decisions with implications for the bus industry:
>
> - an overall 28 per cent reduction in local authority revenue expenditure from 2011–12
> - changes in the formula for concessionary travel reimbursement from 2011–12
> - a 20 per cent reduction in the Bus Service Operators' Grant from 2012–13
>
> The total reduction in revenue for the English bus industry following the Spending Review is still unclear and difficult to predict, but it could be in the region of £200m to £300m per annum.

There is compelling evidence that the central control of local government funding both generally and in the specific case of public transport has produced a system that is far less attractive to users than it is in Zurich, Copenhagen, Lund, Vienna or Bremen. Increasing the budgets available to local authorities and to public transport in the UK is a necessary pre-condition for improving quality of life.

Budgets and central–local government relationships

The issue of budgets in UK local government is deeper than the size of the budget and the gaps between budgets available to UK local authorities and mainland European comparators. The whole system of local government finance in England is widely regarded as unfit for purpose (LGA, 2004; Wilson and Game, 2006).

The basic problem with local government finance is that in the UK local authorities have access to only one tax and this is a property tax. This one tax is also subject to capping so that central government can control how much is raised from the levy of the council tax. This is unusual, and most other countries have a variety of sources of revenue. Wilson and Game (2006) quote Japan, where prefectures and municipalities have taxes on residents, consumption (sales), enterprise (business), automobiles and their purchase, tobacco, property purchase, light oil delivery, and mini-cars and motorcycles. New York has four major taxes: property, personal income, general sales, and a general corporation tax. Hambleton (2005) is clear that the UK system is severely flawed: 'Compare this [the situation in other countries] with the UK, where the council has only one tax – generating a small fraction of revenue spending. And, incredibly, even that is subject to capping by central government. Effective local leadership cannot be expected to prosper in such a constrained setting.'

This comment points very much in the direction of fundamental reform of local government so that its financial base is stronger, less susceptible to central government control and more likely to be able to fund local initiatives that produce high-quality local outcomes. In turn this ability to produce results on the ground is likely to attract a different set of councillors and stimulate a progressive and synergistic process of attitudinal and decision-making change that focus on funded outcomes, link choices to age and gender sensitivity and in a very clear way demonstrate that local government does matter.

Conclusions

Delivering high-quality outcomes in the UK cannot be guaranteed by changes to the age and gender mix of councillors or the budgets they administer. Both these factors are important and are likely on the basis of the evidence we have reviewed to lead to better-quality outcomes. They should be exploited and harvested at the same time in the same place, with a strong commitment to increase the quality of outcomes by reference to mainland European comparators.

We do not underestimate the obstacles to change. In the current UK financial and political climate, arguing for more money to be spent on local government is likely to fall on deaf ears, and yet it is essential if citizens are to enjoy the same high quality of life described in earlier chapters for best practice countries, cities and regions. A recent Cabinet Office report revealed that the cumulative costs of congestion, physical inactivity, CO_2 emissions, pollution, noise and accidents in the UK are approximately £56 billion per annum (Cabinet Office, 2009). These costs can be greatly reduced by interventions recommended in earlier chapters. The costs of not taking action to improve quality of life are higher than the costs of taking action. The costs of significant improvements in the quality of life of UK citizens may well appear to be daunting in comparison with current funding levels, but a wider economic analysis including, for example, the predicted £50 billion per annum cost of obesity identified by the Government Office for Science (2007) would reveal a different picture. Costs can liberate and propagate benefits, and frugality in public spending can store up large costs for the future that will eventually fall on public services or on severely degraded living conditions for groups of citizens.

In the next chapter we turn to the third factor that is likely to contribute to the massive cultural and structural change that is needed in governance in the UK to bring about an improvement in quality of life. This is the degree to which city regions have the power to do the things they want to do and the interrelationships between powers, budgets and the characteristics of councillors.

10 The powers of local government to do things

The UK is an already highly centralised – even hyper-centralised – governmental system, becoming even more centralised, with its reduction in the numbers and powers of elected local authorities and its tight central control of all elements of local finance.

(Wilson and Game, 2006: 157)

The enhancement of local political control is not on the British government's agenda.

(Batley and Stoker, 1991: 218)

The nature of the relationship between the national state and local government has been a constant source of debate for many decades and is still far from resolved. What is clear is that there are large variations in the European Union in the degree to which local authorities are able to raise money, spend money and make their own decisions about how to improve quality of life for their citizens. The suggestion discussed in this chapter is that the UK maintains a strongly centralist control over local government and limits its freedom to innovate, problem-solve and deliver high-quality outcomes.

The *State of European Cities Report* has analysed and mapped the power of cities in the European Union (European Commission, 2007). This is reproduced as Figure 10.1. The index is based on an analysis of quantitative information on EU cities incorporating four main dimensions:

- city size;
- structure and status;
- spending power;
- control over income.

The shading in Figure 10.1 gives an immediate visual impression of the geographical distribution of 'powerful' cities. They are not in the UK. The category 'most powerful' is concentrated in Demark, Sweden, Germany, France and Italy.

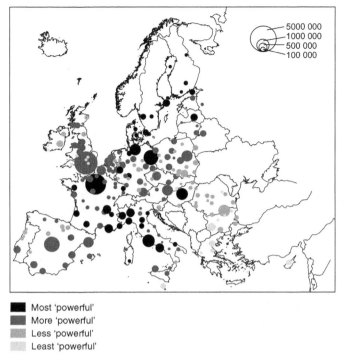

Figure 10.1 The relative power of EU cities: an index of city power

In 2010 the European Commission produced a second edition of *State of European Cities Report* (2010f) and commented on powers as follows: 'Since Scandinavian countries traditionally entrust sub-national levels (e.g. cities) with stronger decision-making powers and greater financial capacity, Scandinavian cities, whether large or small, economically powerful or lagging behind, will, as a matter of course, score high in the index of powers.'

The same report analyses the annual expenditure per resident of over 300 cities and on a one-to-five scale (five is the highest per capita expenditure) categorises the majority of German, Swedish and Danish cities as 'five' and the majority of UK cities as 'three'. UK cities have access to fewer resources than many of their mainland European comparators.

Lower levels of per capita expenditure in the UK are associated with limited powers to do things. These limited powers are very clearly illustrated by the refusal of central government to allow a tram system to be built in Liverpool, contrary to the wishes of the city council and the regional transport authority. The system of central control over budgets exercised through a grant distribution system imposed by central government, very little diversity of funding sources, and rate capping puts English cities in a 'cap in hand' situation and with very little flexibility and ability to pursue political choices backed by the resources to deliver projects. The refusal of central government to allow Lancaster City Council (and many other councils) to become a unitary authority actively denies local elected politicians the opportunity to deliver services and improve the quality of outcomes in the way they think will best serve the interests of local residents. Unitary authorities are not free of central control but are able to deliver a full range of services, with all the opportunities provided by that full range to link housing with planning, planning with transport, social with economic, air pollution with health, and energy with peak oil and climate change. At the moment, these functions in England are often delivered by two levels of government, with very little potential for coordinated and integrated action to improve quality of life across the full spectrum of services that determine quality of life.

We have already discussed two important aspects of reform in governance that we think are needed if we are to bring about a dramatic improvement in quality of life in all our local authorities and localities. These are (1) a closer fit between elected politicians and the populations they represent in terms of age and gender and (2) budgets. These areas are closely linked with powers. If a local authority is to adopt a strongly interventionist policy of place shaping and improvement in quality of life it will need the powers, the budgets and a different set of councillors. We have already argued that creativity and deeper understanding of issues, solutions and actions are more likely to emerge from a group of councillors with a closer fit to the age and gender profile of the locality it serves. The same point can be made about the national level and the degree of fit between the national politicians who sit in Parliament and society as a whole.

We need more young councillors, more female councillors, an improved level of resourcing and greater diversity in income streams. We also need more power to be devolved to local government so that more councillors with a 'can-do' attitude are recruited and more things can be done. The devolution or reallocation of powers to local government on its own will not be enough. All these fundamental structural changes are needed at one and the same time.

The UK is a nation state with a significant amount of control reserved for the centre and relatively little devolved to localities (Gough, 2009). The Local Government Association (LGA, 2008b) quotes a Council of Europe survey of centralisation: 'the UK remains a highly centralised state. A 2006 Council of Europe review of central control over local government placed the UK in the "control/ supervision increasing" category alongside Azerbaijan.'

The devolution of powers to Wales, Scotland and London has altered the geography of power in the UK and has brought about a significant constitutional change but one that still leaves local government without constitutional protection or status (Bogdanor, 2009). It is already clear, for example, that London under its directly elected mayor and exploiting the opportunities provided by the Greater London Authority Act (1999) has far more scope to address important issues and raise revenue than does Birmingham, Manchester or Liverpool. The London congestion charge introduced by mayor Ken Livingstone in 2003 generated £2.4 billion in its first eight years, and the extra income, less operating costs, has been spent on a significant upgrade of buses and a very ambitious cycling strategy. Effective devolution of powers and revenue-raising opportunities to cities will play a large part in improving quality of life in those areas, and the lack of devolution will hinder progress.

One measure of the degree of centralisation is the percentage split on revenue raised by central and local government (OECD, 2011b). The UK split is approximately 90 per cent of revenue collected by central government and 10 per cent by local government. The OECD ranking of countries on this measure puts New Zealand slightly ahead of the UK, and the UK has the highest proportion of centrally collected revenue of all EU countries listed and higher than Japan.

Gough (2009) is very clear about the degree to which the centralisation of power in England is a problem and out of step with other countries: 'Today it is a given that England is among the most centralised – if not the most centralised – of advanced industrial countries.' He compares English local government with Germany, France, Denmark, the Netherlands, Australia, South Africa and Canada ('the peer group') and concludes:

> it is also clear that the English system has distinctive features, many of them inimical to effective local democracy. The comparison with the peer group highlights: English local government's lack of either constitutional protection or of a full place at the national political table; its narrow and inflexible financial base; and the scale of performance management regime to which it is subject.
>
> (Gough, 2009: 48)

The Local Government Association (LGA, 2007), representing 422 local authorities in England and Wales, has recommended major changes in responsibility, funding and freedom of action in its analysis of the current rather dysfunctional system of powers, funding and fragmentation. It argues that the relatively poor performance of UK cities in economic terms is partly the result of constraints on local government, and devolution of powers is one way to fix the problem:

> We have a great global city in London. But the other places in Britain, once world-beaters, have fallen behind. Of the largest English cities apart from the capital, Bristol is the best performing in the European league table – but only in 34th place. Most of our great cities – a century ago the economic powerhouses of the industrialised world – now languish at the bottom of the table. Indeed Manchester, Birmingham, Liverpool and Newcastle have only half the GDP per head of major European cities.
>
> (LGA, 2007)

The LGA added emphasis to this in its weekly publication *First* (*First*, 2007):

> England's economy will continue to lag behind its European neighbours unless Whitehall loosens its grip on the powers it holds over the country, says an LGA report. It says that if central government was willing to devolve powers in areas such as transport, housing, the labour market and planning, more than a million new jobs could be created.

Sandy Bruce-Lockhart, chairman of the LGA, said: British productivity is below the average of G7 countries, lagging behind the US, France and Germany. English cities with the exception of London are not even represented in Europe's wealthiest 30 urban centres . . . politicians of all parties recognise that what distinguishes our local economies from successful places elsewhere is our uniquely centralised system of decision-making and funding. What is needed is a clear devolution of power to make local decisions and put in place local solutions.

The LGA *Prosperous Communities II* report (LGA, 2007) summarises how the new system would work in a hypothetical local authority (Barchester). Barchester would have a single collective plan for land use, transport, employment and skills. It would have enhanced funding from developer contributions (100 per cent of planning gain supplement receipts). The council would have the welfare savings they made by getting local people back into work and business tax receipts produced by the economic growth they had promoted. The LGA report then asks a question and answers it:

Q   To make these changes happen who would they require the permission of?
A   No one.

There is no guarantee that this new model would deliver the significant improvements in quality of life that we have argued for in this book. It is, nevertheless, an important step in an evolutionary progression towards something that loosens the grip of a rather remote central government authority and gives far more flexibility and decision-making powers to those closest to the problems. More importantly it offers the very real possibility that local geographical differences can be taken into account in problem solving and delivery and that local authorities will be more capable of innovation and generating new ways of doing things that can be widely disseminated and copied.

Gough (2009) makes eight recommendations to deal with these problems, including a reformed upper house with local government representation, a more transparent grant distribution system based on the Australian model, and clearer central–local government relationships, with local government an equal partner in financial discussions on the Danish model. Specific recommendations are made for diversifying the financial base of local government. These include the reform of council tax, relocalised business rates and some element of income tax.

The UK government has announced its intention to instigate a radical devolution of power to local level, giving new powers and opportunities to councils, communities, neighbourhoods and individuals (House of Commons, 2011d). This will be delivered through the Localism Bill. The Localism Bill embodies some of the specific changes the government wishes to make to put this into practice, but the select committee has reservations about the degree of commitment to real devolution of powers:

The Government will have to resist temptation to intervene in local affairs – a measure of restraint for which ministers have shown worryingly little appetite thus far. The litmus test of localism will be the Government's reaction to local decisions with which it disagrees. Ministers, civil servants and parliamentarians will all have a part to play if a more localist political culture is to evolve and thrive. A more explicit statement is needed about where the dividing line between a central, light-touch framework and unwarranted interference will be drawn, lest the practice of 'guided localism' become the norm. This would reinforce the impression of mixed messages and unanswered questions about the type of localism the Government wishes to pursue, and how scrupulous it intends to be in living up to its own ideals.

(House of Commons, 2011d)

More importantly there is still no sign of devolution of budgets and changes in local government finance that will strengthen the decision taking and innovation potential of local authorities. This key element of centralisation (the central control of budgets) was identified as crucial for localism to succeed in the submission to the select committee report by Jones and Stewart (2011):

The Treasury has to be as committed to localism and decentralisation as is the Department for Communities and Local Government (CLG). It must champion decentralisation not only of expenditure decisions but also of taxation decisions. It too must reject centralisation. The Treasury controls 96% of taxation, with only council tax as the 4% beyond its direct control, but even it is capped by CLG. The council tax finances only around 25% of local-government expenditure. For decentralisation to be genuine, elected local government should be drawing the lion's share of its revenues from local taxes it levies on its local voters. That shift in the balance of local spending and taxing will enable more responsible, responsive and accountable local government, no longer acting as a supplicant on central government demanding bigger grants, and more involved in interacting with its localities. Citizens, community groups and councillors will behave more responsibly in their use of resources if they know that any demands for higher standards, better services and fewer cuts will have to be paid for by local-taxation increases bearing on them. This local fiscal discipline should be welcomed by the Treasury, since it will no longer be bombarded by local authorities seeking larger grants. Instead local authorities will be their allies in the wise use of resources. These authorities, more reliant on local taxation than central grants, and playing the lead role in place-based budgeting, will help the Treasury avoid its incessant battles with Whitehall spending departments, since decisions on spending and taxing will have been decentralised to local authorities. Cabinet squabbling will be diminished, enabling the Treasury to concentrate on issues of macroeconomic management and international finance.

(Jones and Stewart, 2011, para. 36)

The 2011 House of Commons select committee report followed on from a 2009 House of Commons select committee report examining very much the same area

(House of Commons, 2009). One of the witnesses to this select committee inquiry was very clear about what was important about more local control:

> One of our witnesses, Professor Vernon Bogdanor CBE, Professor of Government, Oxford University, possibly put it most strongly when he argued that decentralisation can 'stimulate a sense of local patriotism which can lead to real improvements in public services. In a decentralised system of government, each local authority will strive to ensure that its own performance is better than that of its competitors.'
>
> (House of Commons, 2009, para. 4)

And:

> The vast majority of our witnesses have argued that this growing centralisation of power, and confining of local government roles, has had far-reaching negative consequences for individuals, for local communities and for democracy. Latterly, successive governments have attempted to move power and decision-making away from the centre and towards localities. However, any government of the day must take account of public and media expectations that demand that it 'do something' about almost any issue of public policy. Moreover, there are additional expectations about fairness and service regulation that cannot be ignored.
>
> (House of Commons, 2009, para. 10)

The 2009 select committee report takes a detailed look at local government responsibilities, powers and revenue-raising options in Denmark and Sweden. It finds that local authorities in these two countries have a greater diversity of funding sources than is the case in the UK and have more autonomy:

> Our hosts in Denmark and Sweden were also clear that the strong position of local government in their countries owed much to the high degree of local government financial autonomy. Danish municipalities raise 60 per cent of their revenue from local taxes (mainly income tax), and a further 14 per cent from charges for services. They are dependent upon central government for only 27 per cent of their funding (12 per cent reimbursements for social expenditure and 13 per cent block grant including an equalisation equation). Similarly, Swedish municipalities raise 69 per cent of their revenue from local tax (mainly income tax), and only 15 per cent in the form of government grant. The local government representatives we spoke to in both countries felt that the clear link between local tax payment and the delivery of local services led to a strong engagement in local democracy. In England, the financial situation is reversed. Local government raises, in total, only 25 per cent of its revenue locally – mainly through the council tax. It is dependent upon central government for the vast majority of its revenue.
>
> (House of Commons, 2009, para. 35)

And even more:

> The relationship between central and local government in England deviates
> from the European norm in at least three areas – the level of constitutional
> protection, the level of financial autonomy, and the level of central govern-
> ment intervention. All serve to tilt the balance of power towards the centre.
>
> (House of Commons, 2009, para. 38)

Seize the moment

It is quite clear from academic analysis, parliamentary select committee scrutiny
and the evidence given by many witnesses to the 2009 and 2011 House of Commons communities and local government select committee investigations that
England suffers from over-centralisation and the overbearing diktat of central
government. This degree of imbalance between central and local government is
at the extreme of European practice, and it damages local democratic vitality,
accountability and the 'can-do' attitude that can deliver effective local solutions
with the budgets necessary to deliver those solutions. It is also clear that the system of local government finance in England is deeply flawed and a barrier to problem solving, vitality and quality-of-life gains. Local authorities need more sources
of finance and more control over those sources, including a local income tax. The
conclusion of the 2009 select committee investigation captures these elements and
points in the direction of a solution:

> Not only should there be a shift in the balance of power, it should be given
> a degree of permanency. To achieve this will require changes not only to
> the balance of funding in England, but also to the constitutional settlement
> and to Parliamentary scrutiny. Only by so consolidating a new balance of
> power between local and central government will local government achieve
> the autonomy it requires to deliver the benefits of local solutions to local
> people and local communities. In so doing, we believe, the groundwork will
> also be laid for a reinvigorated local democracy that will, in time, also help
> to regenerate the national political arena. As our witnesses have noted, the
> central–local relationship is not a zero-sum game. Central and local can gain
> from this process. We are under no illusions: as we have seen, the history
> of reports such as these is not encouraging. But perhaps now is the time for
> the moment to be seized. Building on the small shifts of recent years, central
> government should now be more radical, and local government more ambi-
> tious for itself and the people of its locality. The benefits both to local public
> services and to democracy itself could be immeasurable.
>
> (House of Commons, 2009, para. 149)

The select committee call for a change to the balance of power is well understood and supported by the vast majority of those who have actually experienced
local government at the sharp end. One of the problems in the UK is that the tradi-

tional locus of power and influence lies with civil servants and national politicians who maintain a cultural disdain for local government and the work that goes on at that level of government. Local authorities are regarded as relatively remote outposts of central government whose job it is to implement the diktat of Whitehall. There is no evidence of a close relationship of mutual respect and of an attitude that celebrates the ability and wishes of local government to work out better ways of doing things and keep local democracy alive and well in an atmosphere of serious place shaping, policy formulation, innovation and delivery.

The experience of the author of this book as a district councillor (Lancaster City Council) for eight years, including a brief period on Cabinet with the 'Valuing People' portfolio, is that local government at this level is unable to function in a way that debates, decides and delivers supported by the budgets to deliver. There is almost no point in having 60 councillors meeting once each month to debate views and policy documents that have no chance of being delivered because the local authority does not have the power to deliver and does not have the budget to deliver.

A clear example of the latter is air quality. Lancaster City Council has a legal duty to improve air quality and deliver policies that achieve this objective in its air quality action plan (AQAP). There are no budgets to support the delivery of the AQAP, and the powers to deal with vehicular sources of air pollution (the majority source) are located within Lancashire County Council and the city council is powerless.

Inevitably in these circumstances the job of a councillor becomes one of deliberation on strategy, policy and mission statements that are unrelated to the reality of what can be achieved. In 1903 Lancaster Borough Council generated electricity, collaborated with local entrepreneurs in designing, building and funding a tram system, built the trams at the local 'wagon works' and ran the municipal transport system. In 2012 it empties bins, cleans streets, operates a planning system that can only respond to the whims of developers, and has no demonstrable impact on the health, safety, economy, quality of life and mobility of its 140,000 residents. This place-shaping impotence cannot possibly attract the kind of councillors who actually want to change things and have worked out that the chances of changing things are very low indeed. Why should highly motivated citizens with a desire to improve things in their locality spend years sitting through tedious meetings with very little to show for that time and effort in tangible outcomes?

The whole system of central–local government relationships and the ability of local government to get on with the job in this imbalanced situation are deeply flawed and simply have to change. The time for procrastination is over.

Bringing about change is always difficult, especially in a cultural context where central government jealously guards its powers and local government has deteriorated to the point where it is no longer 'government' in any sense of that word. Nevertheless the basics of what needs to be done are clear:

• The two-tier system of districts and counties in England should be abolished and a system of unitaries put in place. All councils need to be fully responsible for all services or activities and put an end to the 'pass the parcel' culture of local authority communications with citizens.

- All local authorities should be constitutionally enabled through an Act of Parliament with a general power of competence. This means that they can do anything they want to do as long as it is not explicitly forbidden by law. The fact that the ministry of transport, health, housing or whatever does not like it is irrelevant. Central government will have no power to block local government. The Local Government Association (LGA, 2008b) recommends the Italian constitution, Article 118, as a useful model. This article confers wide-ranging powers on councils to provide any public service.
- Local government finance should be reformed so that local authorities can collect a local income tax and keep it. The level of local income tax would be set by discussion between local and central government and would be compensated for by a reduction in national income tax. A local income tax system would be part of a bigger package of revenue-raising possibilities to make sure that local authorities in relatively deprived parts of England were not disadvantaged by comparison with local authorities in relatively affluent areas. We agree with the conclusion set out in House of Commons (2009), though we would go much further in diversifying revenue sources:

> In principle, though, a supplementary local income tax, introduced alongside council tax but with a corresponding reduction in central taxation so that the overall tax burden remained the same, is a potential longer-term solution to the balance of funding problem, and one that Government should seriously consider. It would be possible to replace central funding with such an income tax without any change to the total collected in taxation overall. Councils would then decide at what level to set their local tax.
>
> (House of Commons, 2009, para. 123)

Introducing the three reforms listed above would have the effect of delivering a lively, responsive, democratic, reinvigorated culture of local government in England. It also gives effect to the European Charter of Local Self-Government (Council of Europe, 1985), which has been signed by the UK government. In particular it gives effect to Article 4 (2), Article 8 (2) and Article 8 (3):

> Fundamental to both the Council of Europe and the European Union – as with the related principle of 'subsidiarity' – is the idea that due consideration needs to be given to the appropriate tier of government at which a decision should be taken, and that upper tiers of government should not interfere in matters that are best decided at a lower level. Article 4 (2) of the Charter asserts that 'local authorities shall, within the limits of the law, have full discretion to exercise their initiative with regard to any matter which is not excluded from their competence nor assigned to any other authority'. Article 8 (2) asserts that 'an administrative supervision of the activities of the local authorities shall normally aim only at ensuring compliance with the law and with constitutional principles', whilst article 8 (3) asserts that 'administrative

supervision of local authorities shall be exercised in such a way as to ensure that the intervention of the controlling authority is kept in proportion to the importance of the interests which it is intended to protect.

(House of Commons, 2009, para. 130)

Our three reforms also give effect to Article 9:

Article 9 – Financial resources of local authorities

1   Local authorities shall be entitled, within national economic policy, to adequate financial resources of their own, of which they may dispose freely within the framework of their powers.
2   Local authorities' financial resources shall be commensurate with the responsibilities provided for by the constitution and the law.

(Council of Europe, 1985)

The current system of local–central government relationships and distribution of powers and competence is broken and in urgent need of reform. The balance of evidence is clear about the nature of those reforms, and they should be put into place on the shortest possible time scale. Local authorities should be given constitutional protection and recognition so that they are fully part of government and not junior partners of a strong central government subject to political whims about budgets and powers that are inclined to decline over time. Local authorities should be given a constitutionally guaranteed general power of competence that is positive and encourages them to do whatever they decide to do as long as it is not explicitly ruled out by statute. Should there be any lingering doubts as opposed to a culturally obstructive reluctance to introduce reforms then the doubters can go and experience just what can be done at the local level in Freiburg or Stockholm or Copenhagen or Vienna or any one of dozens of other city regions in Denmark, Sweden, the Netherlands and Germany and reflect on the relative impotence of English local authorities by comparison to their mainland European neighbours.

11 Life in 2030

This book has put forward three interrelated propositions:

1   In terms of quality of life and the daily experience of the majority of UK citizens we are not performing very well when we make comparisons with mainland European cities, regions and nations.
2   In the majority of the indicators and parameters discussed it is not difficult to identify what should be done to improve our performance and to upgrade the UK so that its national performance is near the top of the league and not near the bottom.
3   Identifying what could and should be done does not on its own produce the much needed upgrade. There is a need to explore some important underlying factors that might play a part in our poor performance and then make the kinds of changes in those factors that increase the probability of success. These underlying factors include budgets, the degree to which elected politicians bring a wide variety of experiences and understanding to the decision-making table, and the constitutional powers of local authorities to get on and do the job without obeisance to central government.

There is much we have not discussed, especially under the tantalising heading of 'cultural factors'. It is possible that Swedish politicians and local politicians in Freiburg in southern Germany are 'better' in some way than their UK counterparts. They may have a deeper understanding of the collective good. They may be better at consensus and compromise across political parties based on improving quality of life more than point scoring against the opposition. They may have a more sceptical attitude towards the murky world of privatisation and the introduction of so-called market principles into the design and delivery of health, transport and other public services. An example of this different approach to markets and public services can be found in the contract between the Greater Copenhagen Transport Authority and Arriva, the UK company supplying bus services in this area (HT, 1998). In this example the Danes were more than happy to encourage private sector bus operations, but there are detailed conditions set by HT on the standards to be met. It is possible that Scandinavian countries, Germany, the Netherlands, Switzerland and Austria have a more robust attitude towards public services and actually believe that politicians should set standards for public services (e.g. buses) rather than falling back on the assertion that the 'market will sort it out'. They may be more interventionist in that problems of poor air quality or child welfare or integrated public transport quite simply require bold political direction linked to high-quality outcomes and are too important to be left to the private sector. All of these things are possible and should be debated, but they do not disrupt the fundamental concerns of this book summarised in the three propositions noted above.

Underlying every chapter in this book is the idea that, if we want to, we can take action to remedy poor performance. We have no answer to the possibility that 'we don't want to'. If the prevailing consensus is that it is acceptable for several thousand of our elderly to die each year because they live in energy-inefficient homes and have too little income to pay for both food and high energy bills then that is disgraceful but beyond the scope of this book to take any further. If we are content to have one of the highest rates of child poverty in the European Union when this is so easy to change then we draw a similar conclusion. If we are content for 4,000 people to die in London every year from poor air quality when we know how to improve air quality then once again we draw a similar conclusion. If, on the other hand, there is a shared view that we must sort these things out then we are in business, and we have suggested evidence-based measures that can solve the problems we have identified.

History is on the side of sorting things out. We did this with sanitation and drinking water in all British cities in the period 1840–90 (Trevelyan, 1942). The history of local government in the UK is replete with examples of boldness, initiative, foresight, planning and delivery, and there is no reason to suggest that the DNA of our elected politicians at local or national level in the second decade of the twenty-first century has deteriorated to the extent that these qualities do not exist.

In the period 1873–76 Joseph Chamberlain, mayor of Birmingham, brought about substantial change of great benefit to the citizens of Birmingham (Liberal Democrat History Group, 2011):

> The second Reform Act of 1867 encouraged Chamberlain to become involved in educational provision to educate our new masters, and he contributed £1000 to the Birmingham Education League, founded in 1869. He was elected a town councillor in 1869 and a member of the Birmingham School Board. In 1873 he was elected mayor, a post to which he was re-elected in 1874 and 1875. Chamberlain focused on improving the physical condition of the town and its people. He organised the purchase of the two gas companies and the water works; he appointed a Medical Officer of Health, established a Drainage Board, extended the paving and lighting of streets, opened six public parks, saw the start of the public transport service and personally laid the foundation stone of the new Council House. His Improvement Scheme saw the demolition of ninety acres of slums in the town centre. The council bought the freehold of about half the land to build Corporation Street. His pioneering efforts brought him to national prominence and marked social reform as a Liberal platform.

More recent evidence of the enormous societal capacity for changing direction, restructuring and large-scale social, political, economic and technical change can be found in the Second World War. Brown (2008) makes the connection between contemporary ecological and societal problems and the enormous changes made in the USA as it entered that war:

> As we contemplate mobilizing to save civilization, we see both similarities and contrasts with the mobilization for World War II. In his State of the Union address on January 6th, 1942, one month after the bombing of Pearl Harbor, President Roosevelt announced the country's arms production goals. The United States, he said, was planning to produce 45,000 tanks, 60,000 planes, 20,000 anti-aircraft guns and 6 million tonnes of merchant shipping. He added, 'Let no man say it cannot be done.'
>
> (Brown, 2008: 279)

Roosevelt went on to ban the manufacture and sale of cars for private use, residential and highway construction was halted, and driving for pleasure was banned. The 60,000 aircraft number target was surpassed, and in the 36 months of 1942, 1943 and 1944 the United States produced 229,600 aircraft.

Brown's conclusion is our conclusion. The mobilisation of such enormous resources, energy and sense of purpose tells us that we can mobilise 'to save civilization . . . if convinced of the need to do so'. His definition of saving civilisation is also close to ours: 'Mobilizing to save civilization means restructuring the economy, restoring its natural support systems, eradicating poverty, stabilizing population and climate and, above all, restoring hope.'

In each of the preceding 10 chapters of this book we have tried to paint a picture of what things could be like at some arbitrary point in the future. We can eliminate child poverty, air pollution, death and injury on the roads, and fossil fuel electricity generation, and have a mobility system with most of the work done by bus, train, walking and cycling. We rather like the Freiburg situation as of 2011, with 24 per cent of all trips every day on foot, 28 per cent by bike, 20 per cent by public transport and 28 per cent by car. The Freiburg model is far more important than any discussion about its high-quality trams, car-free residential areas, renewable energy and thousands of jobs created through its pursuit of intelligent local solutions to quality-of-life problems. Freiburg represents a vision of what any British city could be like, and we cannot disguise our disappointment that all British cities are a very long way from this vision and with few exceptions are not even at first base in recognising that things could be improved so dramatically.

There are 48 cities in the UK (excluding London) with a population greater than 100,000 and 20 with a population equal to or greater than Freiburg (240,000). There is no reason at all why all these 48 cities cannot adopt as much of the Freiburg model as possible and if necessary follow the example of Joseph Chamberlain, noted above, who went to Parliament to seek approval to do what he wanted to do in Birmingham if obstacles were put in his path. The enormous failure of English local government and its relationship with central government lies in the lack of initiative and vision at local level and national level and the many constraints imposed by national government on local government that reduce the scope for initiative, boldness and spending. It is very doubtful indeed that a twenty-first-century equivalent of Joseph Chamberlain would have the success of her illustrious predecessor.

Injecting initiative and vision into the political process and thinking, doing and willing is not easy, but there are ways of nurturing this process of attitudinal and cultural change so that a greater level of ambition and resolve can be unleashed. One example is the Sustainable Society Project (SSP) in Canada in the 1990s, described by Robinson (1996).

Robinson (1996) was responsible for a project that set out to establish a vision for Canada in 2030. The subject under discussion was 'defining a coherent and feasible 2030 endpoint and then constructing a convincing scenario to get from now to then'. This is known as visioning and backcasting, and Robinson explains that:

> This . . . is not a forecast of what its authors believe is likely to happen but a backcast from what they would like to see happen. Forecasting takes the trends of yesterday and today and projects mechanistically forward as if humankind were not an intelligent species with the capacity for individual and societal choice. Backcasting sets itself against such predestination and insists on free will, dreaming what tomorrow might be and determining how to get there from today.

The Sustainable Society Project established a detailed set of design criteria and a detailed set of results of what Canada would look like in 2030 if these criteria were incorporated into decision making at all levels aimed at achieving the desired '2030 endpoint'. The criteria reflect a great deal of thinking around sustainability along the lines set out by Brown (2008) and described by Whitelegg *et al.* (2010) in a visioning and backcasting exercise for achieving zero carbon emissions in UK transport by 2050. Robinson sets out 'desired environmental goals' and 'desired socio-political goals', and a selection are summarised below.

Desired environmental goals include the following:

- Minimise resource consumption and waste.
- Curb pollutant emissions at all levels.
- Stop using fossil fuels.
- Develop solar and wind energy.

Desired socio-political goals include the following:

- Reallocate (decentralise) some democratically selected powers from federal and provincial levels to regions and municipalities.
- Ensure equity.
- Foster economic self-reliance to the extent feasible, from the national to the community level, with each level doing only what the level below cannot do.

- Institute full-cost pricing based on cradle-to-grave responsibility of all goods, services and resources.
- Create safeguards for low-income groups who may be disadvantaged by pricing policies.

In total there are 50 environmental goals and 41 socio-political goals.

There then follows a detailed description of what life would actually be like in 2030, ranging over all sectors of the economy and political decision making. The details include:

- 40 per cent fewer trucks (lorries) because of relocalisation of the economy;
- no nuclear-generated electricity, and a huge increase in the percentage generated from wind, sun and hydro;
- increased energy efficiency of homes, and a decline of 60 per cent in energy use for heating as a result of a massive insulation retrofit programme for housing;
- a 10 per cent decrease in the total auto fleet compared with 1990 and a 16 per cent reduction in distance travelled by car;
- urban communities with higher densities of somewhat smaller dwellings, more shared spaces within or between dwellings, and energy-efficient designs;
- public transport playing a considerably larger role in the transportation system, and smaller, lighter and more energy-efficient cars;
- renewable energy providing almost all of the energy needs, and energy efficiency pervading the economy.

It is of more than passing interest that the Sustainable Society Project identifies 'institutional arrangements' as central to achieving this vision of a 'better' Canada. This is also our conclusion and is discussed in some detail in Chapter 10. Robinson takes the view that it is essential to devolve responsibilities 'to the community level', which is the opposite of what is happening in the UK, with greater centralisation and more controls from the centre about what can be done at local level. The recent cuts in grant funding to local government represent yet another reduction in the ability of local authorities to respond to the needs of their communities and to provide leadership, initiative and boldness. As we noted in Chapter 9 in the discussion about councillors in the UK it is increasingly unlikely that clear-thinking, busy people who want to achieve significant improvements in their localities will come forward as councillors. As budgets reduce and as central government ensures that councillors have very little scope to take bold initiatives, it is increasingly unlikely that people who do want to achieve things will opt for the role of councillor. This Darwinian self-selection will deprive the councillor group of precisely those people who are needed to promote a serious upgrade in performance.

The Sustainable Society Project is clear that its desirable future for Canada in 2030 is only one of several futures that are possible. The process of defining the desirable future is just as important as the exact details of the future itself, and this is explained in some detail in Robinson (1996). In our view a serious improvement in outcomes and performance has to begin with a strong vision of what can be achieved and a clear articulation of what the UK could look like in 2030 or at any other end-date.

It is also clear that defining desirable states at some point in the future encapsulates a view about lifestyle and consumption. Robinson's articulation of a 'better' Canada includes references to:

- a healthy lifestyle;
- health policies that emphasise preventative measures;
- considerably reduced consumerism, with durable goods more often shared or rented when needed;
- Canadians increasingly devoting some of the working hours of the week to unpaid activities in the informal economy such as community care or child care;
- 70 per cent of Canadian households with one small electric car, 10 per cent with two, and 20 per cent without a car.

Lifestyle issues were explicitly incorporated into the Whitelegg *et al.* (2010) vision for a zero-carbon transport system for Britain by 2050, and this had the effect of relating rather technical changes in energy sources, spatial planning, taxation and modal shift directly to the kind of world that would be on offer in a zero-carbon transport future. This world would be characterised by much lower levels of kilometres driven, higher levels of walking and cycling, improved health, lower air pollution, reduced obesity, reduced burdens on the taxpayer in funding expensive transport infrastructure, and much improved accessibility to goods, services and community facilities. The local economy would benefit as people would shop more locally, and those who would now find it easier to give up a car would benefit by releasing at least £3,000 per annum per car currently locked up in car outgoings. The absence of these linkages between the technical and the kind of lives we will all be living is, we argued, a block to understanding the advantages of major shifts in mobility. A block of this kind is, in turn, a hindrance to the changes in mindsets that are needed to replace unimaginative bureaucratic cultures in local government with a Chamberlain-like approach to action and initiatives that really do improve real things for real people.

The zero-carbon vision for the UK transport system concluded:

> The transformation of society from having a rather one-dimensional emphasis on economic growth to one based on community growth, increased happiness, reduced pollution, improved health and the creation of jobs that are far more evenly distributed and resilient to potential shocks, will bring enormous benefits to all. Examples of community growth would include more social interaction as people meet each other in a much more pleasant public realm as they walk and cycle. A decline in traffic levels is associated with more friends and acquaintances at the level of an individual street (Appleyard, 1981) and more friends and acquaintances are associated with higher self-reported happiness.

This transformed society, combined with increases in transport choice and improvement in safety and security, all point to the absence of 'losers' in the zero carbon world. Society will be much fairer with much improved access for everyone, much fewer demands on those with constrained budgets through the elimination of the need to own a car as a default option and the availability of many more transport choices.

(Whitelegg *et al.*, 2010)

Visioning is very much enhanced by the experience of seeing what is already in place, and this is why this book has repeatedly returned to Freiburg as a touchstone, benchmark and inspiring vision based on the here and now. This opens up the experiential route to the improvement of UK standards. For those elected politicians and decision makers who do not have the time or inclination to read a 170-page book on the future of Canada in the year 2030 or a 54-page report on the advantages and feasibility of a zero-carbon transport future for the UK by 2050 the answer is very attractive. Go to Freiburg, spend a week there and actually experience high-quality outcomes.

Start with the public transport, the sense of a high-quality public realm, the 28 per cent of trips every day by bike, and the car-free residential areas of Vauban and Rieselfeld. Move on to the large number of photovoltaic installations and the profusion of job-creating research and manufacturing companies devoted to renewable energy. Check out the widespread use of 'Passivhaus' standards to bring about reductions in domestic energy consumption and bills and enjoy the overwhelming sense of a place that actually works and delivers a high quality of life, a buoyant economy and a sense of confidence in the role of city government in achieving high-quality outcomes. Then return to the UK and 'do a Freiburg'. What is actually done in the 48 cities in the UK with a population greater than 100,000 will not be an exact copy of Freiburg. It will change, just as any benchmarking and searching out best practice exercise has to go through a process of transmission and conversion to meet local circumstances. What we are suggesting should not change is the thinking, willing and doing components and an absolute, no-compromise commitment to a serious upgrade in quality of life.

The Freiburg benchmarking point applies with equal force to our discussion about child poverty in Chapter 3. We urgently need to make the UK more like Sweden, Norway, Denmark and Finland. On child pedestrian fatality rates there is no reason why we should accept a rate three times higher than Sweden (Table 3.1). On poverty rates amongst the over 65s there is no reason why the UK should accept the fact that 25 countries out of 29 do better than us. The UK should be in the top three with the lowest rates of poverty in this age group. A similar point can be made for excess winter deaths. The UK performance is poor, and we can learn much from those countries listed in Figure 4.1 (e.g. Finland) that do so much better than we do. On renewables as a percentage of final energy consumption the UK is third from the bottom in the EU (Figure 7.6), and there is no reason why we cannot exploit considerable resources and opportunities to perform at the same level as Denmark, Sweden or Austria.

One of the key messages of this book is that we want everything right in every place and all at the same time. Every locality in the UK can have the very low levels of child poverty to be found in Sweden and Denmark. We can have the very low levels of excess winter deaths amongst older people to be found in Finland. We can have Copenhagen, Muenster, Groningen and Freiburg levels of cycling and associated low levels of car use. We can have Danish and German levels of electricity generation from renewable sources. We can create jobs and move much faster towards a low-carbon economy if we follow the Freiburg model. We can develop new residential areas on brownfield sites with world-class low-energy characteristics, low car ownership and high standards of child-friendly public realm facilities if we adopt the Vauban and Rieselfeld models (Freiburg). We can make all our towns, cities, regions and nations far more resilient than they now are if we actively reduce energy use, switch energy sources away from fossil fuel and nuclear and create a high-quality, safe, secure low-carbon society.

We are confident that in the case of each of the topics covered in earlier chapters of this book there are fully functioning examples of where things are done well and what needs to be done to upgrade our performance so that we are promoted from the laggard group to the best-in-class group. We have also argued that rationality, best practice and pointing to where it is done well may not be enough. The UK has special constitutional problems (Bogdanor, 2009) which have produced weak local authorities and an absence of vision, leadership and boldness at that level. We showed in Chapter 9 that inadequate budgets are one of several possible explanations for poor performance. English local authorities have fewer opportunities to generate revenue and spend that income in ways they choose than is common in other countries. We also think the lack of diversity in our elected politicians is a problem, and getting a more representative age and gender mix would be very helpful in increasing the sense of purpose and will at local level actually to do something to improve the quality of life.

In Chapter 10 we took the view that the centralisation of power and authority in English government is part of the problem and leads to poor-quality outcomes and that the solution lies in real devolution of powers to the local level, together with a greater diversity of income streams, including income streams entirely under the control of the local authority and not controlled by central government.

Bogdanor (2009) has added another consideration to this discussion of the weaknesses and inadequacies of English local government. He says:

> The average population of the lower tier of local government in England, the district council, is, at around 139,300, by far the largest in Western Europe. The next largest is Ireland where the average population size is around 93,300, followed by the Netherlands with 49,900, Portugal with 32,349 and Sweden with 29,200. In Germany the average population of a 'gemeinde' is just 9000 while the average size of a French commune is 1,500. . . . Britain now has the largest average size of local authority in Western Europe and the lowest turnout [in elections] . . . these two facts may well be interconnected.
>
> (Bogdanor, 2009: 246)

We are not suggesting that the recruitment of more female politicians and younger politicians, smaller local authorities, more money and greater powers will guarantee the transformation of a poorly performing system of governance into a high-performing variant. We are saying that these things will be enormously helpful, especially if they can be brought into existence on a short time scale and against a background of real change in self-belief and determination to raise standards. We are also saying that drawing the attention of politicians and others to the existence of impressive places, achievements and outcomes, as in the case of Freiburg, is unlikely, on its own, to have the galvanising effect that we are looking for. If the existence of impressive places was likely to have a galvanising effect there would already be examples of where this has happened and how it was achieved. These examples simply do not exist.

Bogdanor (2009) makes the same point in a slightly different way. He says:

> Perhaps the strongest argument for local government, and indeed for devolution and decentralisation in general, is that it can, at its best, stimulate a sense of local patriotism which can lead to real improvements in the public services. In a decentralised system of government, each local authority will strive to ensure that its own performance is better than that of its competitors.
>
> (Bogdanor, 2009: 268)

The combination of decentralisation, much improved and diversified income streams for local government, and a general power of competence (discussed in Chapter 10), together with greater diversity in the ranks of elected politicians, has the potential to improve things dramatically. We know how 'to do a Freiburg', we know that changes that need to be made to improve quality of life can be made and we know that there is very little possibility of seeing change in action if we cling to the ways we have done things in the last two or three decades. As President Roosevelt said in 1942: 'We must raise our sights along the production line. Let no man say it can't be done. It must be done and we have undertaken to do it.'

References

ADT Europe (2006) *Anti-Social Behaviour across Europe*, Sunbury-on-Thames: ADT Fire and Security. Available online at: http://www.adteurope.com (accessed 29 December 2011).

Al-Riffai, P., Dimaranan, B. and Laborde, D. (2010) *Global Trade and Environmental Impact Study of the EU Biofuels Mandate*, Washington, DC: International Food Policy Research Institute. Available online at: http://trade.ec.europa.eu/doclib/docs/2010/march/tradoc_145954.pdf (accessed 30 December 2011).

Aphekom (2011) *Improving Knowledge and Communication for Decision Making on Air Pollution and Health in Europe: Summary Report, 2008–2011*, Saint-Maurice, France: Aphekom Collaborative Network. Available online at: http://www.aphekom.org/c/document_library/get_file?uuid=5532fafa-921f-4ab1-9ed9-c0148f7da36a&groupId=10347 (accessed 17 November 2011).

Appleyard, D. (1981) *Livable Streets*, Berkeley: University of California Press.

Appleyard, D. and Appleyard, B. (forthcoming) *Livable Streets*, 2nd edn, Abingdon: Routledge.

Arikan, Y., Nuesse, A., Jiang, C., Park, S.J., Spaner, E., Verstraelen, S., Stoffregen, A. and Strickler-Suttle, A. (2011) *carbon*n *Cities Climate Registry 2011 Annual Report*, Bonn: carbon*n*, Bonn Center for Local Climate Action and Reporting. Available online at:http://citiesclimateregistry.org/fileadmin/user_upload/cCCR/cCCR_2011_Annual_Report/cCCR_2011_Annual_Report_www_lo_20111125.pdf (accessed 19 December 2011).

Batley, R. and Stoker, G. (1991) *Local Government in Europe: Trends and Developments*, London: Macmillan.

Ben-Shlomo, Y. and Kuh, D. (2002) 'A life course approach to chronic disease epidemiology: conceptual models, empirical challenges and interdisciplinary perspectives', *International Journal of Epidemiology*, 31: 285–293.

Bertelsmann Foundation (2011a) *Sustainable Governance Indicators 2011: Resources. Environment*, Guetersloh, Germany: Bertelsmann Stiftung. Available online at: http://www.sgi-network.org/pdf/SGI11_Resources_Environment.pdf (accessed 29 December 2011).

Bertelsmann Foundation (2011b) *Sustainable Governance Indicators 2011: Social Justice in the OECD. How Do the Member States Compare?*, Guetersloh, Germany: Bertelsmann Stiftung. Available online at: http://www.sgi-network.org/pdf/SGI11_Social_Justice_OECD.pdf (accessed 29 December 2011).

BESTUFS (2007) *Best Practice Update, 2007*, Part 1: *Road Pricing and Urban Freight Transport. Best Urban Freight Solutions*. Available online at: http://www.bestufs.net/

download/BESTUFS_II/key_issuesII/BPU-2007-I_Road-Pricing_Freight-Platforms. pdf (accessed 29 December 2011).

Boege, S. (1995) 'The well-travelled yoghurt pot: lessons for new freight transport policies and regional production', *World Transport Policy and Practice*, 1 (1): 7–11. Available online at: http://www.eco-logica.co.uk/pdf/wtpp01.1.pdf (accessed 29 December 2011).

Bogdanor, V. (2009) *The New British Constitution*, Oxford: Hart Publishing.

Bringezu, S., Schutz, H., O'Brien, M., Kauppi, L., Howarth, R.W. and McNeely, J. (2009) *Towards Sustainable Production and Use of Resources: Assessing Biofuels*, Paris: United Nations Environment Programme. Available online at: http://www.unep.fr/scp/rpanel/pdf/assessing_biofuels_full_report.pdf (accessed 29 December 2011).

Brisbane City Council (2010) *The River City Project: Liveable City, Connected City, Prosperous City, Sustainable City*. Available online at: http://www.brisbane.qld.gov.au/2010%20Library/2009%20PDF%20and%20Docs/2.%20Planning%20and%20Building/2.1%20About%20planning%20and%20building/About_planning_and_building_RiverCityBlueprint_liveable_presentation.pdf (accessed 30 December 2011).

Bristol City Council (2009) *Building a Positive Future for Bristol after Peak Oil*. Bristol: Bristol City Council. Available online at: https://docs.google.com/viewer?a=v&pid=explorer&chrome=true&srcid=0B_uigthaDDMhMjZmNWQzYjMtYTMyMi00MWIyLWIzNmItMGNkZDkyYWUyZDU5&hl=en_GB (accessed 30 December 2011).

British Medical Association (1997) *Road Transport and Health*, London: British Medical Association.

Brooks, J. (2009) *Proof of Evidence on Air Quality: Canal Corridor North Site, Lancaster*. Available online at: http://www.itsourcity.org.uk/pi/archive/proofs/I-AQ-01%20Air%20Quality%20Proof.pdf (accessed 30 December 2011).

Brown, L. (2008) *Plan B 3.0: Mobilizing to Save Civilization*, New York: W.W. Norton & Company.

Bund fuer Umwelt und Naturschutz Deutschland (BUND) and European Environment Bureau (2011) *European City Ranking: Best Practice for Clean Air*, Berlin: BUND. Available online at: http://www.sootfreecities.eu/ (accessed 29 December 2011).

Cabinet Office (2009) *The Wider Costs of Transport in English Urban Areas in 2009*, London: Cabinet Office Strategy Unit.

Campbell, I. (2011) *Analysis of Portsmouth 20mph Road Casualty Data with Allowance for Random Variation*, IC Statistical Services. Available online at: www.iancampbell.co.uk (accessed 29 December 2011).

Carbon Trust (2006) *Future Marine Energy*, London: Carbon Trust. Available online at: http://www.carbontrust.co.uk/Publications/pages/publicationdetail.aspx?id=CTC601 (accessed 29 December 2011).

Cato, M.S. (2009) *Green Economics: An Introduction to Theory, Policy and Practice*, London: Earthscan.

Centre for Cities (2008) *Cities Outlook*, London: Centre for Cities. Available online at: http://www.centreforcities.org/index.php?id=81 (accessed 29 December 2011).

Citeair (n.d.) *Air Quality Management Guidebook*, Leicester: North East South West Interreg III and Citeair. Available online at: http://citeair.rec.org/downloads/Products/AirQualityManagement.pdf (accessed 29 December 2011).

City of Oakland (2008) *Oil Independent Oakland Action Plan*. Oakland, CA: City of Oakland. Available online at: http://www.oaklandnet.com/Oil/pdfs/OIOactionplan2_08_rev.pdf (accessed 29 December 2011).

City of Portland (2007) *Descending the Oil Peak: Navigating the Transition from Oil and*

Natural Gas. Available online at: http://postcarboncities.net/files/POTF_FinalReport-DescendingTheOilPeak_March07.pdf (accessed 29 December 2011).

Civitas (2008) 'Graz application for 2008 "City of the Year" award', Civitas project. Available online at: http://www.civitas-initiative.org/docs1/CIVITAS_Award_2008_application_form_category_III_GRAZ.pdf (accessed 29 December 2011).

Civitas (2009) 'Nantes application for 2009 "City of the Year" award', Civitas project. Available online at: http://www.civitas-initiative.org/docs1/CIVITAS_Award_2009_Category_III_NantesMetropole.pdf (accessed 29 December 2011).

Civitas (2010) 'Evaluation report on Bremen Civitas projects'. Available online at: http://www.civitas-initiative.org/docs1/Bremen_Evaluation_Results_Report_extract.pdf (accessed 29 December 2011).

Clean Air in London (2011) 'Campaign update', 21 June. Available online at: http://www.cleanairinlondon.org/blog/_archives/2011/6/21/4842298.html (accessed 17 November 2011).

Commission for Architecture and the Built Environment (CABE) (2007) *Spend to Save Thinking*, London: CABE. Available online at: http://www.cabe.org.uk/articles/spend-to-save-thinking (accessed 29 December 2011).

Commission for Architecture and the Built Environment (CABE) (2009) *Future Health: Sustainable Places for Health and Well Being*, London: CABE.

Commission for Integrated Transport (CfIT) (2007) *Are We There Yet? A Comparison of Transport in Europe*, London: CfIT. Available online at: http://webarchive.nationalarchives.gov.uk/20110304132839/http://cfit.independent.gov.uk/pubs/2007/ebp/index.htm (accessed 29 December 2011).

Council of Europe (1985) *European Charter of Local Self-Government*, Strasbourg: Council of Europe. Available online at: http://conventions.coe.int/Treaty/en/Treaties/html/122.htm (accessed 7 September 2011).

Crompton, T. (2010) *Common Cause: The Case for Working with Our Cultural Values*, Godalming: World Wildlife Fund. Available online at: http://assets.wwf.org.uk/downloads/common_cause_report.pdf (accessed 29 December 2011).

Cushman & Wakefield (2011) *European Cities Monitor*, New York: Cushman & Wakefield. Available online at: https://www.cushwake.com/cwglobal/docviewer/2120_ECM_2011_FINAL_10Oct.pdf?id=c50500003p&repositoryKey=CoreRepository&itemDesc=document&cid=c38200001p&crep=Core&cdesc=binaryPubContent&Country=EMEA&Language=EN&just_logged_in=1 (accessed 29 December 2011).

Cyclists' Touring Club (CTC) (2008) Evidence to House of Commons Transport Select Committee, Ev. 180, in House of Commons, *Ending the Scandal of Complacency: Road Safety Beyond 2010*, Transport Select Committee Report, 11th Report of Session 2007–08 (accessed 11 July 2012).

Danmarks Statistik (2010) Befolkning og Valg, Statistiske Efterretninger, 2010:4, 3 March. Available online at: http://www.statistikbanken.dk/statbank5a/default.asp?w=1440.

Davis, A., Valsecchi, C. and Fergusson, M. (2007) *Unfit for Purpose: How Car Use Fuels Climate Change and Obesity*, London: Institute for European Environmental Policy (IEEP).

Davis, S.J. and Caldeira, K. (2010) 'Consumption based accounting of CO_2 emissions', *Proceedings of the National Academy of Sciences, Washington DC*. Available online at: http://www.pnas.org/content/early/2010/02/23/0906974107.full.pdf+html (accessed 29 December 2011).

Demmeler, M. (2004) 'Short paths to efficiency: an ecological and economical approach for a regional food supply', paper presented at the conference Integrated Regional Production and Logistics Management: A Promising Perspective for European Regions?,

Wuppertal, Germany, June. Available online at: http://www.agf.org.uk/cms/upload/pdfs/CR/2004_CR1456_e_regional_production_and_logistics_management.pdf (accessed 29 December 2011).

Demmeler, M. (2009) 'Klimaschutz auf kurzen Wegen. Welchen Beitrag leisten regionale Lebensmittel fuer Umwelt und Verbraucher', Informationsbroschuere. Available online at: http://www.bund-naturschutz.de/uploads/media/PM-058-09-RegionaleWirtschaftskreislaeufe-neue-Studie-LW-mB.pdf (accessed 29 December 2011).

Department of Energy and Climate Change (DECC) (2009) *The UK Renewable Energy Strategy*, CM 7686, London: DECC. Available online at: http://www.decc.gov.uk/assets/decc/What%20we%20do/UK%20energy%20supply/Energy%20mix/Renewable%20energy/Renewable%20Energy%20Strategy/1_20090717120647_e_@@_TheUKRenewableEnergyStrategy2009.pdf (accessed 29 December 2011).

Department of Environment, Food and Rural Affairs (DEFRA) (2009) *Local Air Quality Management: Policy Guidance*, PG09, London: DEFRA. Available online at: http://archive.defra.gov.uk/environment/quality/air/airquality/local/guidance/documents/laqm-policy-guidance-part4.pdf (accessed 30 December 2011).

Department of Environment, Food and Rural Affairs (DEFRA) (2010) *Review of Local Air Quality Management*, London: DEFRA. Available online at: http://archive.defra.gov.uk/environment/quality/air/airquality/local/documents/laqm-report.pdf (accessed 30 December 2011).

Department of Environment, Food and Rural Affairs (DEFRA) (2011) Reply to Freedom of Information Request submitted 9 December 2010. DEFRA reference number RFI 3697. Reply received 9 January 2011.

Department of Trade and Industry (DTI) (2007) *Meeting the Energy Challenge: A White Paper on Energy*, CM 7124, London: DTI. Available online at: http://www.berr.gov.uk/files/file39387.pdf (accessed 29 December 2011).

Department for Transport (DfT) (2008) *Manual for Streets*, London: DfT.

Department for Transport (DfT) (2009) *Analysis and Synthesis of Evidence on the Effects of Investment in the Six Cycling Demonstration Towns*, London: DfT and Cycling England. Available online at: http://www.dft.gov.uk/cyclingengland/site/wp-content/uploads/2010/03/analysis-and-synthesis-report.pdf (accessed 29 December 2011).

Department for Transport (DfT) (2010) *Interim Evaluation of the Implementation of 20mph Speed Limits in Portsmouth: Final Report, September 2010*, London: DfT. Available online at: http://assets.dft.gov.uk/publications/speed-limits-portsmouth/speed-limits-portsmouth.pdf (accessed 21 November 2011).

Derbyshire, D. (2007) 'How children lost the right to roam in four generations', *Daily Mail*, 15 June. Available online at: http://www.dailymail.co.uk/news/article-462091/How-children-lost-right-to-roam-generations.html (accessed 29 December 2011).

De Santi, G., Edwards, R., Szekeres, S., Neuwahl, F. and Mahieu, V. (eds) (2008) *Biofuels in the European Context: Facts and Uncertainties*, Petten, Netherlands: Joint Research Centre, Institute for Energy, European Commission. Available online at: www.ec.europa.eu/dgs/jrc/downloads/jrc_biofuels_report.pdf (accessed 29 December 2011).

Deutscher Staedtetag (2011) 'Frauenanteile in den Kommunalenparlamenten'. Available online at: http://www.staedtetag.de/10/presseecke/daten_fakten/zusatzfenster15.html (accessed 29 December 2011).

Dodson, J. and Sipe, N. (2008a) *Shocking the Suburbs: Oil Vulnerability in the Australian City*, Sydney: University of New South Wales Press.

Dodson, J. and Sipe, N. (2008b) *Unsettling Suburbia: The New Landscape of Oil and*

Mortgage Vulnerability in Australian Cities, Urban Research Programme, Research Paper 17, Brisbane: Griffith University. Available online at: http://www.griffith.edu.au/__data/assets/pdf_file/0003/88851/urp-rp17-dodson-sipe-2008.pdf (accessed 29 December 2011).

Douthwaite, R. (1996) *Short Circuit: Strengthening Local Economies for Security in an Unstable World*, Totnes: Green Books.

Echenique, M., Barton, H., Hargreaves, T. and Mitchell, G. (2010) *Solutions: Sustainability of Land Use and Transport in Outer Neighbourhoods. Final Report*. Available online at: http://www.suburbansolutions.ac.uk/DocumentManager/secure0/SOLUTIONSFinalReport.pdf (accessed 29 December 2011).

Ecofys and Fraunhofer ISI (2010) *Energy Savings 2020: How to Triple the Impact of Energy Saving Policies in Europe*, The Hague: Ecofys and Fraunhofer ISI. Available online at: http://roadmap2050.eu/attachments/files/2EnergySavings2020-ExecutiveSummary.pdf (accessed 29 December 2011).

Economist Intelligence Unit (2011) 'A summary of the Liveability Ranking and Overview'. Available online at: http://www.eiu.com/Handlers/WhitepaperHandler.ashx?fi=NEW_August_liveability_PDF.pdf&mode= wp (accessed 29 December 2011).

Edwards, R., Mulligan, D. and Marelli, L. (2010) *Indirect Land Use Change from Increased Biofuels Demand*, Ispra, Italy: Joint Research Centre, Institute for Energy, European Commission. Available online at: http://re.jrc.ec.europa.eu/bf-tp/download/ILUC_modelling_comparison.pdf (accessed 29 December 2011).

Ekman, B., Rockstrom, J. and Wijkman, A. (2009) *Grasping the Climate Crisis*, Stockholm: Tällberg Foundation. Available online at: http://www.tallbergfoundation.org/MOREACTIVITIES/GlobalStudies/Publications/Graspingtheclimatecrisis/tabid/555/Default.aspx (accessed 29 December 2011).

Ende, M. (1984) *Momo*, London: Puffin Books.

Eurobarometer (2009) *Perception Survey on Quality of Life in European Cities*, Flash EB Series no. 277, Brussels: European Commission.

European Commission (1999) *EU Focus on Clean Air*. Available online at: http://ec.europa.eu/environment/air/pdf/clean_air.pdf (accessed 29 December 2011).

European Commission (2007) *State of European Cities Report: Adding Value to the European Urban Audit*, European Union, Regional Policy, May, Luxembourg: Publications Office of the European Union. Available online at: http://ec.europa.eu/regional_policy/sources/docgener/studies/pdf/urban/stateofcities_2007.pdf (accessed 23 August 2011).

European Commission (2009) *Renewable Energy Directive*, 2009/28/EC, Luxembourg: Publications Office of the European Union.

European Commission (2010a) *Stockholm, European Green Capital 2010*, Luxembourg: Publications Office of the European Union.

European Commission (2010b) *European Green Capital: The Expert Panel's Evaluation Work and Final Recommendations for the European Green Capital Award of 2012 and 2013*. Brussels: European Commission.

European Commission (2010c) *Measuring Urban Sustainability: Analysis of the European Green Capital Award 2010 and 2011 Application Round. European Green Capital*. Brussels: European Commission.

European Commission (2010d) *EU Energy and Transport in Figures: Statistical Pocketbook 2010*, Luxembourg: Publications Office of the European Union. Available online at: http://ec.europa.eu/energy/publications/statistics/doc/2010_energy_transport_figures.pdf (accessed 29 December 2011).

European Commission (2010e) *Energy 2020: A Strategy for Competitive, Sustainable and Secure Energy*, COM (2010) 639 Final, SEC (2010) 1346, Luxembourg: Publications Office of the European Union. Available online at: http://eur-lex.europa.eu/Lex-UriServ/LexUriServ.do?uri=COM:2010:0639:FIN:EN:PDF (accessed 29 December 2011).

European Commission (2010f) *Second State of European Cities Report*, Luxembourg: Publications Office of the European Union. Available online at: http://ec.europa.eu/regional_policy/sources/docgener/studies/pdf/urban/stateofcities_2010.pdf (accessed 23 August 2011).

European Commission (2011) *White Paper on Transport: Roadmap to a Single European Transport Area – Towards a Competitive and Resource Efficient Transport System*, Luxembourg: Publications Office of the European Union. Available online at: http://ec.europa.eu/transport/strategies/doc/2011_white_paper/white-paper-illustrated-brochure_en.pdf (accessed 23 November 2011).

European Environment Agency (EEA) (2008a) *Maximising the Environmental Benefits of Europe's Bioenergy Potential*, Technical Report no. 10, Copenhagen: EEA. Available online at: http://www.eea.europa.eu/publications/technical_report_2008_10 (accessed 30 December 2011).

European Environment Agency (EEA) (2008b) *Energy and Environment Report*, Report 6/2008, Copenhagen: EEA. Available online at: http://www.eea.europa.eu/publications/eea_report_2008_6 (accessed 29 December 2011).

European Environment Agency (EEA) (2009) *Ensuring Quality of Life in Europe's Cities and Towns: Tackling the Environmental Challenges Driven by European and Global Change*, Technical Report 5/2009, Copenhagen: EEA.

European Environment Agency (EEA) (2010) *The European Environment: State and Outlook 2010*, Copenhagen: EEA. Available online at: http://www.eea.europa.eu/soer (accessed 29 December 2011).

European Environment Agency (EEA) (2011) *Mapping the Impact of Natural Hazards and Technological Accidents in Europe*, Technical Report 13/2010, Copenhagen: EEA. Available online at: http://www.eea.europa.eu/publications/mapping-the-impacts-of-natural (accessed 29 December 2011).

European Environment Agency (EEA) and World Health Organization (WHO) (2002) *Children's Health and Environment: A Review of Evidence*, Copenhagen: EEA and WHO European Office.

European Local Transport Information Service (ELTIS) (2011) 'City staff support police in speed enforcement in Graz (Austria)'. Available online at: www.eltis.org/index.php (accessed 29 December 2011).

European Partnership for Energy and the Environment (EPEE) (n.d.a) *Evaluation of Fuel Poverty in Belgium, Spain, France, Italy and the UK: European Fuel Poverty and Energy Efficiency*, WP2, Deliverable 6, European Commission: Brussels.

European Partnership for Energy and the Environment (EPEE) (n.d.b) *Definition Evaluation of Fuel Poverty in Belgium, Spain, France, Italy and the UK: European Fuel Poverty and Energy Efficiency*, WP2, Deliverable 7, European Commission: Brussels.

European Platform on Mobility Management (EPOMM) (2011) 'The EPOMM modal split tool'. Available online at: http://www.epomm.eu/tems/index.phtml (accessed 29 December 2011).

European Road Safety Observatory (ERSO) (2008) *EU Safety Net, Annual Statistical Report, Safety 2008*, Brussels: ERSO. Available online at: www.erso.eu (accessed 30 December 2011).

European Study of Adult Well-Being (ESAW) (2001) *Physical Health and Functional*

Status, Research Summary Series no. 3, ESAW. Available online at: http://www.bangor. ac.uk/esaw/ (accessed 29 December 2011).

Eurostat (2008) *Living Conditions in Europe, 2003–2006*, Eurostat Pocket Book, Brussels: European Commission. Available online at: http://epp.eurostat.ec.europa.eu/cache/ITY_ OFFPUB/KS-DZ-08-001/EN/KS-DZ-08-001-EN.PDF (accessed 29 December 2011).

Eurostat (2009) *Statistics in Focus: Population and Social Conditions*, Eurostat Report 46/2009, Brussels: European Commission.

Eurostat (2010) *Social Protection Backgrounds*, Brussels: European Commission. Available online at: http://epp.eurostat.ec.europa.eu/statistics_explained/index.php/Social_ protection_backgrounds (accessed 29 December 2011).

Eurostat (2011) *Statistics in Focus: Populations and Social Conditions*, Brussels: European Commission. Available online at: http://epp.eurostat.ec.europa.eu/cache/ITY_OFFPUB/ KS-SF-11-017/EN/KS-SF-11-017-EN.PDF (accessed 23 December 2011).

Ewing, R., Bartholomew, K., Winkelman, S., Walters, J. and Chen, D. (2008) *Growing Cooler: The Evidence on Urban Development and Climate Change*, Washington, DC: Urban Land Institute.

First (2007) *First: Weekly Journal of the Local Government Association*, 325, 10 February.

First (2008) 'Parties responsible for candidate clones', *First: Weekly Journal of the Local Government Association*, 392, 13 September. Available online at: http://www.lga.gov. uk/lga/aio/989082 (accessed 29 December 2011).

Fishman, E. (2009) *Peak Oil Contingency Plan*, Melbourne: Maribyrnong City Council. Available online at: http://www.maribyrnong.vic.gov.au/Files/Final_PeakOil_25_ August_Website.pdf (accessed 30 December 2011).

Frank, L., Andersen, M. and Schmid, T. (2004) 'Obesity relationships with community design, physical activity and time spent in cars', *American Journal of Preventive Medicine*, 27 (2): 87–96.

Freeman, C. and Tranter, P. (2011) *Children and Their Urban Environment*, London: Earthscan.

Friedrich Ebert Stiftung (FES) (2010) *Neuordnung der Finanzierung des Öffentlichen Personennahverkehrs*, Bonn: Friedrich Ebert Stiftung. Available online at: http://library.fes. de/pdf-files/wiso/07641.pdf (accessed 26 August 2011).

Gallagher, E. (2008) *The Gallagher Review of the Indirect Effects of Biofuel Production*, St Leonards-on-Sea: Renewable Fuels Agency. Available online at: www.dft.gov.uk/rfa/_ db/_documents/Report_of_the_Gallagher_review.pdf (accessed 29 December 2011).

Garrard, J. (2008) *Safe Speed: Promoting Safe Walking and Cycling by Reducing Traffic Speed*, Melbourne: Heart Foundation.

Garrard, J. (2009) *Active Transport: Children and Young People. An Overview of Recent Evidence*, Melbourne: Vic Health. Available online at: http://www.vichealth.vic.gov. au/en/Publications/Physical-Activity/Active-transport/Active-Transport-Children.aspx (accessed 29 December 2011).

Garrard, J. (2011) *Active Travel to School: A Literature Review*, Canberra: ACT Health.

Gehl Architects (2007) *Report to Sydney City Council, 2007*, Copenhagen: Gehl Architects. Available online at: http://www.cityofsydney.nsw.gov.au/Council/documents/ meetings/2007/Committee/Environment/031207/071203_EHC_ITEM04_ATTACH-MENTA2.PDF (accessed 29 December 2011).

Gehl Architects (2008) *Brisbane: Smart City Strategies. A People-Oriented Vision for Brisbane*, Copenhagen: Gehl Architects. Available online at: http://www.dlgp.qld.gov. au/resources/report/river-city-blueprint/gehl-part-1-intro.pdf (accessed 29 December 2011).

Gilbert, R. and O'Brien, C. (2005) *Child and Youth Friendly Land Use and Transport Planning Guidelines*, Toronto: Centre for Sustainable Transportation.

Gilbert, R. and Perl, A. (2008) *Transport Revolutions: Moving People and Freight Without Oil*, London: Earthscan.

Giuliani, R. (2002) *Leadership*, New York: Hyperion.

Glasgow Centre for Population Health (2010) *The Psychological, Social and Biological Determinants of Health: A Review of the Evidence*, Briefing Paper no. 8, Concepts Series, Glasgow: Glasgow Centre for Population Health. Available online at: http://www.gcph.co.uk/assets/0000/0406/GCPH_BP_8_concepts_web.pdf (accessed 29 December 2011).

Glotz-Richter, M. (2010) 'To bring it all together in the real world: walking, cycling, public transport and the role of car sharing', paper presented at the World Car-Free City Conference, York, July.

Gough, R. (2009) *With a Little Help from Our Friends: International Lessons for English Local Government*, London: Localis. Available online at: http://www.localis.org.uk/images/articles/Jan%2009_With%20a%20Little%20Help%20From%20Our%20Friends.pdf (accessed 21 August 2011).

Government Office for Science (2007) *Foresight Tackling Obesities: Future Choices. Project Report*. London: Government Office for Science.

Grundy, C., Steinbach, R., Edwards, P., Wilkinson, P. and Green J. (2008) *20mph Zones and Road Safety in London: A Report to the London Road Safety Unit*, London: Transport for London. Available online at: http://www.tfl.gov.uk/assets/downloads/20-mph-zones-and-road-safety-in-london.pdf (accessed 29 December 2011).

Haines, A., McMichael, A.J., Smith, K.R., Roberts, I., Woodcock, J., Markandya, A., Armstrong, B.G., Campbell-Lendrum, D., Dangour, A.D., Davies, M., Bruce, N., Tonne, C., Barrett, M. and Wilkinson, P. (2009) 'Public health benefits of strategies to reduce greenhouse-gas emissions: overview and implications for policy makers', *Lancet*, 374: 2104–2114.

Hambleton, R. (2005) 'Biting the big apple', *Municipal Journal*, 30 June, p. 23.

Hanlon, P., Walsh, D. and Whyte, B. (2006) *Let Glasgow Flourish*, Glasgow: Glasgow Centre for Population Health.

Haq, G., Minx, J., Whitelegg, J. and Owen, A. (2007) *Greening the Greys: Climate Change and the Over 50s*, York: Stockholm Environment Institute.

Haq, G., Whitelegg, J. and Kohler, M. (2008) *Growing Old in a Changing Climate: Meeting the Challenges of an Ageing Population and Climate Change*, York: Stockholm Environment Institute.

Hart, J. and Parkhurst, G. (2011) 'Driven to excess: a study of motor vehicle impacts on three streets in Bristol, UK', *World Transport Policy and Practice*, 17 (2): 12–30. Available online at: http://www.eco-logica.co.uk/pdf/wtpp17.2.pdf (accessed 29 December 2011).

Health Is Wealth Commission (2008) *Health Is Wealth: Final Report*, Liverpool: Liverpool City Region Health Is Wealth Commission. Available online at: http://www.liv.ac.uk/ihia/IMPACT%20Reports/HIW_Final_Report_sml.pdf (accessed 29 December 2011).

Healy, J.D. (2003) 'Excess winter mortality in Europe: a cross-country analysis identifying key risk factors', *Journal of Epidemiology and Community Health*, 57: 784–789.

Heaps, C., Erickson, P., Kartha, S. and Kemp-Benedict, E. (2009) *Europe's Share of the Climate Challenge: Domestic Actions and International Obligations to Protect the Planet*, Boston, MA: Stockholm Environment Institute, US Centre. Available online at: http://sei-us.org/Publications_PDF/SEI-EuropeShareOfClimateChallenge-09.pdf (accessed 30 December 2011).

Heinberg, R. (2003) *The Party's Over: Oil, War and the Fate of Industrial Societies*, Forest Row, East Sussex: Clairview.

Herrstedt, L. (1992) 'Traffic calming design: a speed management method: Danish experiences on environmentally adapted through roads', *Accident Analysis and Prevention*, 24: 3–16.

Hillman, M. (1993) *Children, Transport and the Quality of Life*, London: Policy Studies Institute.

Hillman, M., Adams, J. and Whitelegg, J. (1990) *One False Move: A Study of Children's Independent Mobility*, London: Policy Studies Institute.

Hills, J. (2011) *Fuel Poverty: The Problem and Its Measurement. Interim Report of the Fuel Poverty Review*, London: Department of Energy and Climate Change. Available online at: http://www.decc.gov.uk/assets/decc/11/funding-support/fuel-poverty/3226-fuel-poverty-review-interim-report.pdf (accessed 29 December 2011).

Holzapfel, H. (1995) 'Potential forms of regional economic co-operation to reduce goods transport', *World Transport Policy and Practice*, 1: 34–39. Available online at: http://www.eco-logica.co.uk/pdf/wtpp01.2.pdf (accessed 29 December 2011).

Holzapfel, H. (2012) *Urbanismus und Verkehr*, Wiesbaden: Vieweg und Teubner.

Hopkins, R. (2008) *The Transition Handbook: From Oil Dependency to Local Resilience*, Totnes: Green Books. Available online at: http://transitionculture.org/shop/the-transition-handbook/ (accessed 29 December 2011).

House of Commons (2008) *Ending the Scandal of Complacency: Road Safety Beyond 2010*, Transport Select Committee Report, 11th Report of Session 2007–08, London: Stationery Office.

House of Commons (2009) *The Balance of Power: Central and Local Government*, Communities and Local Government Select Committee Report, HC 33-1, 2008–09, 20 May. Available online at: http://www.publications.parliament.uk/pa/cm200809/cmselect/cmcomloc/33/3304.htm (accessed 5 September 2011).

House of Commons (2011a) *Report on the Strategic Case for High Speed Rail*, Select Committee on Transport, 10th Report, 1 November. Available online at: http://www.parliament.uk/business/committees/committees-a-z/commons-select/transport-committee/news/hsr---substantive/ (accessed 29 December 2011).

House of Commons (2011b) *Air Quality: A Follow-Up Report*, Environmental Audit Committee, 14 November. Available online at: http://www.publications.parliament.uk/pa/cm201012/cmselect/cmenvaud/1024/102402.htm (accessed 29 December 2011).

House of Commons (2011c) *Bus Services after the Spending Review*, Select Committee on Transport, 8th Report, July. Available online at: http://www.publications.parliament.uk/pa/cm201012/cmselect/cmtran/750/75003.htm (accessed 29 December 2011).

House of Commons (2011d) *Localism*, Communities and Local Government Select Committee Report, July. Available online at: http://www.publications.parliament.uk/pa/cm201012/cmselect/cmcomloc/547/54702.htm (accessed 22 August 2011).

House of Lords (2011) *Behaviour Change*, Report of the Science and Technology Select Committee, 2nd Report of Session 2010–12, HL Paper 179, London: Stationery Office. Available online at: http://www.publications.parliament.uk/pa/ld201012/ldselect/ldsctech/179/179.pdf (accessed 29 December 2011).

Hovedstadsomradets Trafikselskab (HT) (1998) *Tender Condition and Specifications: 8th Invitation to Tender, June 9th 1998*, Copenhagen: HT.

Howarth, R.W. and Bringezu, S. (eds) (2009) 'Biofuels: environmental consequences and interactions with changing land use', *Proceedings of the SCOPE International Biofuels Project Rapid Assessment on Biofuels*, Gummersbach, Germany, September, Ithaca,

NY: Cornell University Press and Wuppertal: Wuppertal Institute. Available online at: http://cip.cornell.edu/biofuels/ (accessed 29 December 2011).

Hutton, W. (2010) *Them and Us: Changing Britain – Why We Need a Fair Society*, London: Little, Brown.

Illich, I. (1974) *Energy and Equity*, London: Calder & Boyars.

Inrix (2011) 'Traffic congestion in Europe: INRIX U.K. traffic scorecard provides revealing look at traffic congestion in cities across the country'. Available online at: http://www.inrix.com/pressrelease.asp?ID=107 (accessed 29 December 2011).

Institute for Transportation and Development Policy (ITDP), Gehl Architects and Nelson Nygaard (2010) *Our Cities Ourselves: 10 Principles for Transport in Urban Life*, New York: ITDP. Available online at: http://www.itdp.org/documents/2010-OurCitiesOurselves_Booklet.pdf (accessed 29 December 2011).

Intergovernmental Panel on Climate Change (IPCC) (2007) *Fourth Assessment Report: Climate Change. Synthesis Report*, Geneva: IPCC. Available online at: http://www.ipcc.ch/publications_and_data/ar4/syr/en/mains3-3-5.html (accessed 29 December 2011).

International Energy Agency (IEA) (2009) *Cities, Towns and Renewable Energy: Yes in My Front Yard*, Paris: IEA. Available online at: http://www.iea.org/textbase/nppdf/free/2009/cities2009.pdf (accessed 29 December 2011).

International Energy Agency (IEA) (2010) *World Energy Outlook Executive Summary*, Paris: IEA. Available online at: http://www.worldenergyoutlook.org/docs/weo2010/WEO2010_ES_English.pdf (accessed 29 December 2011).

International Idea (n.d.) *Sweden: Women's Representation in Parliament*, Stockholm: IDEA. Available online at: http://www.idea.int/news/upload/sweden_women.pdf (accessed 30 December 2011).

Ipsos MORI (2009) *Public Attitudes to the Nuclear Industry*. Available online at: http://www.ipsos-mori.com/Assets/Docs/Polls/public-attitudes-to-the-nuclear-industry-slides-december-2009.pdf (accessed 29 December 2011).

Italian National Institute of Statistics (ISTAT) (2010) *Air Quality in European Cities, 2004–08*, Rome: ISTAT.

Jagger, C., Gillies, C., Moscone, F., Cambois, E., Oyen, H. van, Nusselder, W. and Robine, J.M. (2008) 'Inequalities in healthy life years in the 25 countries of the EU in 2005: a cross-national meta-regression analysis', *Lancet*, 372: 2124–2131.

Jones, G. and Stewart, J. (2011) 'Memorandum to House of Commons Select Committee on Communities and Local Government'. Available online at: http://www.publications.parliament.uk/pa/cm201012/cmselect/cmcomloc/547/547we02.htm (accessed 22 August 2011).

Jordan, A., Hiutema, D., Asselt, H. van, Rayner, T. and Berkhout, F. (2010) *Climate Change Policy in the European Union: Confronting the Dilemmas of Mitigation and Adaptation*, Cambridge: Cambridge University Press.

Kampman, B. (2011) Personal communication, 13 December.

Kampman, B., Leguijt, C., Bennink, D., Wielders, L., Rijkee, X., Buck, A. de and Braat, W. (2010) *Green Power for Electric Cars: Development of Policy Recommendations to Harvest the Potential of Electric Vehicles*, Delft: CE Delft. Available online at: http://www.cedelft.eu/publicatie/green_power_for_electric_cars/1011 (accessed 29 December 2011).

Kenworthy, J. (2008) 'The world oil production peak and its impact on cities', in C. Condak, G. Heindl, L. Schmidt-Colinet and N. Seraji, *Review VI: Five Platforms, Five Ecologies*, Salzburg: Verlag Anton Pustet.

Kenworthy, J. and Laube, F. (2001) *The Millennium Cities Database for Sustainable Transport*, Brussels: UITP and Perth, Western Australia: ISTP, Murdoch University.

Keynes, J.M. (1933) 'National self-sufficiency', *Yale Review*, 22 (4): 755–769. Reprinted in D. Mogridge (ed.), *The Collected Works of J.M. Keynes*, vol. 21, London: Macmillan.

Kirklees Council (2010) *Development of Renewable Energy*, Huddersfield: Kirklees Council. Available online at: http://www.kirklees.gov.uk/you-kmc/priorities/storyboards/pdf/climate-change/CC12-RenewableEnergy.pdf (accessed 29 December 2011).

Layard, R. (2005) *Happiness: Lessons from a New Science*, London: Allen Lane.

Lewes Pound Group (2011) 'The Lewes pound: what is it?' Available online at: http://www.thelewespound.org/what.html (accessed 29 December 2011).

Liberal Democrat History Group (2011) *The Biography of Joseph Chamberlain, 1836–1914*. Available online at: http://www.liberalhistory.org.uk/item_single.php?item_id=42&item=biography (accessed 29 December 2011).

Lindert, P. (2004) *Growing Public*, vol. 1: *The Story: Social Spending and Economic Growth since the 18th Century*, Cambridge: Cambridge University Press.

Lindert, P. (2007) 'Welfare states, markets and efficiency: the free lunch puzzle continues', paper presented at the Van Leer Jerusalem Institute, Jerusalem, December. Available online at: http://lindert.econ.ucdavis.edu/Docs/17/Welfare%20States%20Paper.pdf (accessed 29 December 2011).

Liverpool Vision (2009) *Business Plan, 2009/10–2011/12*. Available online at: http://www.liverpoolvision.co.uk/Docs/DownloadDocs/LIVERPOOL%20VISION%20BUSINESS%20PLAN%202009(4).pdf (accessed 29 December 2011).

Living Streets (2009) *Inquiry into Active Travel: Submission from Living Streets, Scotland*. Available online at: http://www.livingstreets.org.uk/search-result?cx=00966077260358 1942210%3Ace7y6rbvlfa&cof=FORID%3A10&ie=UTF-8&q=Inquiry+into+active+travel (accessed 30 December 2011).

Local Government Association (LGA) (2004) *The Balance of Funding: A Combination Option*, London: LGA.

Local Government Association (LGA) (2007) *Prosperous Communities II: Vive la Devolution*, London: LGA. Available online at: http://www.lga.gov.uk/lga/aio/21918 (accessed 21 August 2011).

Local Government Association (LGA) (2008a) *Volatile Times: Transport, Climate Change and the Price of Oil*, London: LGA. Available online at: http://www.lga.gov.uk/lga/aio/1335142 (accessed 29 December 2011).

Local Government Association (LGA) (2008b) *One Country, Two Systems? How Central and Local Democracy Can Work Together to Improve Britain's Political Culture*, London: LGA. Available online at: http://www.lga.gov.uk/lga/aio/1314639 (accessed 19 October 2011).

London Evening Standard (2008) 'Traffic lights across the capital will be re-phased to cut jams', *London Evening Standard*, 21 May. Available online at: http://www.thisislondon.co.uk/standard-mayor/article-23486398-traffic-lights-across-the-capital-will-be-rephased-to-cut-jams.doc (accessed 29 December 2011).

Louv, R. (2008) *Last Child in the Woods*, Chapel Hill, NC: Algonquin Books.

Lynch, J.W., Kaplan, G.A., Cohen, R.D., Kauhansen, J., Wilson, T.W., Smith, N.L. and Salonen, J.T. (2004) 'Childhood and adult socioeconomic status as predictors of mortality in Finland', *Lancet*, 343: 524–527.

Marmot, M. (2010) *Fair Society, Healthy Lives: Strategic Review of Health Inequalities in England, Post 2010*, London: Department of Health.

Mees, P. (2010) *Transport for Suburbia: Beyond the Automobile Age*, London: Earthscan.

Melillo, J., Reilly, J., Kicklighter, D.W., Gurgel, A.C., Cronin, T.W., Paltsev, S., Wang, X., Sokolov, A.P. and Schlosser, C.A. (2009) 'Indirect emissions from biofuels: how important?', *Science*, 326 (4): 1397–1399. Available online at: http://www.sciencemag. org/cgi/reprint/326/5958/1397.pdf (accessed 29 December 2011).

Mercer Consulting (2010) 'Quality of Living Index', *CityMayors.com*. Available online at: http://www.citymayors.com/features/quality_survey.html (accessed 29 December 2011).

Metz, D. (2008) *The Limits to Travel: How Far Will You Go?*, London: Earthscan.

Mingado, G., Berg, L. van den and Haaren, J. van (2008) *Transport, Economy and Environment at the Urban Level: The Need for Decoupling. A Comparative Study of Four European Cities – Rotterdam, London, Goteborg and Hamburg*, Rotterdam: European Institute for Comparative Urban Research (EURICUR), Erasmus University. Available online at: http://www.euricur.nl (accessed 29 December 2011).

Momo (2010) *The State of European Car-Sharing: Final Report D2.4 Work Package 2*, Berlin: Momo Car-Sharing, Intelligent Energy Europe (IEE). Available online at: http://www.motiva.fi/files/4138/WP2_Final_Report.pdf (accessed 18 November 2011).

Munich RE (2012) *Natural Catastrophes, 2011*. Available online at: http://www.munichre. com/app_pages/www/@res/pdf/media_relations/press_releases/2012/2012_01_04_ munich_re_natural-catastrophes-2011_en.pdf (accessed 5 May 2012).

National Foundation for Educational Research (NFER) (2009) *National Census of Local Authority Councillors 2008*, Slough: NFER. Available online at: http://www.lga.gov. uk/lga/aio/1399651 (accessed 29 December 2011).

National Institute for Health and Clinical Excellence (NICE) (2008) *Promoting and Creating Built and Natural Environments that Encourage and Support Physical Activity*, Public Health Guidance no. 8, London: NICE.

New Economics Foundation (NEF) (2009) *The (Un)Happy Planet Index: Why Good Lives Do Not Have to Cost the Earth*, London: NEF. Available online at: http://www.happyplanetindex.org/public-data/files/happy-planet-index-2-0.pdf (accessed 29 December 2011).

Newman, P., Beatley, T. and Boyer, H. (2009) *Resilient Cities: Responding to Peak Oil and Climate Change*, Washington, DC: Island Press.

Newman, P. and Kenworthy, J. (1989) 'Gasoline consumption and cities: a comparison of US cities with a global survey', *Journal of the American Planning Association*, 5 (1): 24–37.

NHS Greater Glasgow and Clyde (2008) *The Director of Public Health Annual Report, 2007–08: A Call to Debate, a Call to Action*, Glasgow: NHS Greater Glasgow and Clyde.

North West Public Health Observatory (NWPHO) (2011) *Health Profiles, Liverpool*, Liverpool: NWPHO. Available online at: http://www.apho.org.uk/resource/view. aspx?QN=HP_RESULTS&GEOGRAPHY=C0 (accessed 29 December 2011).

Oil Depletion Analysis Centre (ODAC) (2008) *Preparing for Peak Oil: Local Authorities and the Energy Crisis*, London: ODAC. Available online at: http://www.odac-info.org/ sites/default/files/Preparing_for_Peak_Oil_0.pdf (accessed 29 December 2011).

Organisation for Economic Co-operation and Development (OECD) (2006) *Decoupling the Environmental Impacts of Transport from Economic Growth*, Paris: OECD.

Organisation for Economic Co-operation and Development (OECD) (2011a) 'Child poverty', OECD Family Database. Available online at: http://www.oecd.org/dataoecd/52/43/41929552.pdf (accessed 29 December 2011).

Organisation for Economic Co-operation and Development (OECD) (2011b) 'Government at a glance, 2011: revenue structure by level of government'. Available online at: http://www.oecd.org/document/33/0,3746,en_2649_33735_43714657_1_1_1_1,00. html (accessed 30 December 2011).

Oxera (2009) *Subsidising Buses: How to Get the Best from Taxpayers' Money*, Report prepared for the Local Government Association, Oxford: Oxera.

Passivhaus Institut (2010) *What is a Passive House?*, Darmstadt: Passivhaus Institut. Available online at: http://www.passiv.de/07_eng/index_e.html (accessed 29 December 2011).

Passivhaus Institut (2011) *Passivhaus Primer*, Darmstadt: Passivhaus Institut. Available online at: http://www.passivhaus.org.uk/filelibrary/Passivhaus%20Standards/BRE_Passivhaus_Primer.pdf (accessed 29 December 2011).

Paxton, P. and Hughes, M. (2007) *Women, Politics and Power: A Global Perspective*, Thousand Oaks, CA: Sage Publications. Available online at: http://www.sagepub.com/upm-data/14346_Chapter1.pdf (accessed 29 December 2011).

Peak Oil Centre (2011) 'Facts and data'. Available online at: http://members.home.nl/peak-oil/facts.html (accessed 29 November 2011).

Pinfield, G. (2010) Personal communication from Graham Pinfield, Principal Policy Officer, Manchester City Council, 9 March.

Play England (2011) *Creating Playful Communities: Lessons from the Emerging Communities in Play Programme*, London: Play England. Available online at: http://www.playengland.org.uk/media/283281/ecp%20final%20report%20-%20final.pdf (accessed 29 December 2011).

Power, C., Atherton, K., Strachan, D.P., Shepherd, P., Fuller, E., Davis, A., Gibb, I., Kumari, M., Lowe, G., MacFarlane, G., Rahi, J., Rodgers, B. and Stansfield, S. (2007) 'Life-course influences on health in British adults: effects of socioeconomic position in childhood and adulthood', *International Journal of Epidemiology*, 36: 532–539.

Pucher, J. and Buehler, R. (2007) 'At the frontiers of cycling: policy innovation in the Netherlands, Denmark and Germany', *World Transport Policy and Practice*, 13 (3): 8–57. Available online at: http://www.eco-logica.co.uk/pdf/wtpp13.3.pdf (accessed 30 December 2011).

Pucher, J. and Buehler, R. (2008) 'Making cycling irresistible: lessons from the Netherlands, Denmark and Germany', *Transport Reviews*, 28 (4): 495–528.

Pucher, J. and Buehler, R. (eds) (2012) *City Cycling*, Cambridge, MA: MIT Press.

Pucher, J., Buehler, R., Bassett, D.R. and Dannenberg, A.L. (2010a) 'Walking and cycling to health: a comparative analysis of city, state and international data', *American Journal of Public Health*, online edn, 19 August. Available online at: http://ajph.aphapublications.org/cgi/content/abstract/AJPH.2009.189324v1 (accessed 29 December 2011).

Pucher, J., Dill, J. and Handy, S. (2010b) 'Infrastructure, programs, and policies to increase bicycling: an international review', *Preventive Medicine*, 50: S106–S125. Available online at: http://policy.rutgers.edu/faculty/pucher/Pucher_Dill_Handy10.pdf (accessed 29 December 2011).

Redelmeier, D.A. and Bayoumi, A.M. (2010) 'Time lost by driving fast in the United States', *Medical Decision Making*, published online 26 February. Available online at: http://mdm.sagepub.com/content/early/2010/03/29/0272989X09357476 (accessed 29 December 2011).

Roadpeace (2011) *Stricter Liability: The Civilised System for Civil Compensation*, London: Roadpeace. Available online at: http://www.roadpeace.org/change/safer_streets/stricter_liability/ (accessed 29 December 2011).

Robinson, J.B. (1996) *Life in 2030: Exploring a Sustainable Future for Canada*, Vancouver: University of British Columbia Press.

Rockstrom, J., Steffen, W., Noone, K., Persson, A., Chapin, F., Lambin, E., Lenton, T., Scheffer, M., Folke, C., Schnellhuber, H., Nykvist, B., Wit, C. de, Hughes, T., Leeuw, S. van der, Rodhe, H., Sorlin, S., Snyder, P., Costanza, R., Swedin, U., Falkenmark, M., Karlberg, L., Corell, R., Fabry, V., Hansen, J., Walker, B., Liverman, D., Richardson, K., Crutzen, P. and Foley, J. (2009) 'Planetary boundaries: exploring the safe operating space for humanity', *Ecology and Society*, 14 (2): 32. Available online at: http://www.stockholmresilience.org/download/18.8615c78125078c8d3380002197/ES-2009-3180.pdf (accessed 29 December 2011).

Roosevelt, F.D. (1942) *State of the Union Address, 6th January 1942*. Available online at: http://www.ibiblio.org/pha/7-2-188/188-35.html (accessed 29 December 2011).

Ros, J.P.M., Overmars, K.P., Stehfest, E., Prins, A.G., Notenboom, J. and Oorschot, M. van (2010) *Identifying the Indirect Effects of Bio-energy Production*, Bilthoven, Netherlands: Netherlands Environmental Assessment Agency. Available online at: http://www.pbl.nl/en/publications/2010/Identifying-the-indirect-effects-of-bio-energy-production.html (accessed 29 December 2011).

Sachs, W. (1992) *For the Love of the Automobile: Looking Back into the History of Our Desires*, Berkeley: University of California Press.

Salomon, D. (2010) Interview with Dr Dieter Salomon, Oberburgermeister of Freiburg, 25 November.

Schubert, R., Schnellhuber, H.J., Buchmann, N., Epiney, A., Griesshammer, R., Kulessa, M., Messner, D., Rahmstorf, S. and Schmid, J. (2010) *Future Bioenergy and Sustainable Land Use*, London: Earthscan.

Searchinger, T., Heimlich, R., Houghton, R.A., Dong, F., Elobeid, A., Fabiosa, J., Tokgoz, S., Hayes, D. and Yu, T.H. (2008) 'Use of US croplands for biofuels increases greenhouse gases through emissions from land use change', *Science*, 319: 1238–1240. Available online at: www.sciencemag.org/cgi/content/abstract/1151861 (accessed 29 December 2011).

Seifried, D. (1990) *Gute Argumente: Verkehr, Beck'sche Reihe*, Munich: C.H. Beck.

Shaheen, F. (2008) *Empowering Our Cities to Tackle Worklessness*, London: Centre for Cities. Available online at: http://www.centreforcities.org/index.php?id=537 (accessed 29 December 2011).

Shaw, B., Watson, B., Frauendienst, B., Redecker, A. and Hillman, M. (2012) *The Erosion of Children's Independent Mobility: A Comparative Study in England and Germany (1971 to 2010)*, London: Policy Studies Institute.

Shears, M. (2008) 'Equal opportunities and equality of representation for women in Europe', paper presented at the 58th Political Studies Association Conference, Swansea, April. Available online at: http://www.psa.ac.uk/journals/pdf/5/2008/Shears.pdf (accessed 29 December 2011).

Sloman, L. (2003) *Rural Transport Futures: Transport Solutions for a Thriving Countryside*, London: Transport 2000 Trust (now renamed Campaign for Better Transport).

Smith, M., Whitelegg, J. and Williams, N.J. (1998) *Greening the Built Environment*, London: Earthscan.

Social Exclusion Unit (SEU) (2003) *Making the Connections: Final Report on Transport and Social Exclusion*, London: SEU.

Social Trends (2010) *Number 40*, London: Office for National Statistics.

Stadt Bochum (2011) Personal communication from Constanze Mozarski, Stadt Bochum, Büro für Angelegenheiten des Rates und der Oberbürgermeisterin, 14 July.

Stadt Darmstadt (2011) 'Stadtverordnetenversammlung und Magistrat der Wissenschaftsstadt Darmstadt'. Available online at: http://www.darmstadt.de/fileadmin/Bilder-Rubriken/Rathaus/Politik/stadtverordnetenversammlung/einladungen2010/stavoliste2011_-_2016_November_2011.pdf (accessed 1 January 2012).

Stadt Freiburg (2005) *Solarfuehrer Region Freiburg*, Stadt Freiburg im Breisgau. Available online at: http://www.energieagentur-regio-freiburg.de/verlag/broschueren/solarfuehrer/ (accessed 23 November 2011).

Stadt Freiburg (2007) *Klimaschutz-Strategie der Stadt Freiburg*, Stadt Freiburg im Breisgau. Available online at: http://www.freiburg.de/servlet/PB/show/1173335/Umwelt_Klimaschutz-Strategie.pdf (accessed 29 December 2011).

Stadt Freiburg (2009) *Freiburg Green City: Approaches to Sustainability*, Stadt Freiburg im Breisgau, Sustainability Office. Available online at: www.freiburg.de/greencity (accessed 29 December 2011).

Stadt Freiburg (2010) *Umweltpolitik in Freiburg*, Dezernat fuer Umwelt, Schule, Bildung und Gebäudemanagement, Stadt Freiburg im Breisgau. Available online at: http://www.freiburg.de/servlet/PB/show/1225049_11/Broschuere_Umweltpolitik.pdf (accessed 29 December 2011).

Stadt Freiburg (2011) Personal communication from Dr Dieter Wörner, Stadt Freiburg Umweltschutzamt, 24 October.

Standing Advisory Committee on Trunk Road Assessment (SACTRA) (1999) *Transport and the Economy*, London: SACTRA, Department of the Environment, Transport and the Regions.

Statistics Sweden (2011) 'Allmänna val, valresultat'. Available online at: http://www.scb.se/Pages/TableAndChart____302585.aspx (accessed 14 January 2012).

Stern Review (2006) *The Economics of Climate Change*, London: HM Treasury. Available online at: http://webarchive.nationalarchives.gov.uk/+/http://www.hm-treasury.gov.uk/stern_review_report.htm (accessed 29 December 2011).

Sustainable Development Commission (SDC) (2006) *Is Nuclear the Answer?*, London: SDC. Available online at: http://www.sd-commission.org.uk/publications/downloads/IsNuclearTheAnswer.pdf (accessed 29 December 2011).

Swedish Government (2006) *Making Sweden an Oil Free Society*, Stockholm: Commission on Oil Independence. Available online at: http://www.sweden.gov.se/sb/d/574/a/67096 (accessed 29 December 2011).

Therivel, R. and Whitelegg, J. (2005) *Thames Gateway Bridge Public Inquiry: Case for the Objectors on Regeneration*. Available online at: http://www.persona.uk.com/thames-gateway/Objector_docs/OBJ-4983/4983-1-A1.pdf (accessed 29 December 2011).

Tingvall, C. and Haworth, N. (1999) 'Vision Zero: an ethical approach to safety and mobility', paper presented to the 6th International Conference on Road Safety and Traffic Enforcement beyond 2000, Melbourne, September.

Transition Network (2011) Main website. Available online at: http://www.transitionnetwork.org/about/principles (accessed 29 December 2011).

Transition Town Totnes (2010) *Transition in Action. Totnes and District 2030: An Energy Descent Action Plan*, Totnes: Transition Town Totnes. Available online at: http://totnesedap.org.uk/book/ (accessed 29 December 2011).

Transport and Environment (2011) 'Car free Milan after PM pollution', *Bulletin*, 202, October.

Transport for London (TfL) (2008) *London Low Emission Zone Impacts Monitoring*, London: TfL. Available online at: http://www.tfl.gov.uk/assets/downloads/roadusers/lez/lez-impacts-monitoring-baseline-report-2008-07.pdf (accessed 29 December 2011).

Tranter, P.J. (1996) 'Children's independent mobility and urban form in Australasian, English and German cities', in D. Hensher, J. King and T. Oum (eds), *World Transport Research: Proceedings of the Seventh World Conference on Transport Research*, vol. 3: *Transport Policy*, Oxford: Pergamon, pp. 31–44.

Tranter, P.J. (2006) 'Overcoming social traps: a key to creating child friendly cities', in B.J. Gleeson and N. Sipe (eds), *Creating Child Friendly Cities: Reinstating Kids in the City*, London: Routledge.

Tranter, P.J. (2010) 'Speed kills: the complex links between transport, lack of time and urban health', *Journal of Urban Health: Bulletin of the New York Academy of Medicine*, 87 (2): 155–166.

Tranter, P.J. and Ker, I. (2007) 'A wish called $quander: (in)effective speed and effective wellbeing in Australian cities', in *Proceedings of the State of Australian Cities 2007 National Conference*, 28–30 November 2007, Adelaide: University of South Australia. Available online at: http://s3.amazonaws.com/zanran_storage/www.fbe.unsw.edu.au/ContentPages/744449240.pdf (accessed 30 December 2011).

Tranter, P.J. and Malone, K. (2008) 'Out of bounds: insights from Australian children to support sustainable cities', *Encounter: Education for Meaning and Social Justice*, 21 (4): 20–26.

Trevelyan, G.M. (1942) *English Social History: A Survey of Six Centuries, Chaucer to Queen Victoria*, London: Longmans, Green & Co.

Unger, N., Bond, T.C., Wang, J.S., Koch, D.M., Menon, S., Drew, T.S. and Bauer, S. (2010) 'Attribution of climate forcing to economic sectors', *Proceedings of the National Academy of Sciences*, Washington, DC, online edn. Available online at: http://www.pnas.org/content/early/2010/02/02/0906548107.abstract (accessed 29 December 2011).

United Kingdom Energy Research Centre (UKERC) (2009) *Global Oil Depletion: An Assessment of the Evidence for a Near-Term Peak in Global Oil Production*, London: UKERC.

United Nations Children's Fund (UNICEF) (2000) *A League Table of Child Poverty in Rich Nations*, UNICEF Innocenti Report Card 1, Florence: UNICEF.

United Nations Children's Fund (UNICEF) (2004) *The State of the World's Children, 2005*, Florence: UNICEF. Available online at: http://www.unicef.org/sowc05/english/sowc05.pdf (accessed 29 December 2011).

United Nations Children's Fund (UNICEF) (2007) *Child Poverty in Perspective: An Overview of Child Well-Being in Rich Countries*, UNICEF Innocenti Report Card 7, Florence: UNICEF. Available online at: http://www.unicef-irc.org/publications/pdf/rc7_eng.pdf (accessed 29 December 2011).

Vaxjo Kommun (2011) *The Greenest City in Europe*, Sweden: Vaxjo Kommun. Available online at: http://www.vaxjo.se/upload/www.vaxjo.se/Kommunledningsf%C3%B6rvalt ningen/Planeringskontoret/10%20VEGS_eng_webb.pdf (accessed 29 December 2011).

Victoria Transport Policy Institute (VTPI) (2011) *Road Pricing*, Vancouver: VTPI. Available online at: http://www.vtpi.org/tdm/tdm35.htm (accessed 29 December 2011).

Waengnerud, L. (n.d.) *Sweden: A Step Wise Development*, Stockholm: IDEA. Available online at: http://www.idea.int/publications/wip2/upload/Sweden.pdf (accessed 28 December 2011).

Walk 21 (2011) 'International Charter for Walking'. Available online at: http://www.walk21.com/papers/International%20Charter%20for%20Walking.pdf (accessed 29 December 2011).

Webber, M. (1964) 'The urban place and non-place urban realm', in M. Webber, J. Dyckman, D. Foley, A. Guttenberg, W. Wheaton and C. Bauer Wurster (eds), *Explorations into Urban Structure*, Philadelphia: University of Pennsylvania Press, pp. 79–153.

Whitelegg, J. (1983) 'Road safety: defeat, complicity and the bankruptcy of science', *Accident Analysis and Prevention*, 15 (2): 153–160.

Whitelegg, J. (1993a) 'Time pollution', *Ecologist*, 23 (4): 132–134. Available online at: http://www.eco-logica.co.uk/pdf/TimePollution.pdf (accessed 29 December 2011).

Whitelegg, J. (1993b) *Critical Mass: Transport, Environment and Society in the 21st Century*, London: Pluto Press.

Whitelegg, J. (1994) *Roads, Jobs and the Economy*, Lancaster: Eco-Logica.

Whitelegg, J. (2005) *London Sustainable Food Hub: Opportunities for a Sustainable Food Logistics Centre in London*, London: London Development Agency.

Whitelegg, J. (2007a) *Heysham–M6 Link: Evidence to Public Inquiry on Air Quality*, Transport Solutions for Lancaster and Morecambe. Available online at: http://heysham-m6link.info/Evidence_on_Air_quality.pdf (accessed 29 December 2011).

Whitelegg, J. (2007b) *Heysham–M6 Link: Evidence to Public Inquiry on Climate Change*, Transport Solutions for Lancaster and Morecambe. Available online at: http://www.heyshamm6link.info/Evidence_on_Climate_change.pdf (accessed 29 December 2011).

Whitelegg, J. (2009a) *Less Carbon More Jobs: A Vision for the Liverpool City Region*, Report for the Local Transport Plan Partnership, Liverpool: Merseytravel.

Whitelegg, J. (2009b) On the wrong track: why high speed trains are not such a green alternative, *Guardian*, 29 April. Available online at: http://www.guardian.co.uk/environment/2009/apr/29/high-speed-rail-travel-europe-uk (accessed 29 December 2011).

Whitelegg, J. (2011a) 'A beginner's guide to sustainable transport and how to get it right', *Environment Industry Magazine*, October/November, pp. 153–155.

Whitelegg, J. (2011b) *Pay as You Go: Managing Traffic Impacts in a World-Class City*, Lancaster: Eco-Logica. Available online at: http://www.london.gov.uk/profile/darren-johnson/reports (accessed 17 December 2011).

Whitelegg, J. (2011c) 'Evidence to House of Commons Select Committee on Transport investigation into the strategic case for high speed rail', HSR 34, p. 135. Available online at: http://www.publications.parliament.uk/pa/cm201012/cmselect/cmtran/1185/1185vw32.htm (accessed 30 December 2011).

Whitelegg, J. and Haq, G. (2004) *The York Intelligent Travel Project: Final Report*, York: Stockholm Environment Institute.

Whitelegg, J. and Haq, G. (2006) *Vision Zero: Adopting a Target of Zero for Road Traffic Fatalities and Serious Injuries*, York: Stockholm Environment Institute.

Whitelegg, J., Haq, G., Cambridge, H. and Vallack, H. (2010) *Towards a Zero Carbon Vision for UK Transport*, York: Stockholm Environment Institute. Available online at: http://www.sei-international.org/mediamanager/documents/Publications/SEI-ProjectReport-Whitelegg-TowardsAZeroCarbonVisionForUKTransport-2010.pdf (accessed 8 August 2011).

Whitelegg, J. and Holzapfel, H. (1993) 'The conquest of distance by the destruction of time', in J. Whitelegg, S. Hulten and T. Flink (eds), *High Speed Trains: Fast Tracks to the Future*, Hawes: Leading Edge Press in association with the Stockholm School of Economics.

Whitelegg, J. and Pye, W. (2009) 'Traffic and transport: evidence presented to public inquiry into proposals for a new shopping centre and associated developments in Lancaster', *It's Our City*. Available online at: http://www.itsourcity.org.uk/pi/archive/proofs/I-TR-01%20Transport%20Proof.pdf (accessed 29 December 2011).

Whyte, B. and Livingston, M. (2009) 'Analysis of children's travel patterns', paper presented at Glasgow School for Population Health conference on active travel, October.

Wiedman, T., Wood, R., Lenzen, M., Minx, J., Guan, D. and Barrett, J. (2008) *Development of an Embedded Carbon Emissions Indicator*, York: Stockholm Environment Institute and University of Sydney. Available online at: http://randd.defra.gov.uk/Document.aspx?Document=EV02033_7331_FRP.pdf (accessed 30 December 2011).

Wilkinson, R. and Pickett, K. (2009) *The Spirit Level: Why Equality Is Better for Everyone*, London: Penguin Books.

Wilson, D. and Game, C. (2006) *Local Government in the United Kingdom*, Basingstoke: Palgrave Macmillan.

Woodcock, J., Edwards, P., Tonne, C., Armstrong, B., Ashiru, O., Banister, D., Beevers, S., Chalabi, Z., Chowdhury, Z., Cohen, A., Franco, O., Haines, A., Hickman, R., Lindsay, G., Mittal, I., Mohan, D., Tiwari, G., Woodward, A. and Roberts, I. (2009) 'Public health benefits of strategies to reduce greenhouse gas emissions: urban land transport', *Lancet*, 374: 1930–1943.

World Bank (2011) 'GDP rankings by country'. Available online at: http://databank.worldbank.org/databank/download/GDP.pdf.

World Health Organization (WHO) (2004) *World Report on Road Traffic Injury and Prevention*, Geneva: WHO.

World Health Organization (WHO) (2007) *The Challenge of Obesity in the European Region and the Strategies for Response*, Copenhagen: WHO, Regional Office for Europe.

World Health Organization (WHO) (2008) *Closing the Gap: Health Equity through Action on the Social Determinants of Health*, Geneva: WHO.

World Health Organization (WHO) (2009) *European Status Report on Road Safety: Towards Safer Roads and Healthier Transport Choices*, Copenhagen: WHO, Regional Office for Europe.

World Health Organization (WHO) (2011a) 'Air pollution database', 27 September 2011. Available online at: http://www.who.int/phe/health_topics/outdoorair/databases/OAP_database_8_11.xls (accessed 29 December 2011).

World Health Organization (WHO) (2011b) 'Air quality and health', Fact Sheet 313. Available online at: http://www.who.int/mediacentre/factsheets/fs313/en/index.html (accessed 18 November 2011).

Wuppertal Institute (2009) *Sustainable Urban Infrastructure, Munich Edition: Paths towards a Carbon Free Future*, Munich: Siemens. Available online at: http://www.mobility.siemens.com/shared/data/pdf/www/corporate/sustainable_munich_2009_e.pdf (accessed 29 December 2011).

York City Council (2011) Personal communication via e-mail from Tom Horner, Local Transport Plan Team, York City Council, 2 August.

Zeibots, M. (2010) Personal communication, 6 December.

Index